Emotional Honesty
& Self-Acceptance

1001-BRIL

Emotional Honesty
& Self-Acceptance

Education Strategies for Preventing Violence

Ronald R. Brill

To order additional copies of this book, contact:
Xlibris Corporation
1-888-7-XLIBRIS
www.Xlibris.com
Orders@Xlibris.com

CONTENTS

FOREWORD

Violence prevention? Everybody's talking about it, but few people offer new strategies. Now comes along a refreshing perspective on this troubling issue. Ronald Brill conceptualizes and names the process by which hurt feelings are converted into destructive behavior. His idea of what causes "good kids with bad feelings" to erupt into murderous revenge against their classmates is a good start toward rethinking conventional approaches for preventing violence in schools, homes and workplaces. He describes "acquired emotional disabilities" that keep people of all ages from dealing effectively with painful feelings. This book offers a creative approach using education as a primary violence prevention strategy. Here is a message of hope that we can teach and learn skills for dealing more honestly and successfully with inevitably painful, wounding experiences. This book can be richly rewarding for a society desperately searching for new ideas to solve one of its most perplexing problems.

J.M. Stubblebine, M.D.
Chairman, Violence Prevention Forum
Former California Director of Health and
Director of Mental Hygiene

INTRODUCTION

I've written this book to offer a conceptual framework as well as practical strategies for self-awareness training, group discussions, and structured education programs. The book is designed to be used in programs for parents, adolescents and all who can benefit by strengthening their self-acceptance and personal relationships. A major objective is to help prevent hurt feelings from turning into harmful acts.

I call this process of accepting our feelings, emotional honesty. Accepting our emotional truth is essential for self-acceptance. In turn, self-acceptance is necessary for accepting others. Learning the principles of emotional honesty enables us to stop punishing ourselves and others for our emotional pain. By acknowledging our emotional vulnerability we also increase emotional intimacy. I believe we can learn to develop emotional honesty, just as we have learned to use emotional *dishonesty* to protect ourselves from painful feelings.

The well-worn axiom that "Sticks and stones may break my bones, but words can never hurt me" is commonly learned in childhood. This is one way parents innocently teach their children to deny their emotional pain. The saying could be described as a mantra for emotional dishonesty.

It is human nature to avoid what is painful. Yet, being alive in the world means being vulnerable and experiencing emotional wounds. This is the dilemma that confronts us all. We may flee from painful feelings through self-deception and emotional dishonesty. But what if doing so results in even more emotional distress and suffering? I believe parents can be equipped with knowledge that can help keep their children from turning normal hurt feelings into an emotional disability. I believe we can give adolescents a much needed emotional road map for understanding the predictable causes and preventable effects of their emotional confusion and painful social experiences. I believe we and our children can learn to recover from wounding events without expressing our pain through anger or depression. Our challenge is this: *Learning to become more aware of the hidden defenses and pretenses that keep us trapped in pain and prevent us from honestly dealing with our hurt feelings.*

The methods for accomplishing these goals are contained in principles few of us learned at home or school. In this book I've attempted to describe some of the basic principles that enable us to understand and practice emotional honesty.

This book is for those seeking greater emotional freedom and fulfillment for themselves, their children, students, and loved ones. I welcome fellow voyagers as companions on this odyssey that explores the anatomy of our feelings. We all need companions on this voyage, for it takes us into uncomfortable areas many would rather not visit. It takes courage to end our denial and examine why we suffer needlessly from emotional distress.

One way to release our pain is to stop hiding it under shameful pretenses, secrecy and rigid defenses. We can learn how to recognize self-deception that sentences perfectly innocent, normal people to suffer more from their *reactions* to painful feelings than from the original wounding events. Emotional dishonesty typically involves *under-reacting* to the original wounding event and *over-reacting* to the inner pain resulting from hurt feelings.

Many of us were not fortunate to have parents who exemplified or taught us how to accept and honor our hurt feelings, particularly the pain we felt when wounded by loss, rejection, betrayal, or humiliation. Because we learned to hide and feel ashamed of hurt feelings, we became handicapped in our struggle to recover from life's predictable misfortunes and disappointments. These ordinary wounding experiences happen without our necessarily deserving them. Only we give them meaning by connecting them to our fear of being unlovable or unacceptable.

This book is a foundation work rather than a definitive study. It is intended to stimulate further inquiry and discussions about a subject too long held in secrecy as "a private matter." Unfortunately, we suffer from a cultural myth that feeling hurt and vulnerable is wrong: For men it is a sign of weakness and unacceptability. For women, it means risking rejection and feeling undesirable or unlovable. For adolescents, it leads to agonizing despair or rage about feelings they can neither understand nor control. How is it that defenses, which we believe protect us from emotional devastation, actually deepen and lengthen our distress? How does emotional dishonesty destroy intimacy and undermine relationships? These are some of the questions this book attempts to address.

Once we learn how our instinctive survival needs ensnare us in this trap, we can begin working to free our true feelings from our self-made prison. We can learn ways to manage powerful defenses that prevent us from being emotionally honest and present – defenses that sentence us to deny *past,* painful experiences and live in fear of *future* ones. If we cannot accept our feelings, we cannot accept ourselves. On the other hand, if there is nothing "wrong" with what we feel, then there is no need to shame ourselves or blame others for our pain.

Emotional honesty is a no-fault system for accepting our feelings and accepting ourselves. Emotional dishonesty traps us in emotional distress that can deepen and lead to violent and/or self-destructive behavior. These are the twin tragedies of emotional dishonesty. It is the threat of these tragic outcomes that forces us to bring the "private matter" of hurt feelings out of the closet and into our homes, schools and communities.

Ronald Brill
Novato, California
February 2000

Notes on using this book:

Most chapters of this book were originally written as separate elements for education and training programs. While this creates some unavoidable repetition, the advantage is that the book can be read selectively rather than from front to back. I suggest reviewing the table of contents, which lists both chapter titles and main topics within chapters. As you leaf through chapters, you will find both main-topic headings (the same as listed under chapters in the table of contents), and sub-headings, which help you to locate specific subjects. Chapter 15 also serves as a conclusion and summary.

Rather than use one conventional bibliography, there are two types of references noted. There are general references, and references that are "Recommended Reading." General references are noted in the text with author, title and date. The recommended reading references are listed alphabetically in Appendix IV, as well as noted as such in the text.

PERSONAL PROLOGUE:

Why I Wrote This Book

My motivation for writing this book grew out of four separate experiences that have become welded into a personal conviction that emotional education should become a national priority.

• The most relevant incident occurred when my youngest daughter (now 21) was entering adolescence. Her middle school invited parents to preview the standard audiovisual materials to be used in their life (sex) education unit. I watched and listened to the audiovisual material about *physical* changes and challenges during adolescence. I waited anxiously to see how the program would explain normal adolescent *emotional* changes and challenges during this tumultuous period that commonly confuse and often overwhelm parents, students, and even teachers. I was shocked and dismayed that emotional issues during adolescence were scarcely mentioned in the program. How could any school, filled with emotionally insecure youngsters entering the most stormy period of life, not address their inevitable emotional struggles and traumas? I registered my concern with the school nurse presenting the material, only to hear excuses about a lack of resources to address emotional development issues. I then realized that while our society has overcome the taboo of discussing and teaching physiological aspects of sexual development, we are still in the Middle Ages when it comes to teaching our children healthy ways of dealing with their troubling feelings.

• A second experience occurred 25 years ago, and had a powerful and personal impact on my need to understand and write about the origins of emotional distress. My first marriage ended as a result of my ex-wife developing a serious psychosis during midlife that not only was disabling for her, but was devastating to me and our three children. My children and I struggled for over 10 years, with the aid of therapy, to survive and overcome our sense of powerlessness as mental illness transformed the person we knew and loved into a virtual stranger.

• The third experience that triggered my interest in preventable aspects of emotional distress was my own, unbearable adolescence. In high school I was fortunate to have a compassionate biology teacher, who on several occasions tried to console her shy and confused student by talking to me after class about my noticeable adolescent angst. Then one day she devoted her classroom lecture to "the emotional crisis of adolescence." I still recall my mortifying embarrassment that here, before all my classmates, *my* private, shameful pain and flaws were being discussed. Though my teacher never mentioned my name, I felt humiliated by just the hint that *my* secret problems were so bad, that they were being used as an example, put on public display.

Now, nearly 50 years later as I write this book, I realize that the inevitable problem of having hurt feelings and being emotionally vulnerable remains very much a private, secret subject shunned in public life. I recall in my 20's, wanting to lift the veil shrouding the secret, torturous feelings of adolescence so the next generation would not have to endure the pain and confusion I had experienced. This motivated me to start college as a psychology major. In writing this book I have revisited many painful experiences in my own rather typical, but nonetheless tormenting adolescence. I now know why each wounding experience at that time seemed so overwhelming. My relatively normal adolescence was so unbearable that I recall living in utter terror that my secret feelings of being a flawed person would be exposed. Writing this book has helped to shine a light back into those dark and nameless fears that haunted me through much of my youth. I recall searching for "what was wrong with me," yet being terrified of finding it out. As I think about this puzzling and painful period of my life, I cannot help but think how many millions of confused and tormented adolescents today could be helped by school emotional health education programs.

• The fourth and final triggering factor behind my writing this book is the horrifying series of shootings during the last several years by good kids with bad feelings killing innocent classmates in America's schools. I could wait no longer in silence. These tragic, desperate acts compelled me to write a series of newspaper articles calling for emotional education in schools. I began writing this book after the first three shocking incidents of teen killings in typical, suburban American schools. While I have been writing this book these indiscriminate killings continue. They culminated in the Littleton, Colorado tragedy in April, 1999. Certainly the pain of our emotionally wounded youth crying out through murderous rage must awaken us to address our society's need for emotional education in schools and in our homes.

Beyond this book

This book is written in nontechnical terms for the subject it deals with is every person's responsibility. We need a common, easily understood language for stating the disabling effects of emotional dishonesty. And we need a clear set of principles for learning how to use emotional honesty to recognize and better manage inner reactions to emotional wounds so hurt feelings don't lead to further punishing ourselves or others.

I recognize that this book is but a beginning of a much larger task to develop and put into place emotional health education programs at school, at home, at our places of worship, and at work. To accomplish this we need more public dialogue on this subject. We must begin to test and determine the most effective emotional educational principles for enabling children to resolve painful wounds so they are not lured to violence nor commit self-destructive acts. We need to train more emotional health educators who can reach out to schools and community agencies to ensure that this critical subject receives the public attention it deserves. Educators, parents, therapists and teenagers are encouraged to participate in Emotional Honesty Discussion Groups. These creative and supportive networks–which can operate in homes, schools, churches or synagogues–are explained in the appendix.

In addition, readers are referred to the author's newsletter, *Emotional Education Perspective*, as a source of information about new programs and resources that address the education needs described in this book. The author plans a series of books based on this foundation work. Announcements and descriptions of publications and books on this subject can be found on the author's web site, emotionalhonesty.com.

Readers' questions, comments and suggestions are important for the continuing development and refinement of emotional honesty concepts and applications. These may be e-mailed to rbrill@earthlink.net. Reviews of this book are also found on the website: emotionalhonesty.com.

WHAT IS EMOTIONAL HONESTY?

By being honest with ourselves about what we feel when we are hurt, we learn to accept our feelings and to recover from emotional distress.

Emotional *dishonesty* is a self betrayal which keeps us from healing emotional wounds and experiencing the inner peace of self-acceptance. Self-acceptance comes from honoring and accepting what we feel rather than judging feelings, blaming others or shaming ourselves. *Self-accepting persons have no need to harm themselves or others.* Self-accepting persons are more capable of accepting others.

Emotional *honesty* is listening to the meaning of each hurt feeling and attending to the resulting distress that occurs. By naming and thus disarming emotional wounds, they do not accumulate and become infected with shame, fear, hate and anger. Emotional honesty is an individual process by which we learn how to prevent the violent and self-destructive responses to emotional pain that threaten to tear apart ourselves and our society.

Emotional honesty is taking responsibility for what we feel. What tends to prevent awareness and acceptance of our true feelings is a prevalent cultural misbelief that emotional pain is shameful and *"someone must be to blame if I'm in pain!"* Being vulnerable to painful wounding experiences is seen as a weakness rather than a sign of being human.

Emotional honesty does not mean escaping from being emotionally wounded. Rather it is taking responsibility for what *we* feel, including our pain. *One reason our society seems so incapable of finding preventive strategies that can stem the growth of child and adult violence and depression is our tendency to place blame, rather than look inside ourselves for the trigger that detonates destructive acts upon ourselves or others.* Rather than focus on violence-proofing our schools, we should use schools to violence-proof our children. Similarly, rather than employers trying to reduce violent incidents by trying to violence-proofing the workplace employers should violence-proof their employees.

Blaming violence on entertainment media, too many guns, or attributing destructive behavior to mental illness, or saying that it is genetically acquired, or that perpetrators are evil persons–all relieve us of the responsibility and opportunity for *educating our children, parents and workers about human, self-deceptive emotional processes which convert hurt feelings into destructive acts.*

PART ONE

*Exploring the Mysterious
Realm of Feelings*

CHAPTER 1

Feelings Linked to Destructive Behavior

I. Good Kids with Bad Feelings

Observe children. Being more emotionally transparent than adults, they more clearly reveal the self-deception and secrets we dare not discuss. Observe children, for they more accurately reflect what we avoid in our society.

Why do we avoid using education, for example, as a means of teaching youth how to safely recover from emotionally wounding experiences? Why are we then surprised that they express their pain through violence or self-destructive behavior? Despite the recent rash of school shootings by adolescents, schools continue to consider emotional health education a foreign language, rather than an essential part of human development. What drives good kids with bad feelings to kill other children? Why, in some cases, do they choose to end their young lives as well as the lives of their innocent classmates? What do these tragedies tell us about our failure as a society to deal with the crushing effects of being rejected or humiliated? These children reveal our collective inability to honor and accept ourselves when we are emotionally wounded.

I am perplexed and disappointed by our society's reluctance to provide adolescents with information and teach emotional skills that could enable them to better deal with their normal angst. It is obvious that teens are ill-equipped to handle the torturous emotional distress so characteristic of their confusing period of life. What most bothers me, as much as the unnecessary snuffing out of young lives, is that after each school shooting we continue to look in all the wrong places for ways of preventing the recurrence of this tragic violence.

Until I began writing this book, I was hesitant to suggest any particular type of emotional education curriculum that might help prepare children with safe ways of handling troubling feelings. All I did know, as a parent, a former director of health education campaigns, a college teacher, and a consultant to private schools was that there seemed to be little interest in using education to prevent both violent and self-destructive behavior. I knew that most schools were certainly capable of assembling and presenting basic information about healthy ways of recovering from disturbing feelings. What I had failed to realize, however, until delving into the subject for this book, was our *cultural unwillingness* to deal with the subject of hurt feelings – particularly their powerful influence during adolescence.

Teachers and parents appear reluctant to address this subject with children because it has been a taboo topic. It has taken the recent and tragic series of school killings to force us as a society to re-examine our reluctance to broach the subject of educating children about safe and healthy ways of dealing with their hidden and shameful hurt feelings. Brutality against innocent classmates by children from relatively affluent and educated families means there are no schools where adolescents are safe. There is obviously some factor that neither adolescents, their parents, nor schools know about that drives otherwise good kids with bad feelings to avenge their emotional suffering by killing classmates whom they hold responsible for their pain.

Distraught teens are unable to turn to parents or schools to ask why they can't recover from the chronic pain from emotional wounds – wounds suffered from the ordinary experiences of *losses, rejection, betrayal and humiliation.* Parents are silent because they too often suffer from the same disability. And so schools are not urged to take action through preventive education programs. By our society's silent acquiescence to the cultural denial of hurt feelings, we seem incapable to help our children more effectively cope with their pain.

And so, we remain frightened and ashamed of having hurt feelings. By default, we are teaching our children to also ignore the issue. Rather than help teens understand how to recover from the punishing effects of their painful feelings, we tacitly teach them to ignore these wounds. They are left to accumulate and deepen, fester in hate, and then erupt as murderous rage or self-destructive behavior. Rather than learning honest and safe ways of dealing with their pain, teens blame other emotionally insecure classmates for their suffering they cannot understand. And what of the taunting and jeering children who relish upsetting their peers? Don't they also lack the necessary knowledge and experience to deal with their emotional pain – and the resulting sense of feeling unlovable or unacceptable – which leads to rejecting, humiliating and punishing their peers?

Violence, however, is only part of the destructive legacy from the emotional disability that our children carry. Far more common than violence toward others is their silent suffering caused by self-punishing acts of emotional withdrawal, depression, suicide, self-injury, etc., which stem from the same inability to recover from their accumulated painful experiences – experiences that are a normal part of life.

It seems that we will do *anything* rather than deal directly with our hurt feelings. We punish ourselves by hiding emotional pain rather than learning how to honestly deal with it. We use drugs, prescription and illegal, to control or diminish our inner pain. The U.S. Surgeon General estimates 19 million children and adults today suffer from the energy-robbing effects of chronic depression. Anti-depressants are the most widely prescribed medication in America. The U.S. Centers for Disease Control and Prevention report the teenage rate of depression has tripled over the last 30 years. Over 250,000 U.S. teens, who feel hopeless to recover from emotional pain, attempt suicide every year – that's nearly 700 suicide attempts per day! Each day five American teens kill themselves. Suicide is second only to accidents as the leading cause of death for teenagers.

This book examines why we have compelling needs to punish *ourselves* and *others* for the painful feelings *we* cannot name or disarm. Understanding the connection between hurt feelings and harmful behavior is critical not only for teens but also for their parents and teachers and society as a whole. Parents also need to learn ways of dealing with their own hurt feelings in honest ways so they don't inadvertently teach their children unhealthy ways of dealing with their pain. Both teens and adults who engage in violent or self-destructive behavior may use these acts in a ritualistic manner to express otherwise unspeakable, emotional pain. Chapter Nine examines the origins of this problem and Chapter 14 addresses its prevention.

In the following chapters we will see how adolescents become more agitated by wounding experiences because of their naturally high level of emotional vulnerability and insecurity. What better time and place than middle and high school to introduce emotional health education programs to help teens navigate the perilous passage from childhood to adult. Adolescents and their parents need to learn a common language other than destructive acts – from depression to violence – for expressing their anguish. Emotional pain from common events like rejection or humiliation, losses, or betrayal echo within us if it is unattended and allowed to accumulate. The accumulated pain may eventually ignite into a desire for retaliation or become twisted into a compelling need to punish one's self for being in pain.

The cry from Littleton

One of the most shocking events in recent American history occurred April 20, 1999 – the killing of 12 students, a teacher and the wounding of others at Columbine High School in the quiet, upscale, suburb of Littleton, Colorado. The teenage killers' need to avenge and end their pain tragically symbolizes our youth's inability to deal with painful feelings from everyday wounding events. Not since the assassination of President Kennedy nearly 40-years earlier has our nation's innocence been so shattered. Suddenly schoolyards have become killing fields for distraught teens.

The shocking scenario is played out again and again by good kids with bad feelings – teenagers from quiet, suburban neighborhoods. Observe our children for they ask us to listen to their cry for help.

These incidents make us confused, angry and, beneath it all, somehow ashamed. We see in our children's acts of murderous rage against taunting classmates a shameful sign of our general inability to deal with emotional wounds. School children – incapable of handling the normal, tormenting feelings of adolescence – mirror distressed adults who beat or abuse their mates and children to punish them for the wounded adult's own painful feelings. They echo the growing incidence of adult drivers who, unable to deal with their everyday emotionally wounding experiences, erupt in "road rage" or explode violently against co-workers. Why are so many good people unable to deal with their bad feelings? What is the emotional disability they share? This book will help to explore this mystery.

II. Asking the Right Questions to Prevent Violence

Following the rash of school shootings, a growing chorus of demands are heard for stronger gun control measures, tighter school security measures, and tougher school policies that assume all teenagers are potential murderers. We voice growing concern about the influence upon teens of graphic portrayals of violence in our entertainment media. What we don't ask is: "Why are youngsters so attracted to violence in the first place?" Why not counter the portrayals of violence in the media by using television and educational programs to show parents how to model emotional honesty so children learn how to safely handle their emotional pain?

All of the conventional, so-called "prevention" strategies fail to recognize that *schools, like our children, are reflections of our cultural denial of the importance of hurt feelings.* Is it any wonder that we resist discussing hurt feelings in school? Parents demand that schools focus on behavior, thinking skills and values, carefully avoiding the taboo subject of feelings. Do schools have an educational responsibility for stemming the tide of youth violence? If so, how can middle and high schools help teenagers understand their confusing, embarrassing and mysterious inner reactions to being emotionally hurt? Parents, themselves, often have difficulty talking about these very issues with their children, as did their parents before them. Each new generation typically inherits the tendency to avoid discussing hurt feelings. Perhaps we fear that doing so makes us even more vulnerable.

Wounding experiences are as troubling as they are inevitable. So why do we not provide teenagers with skills for coping with them? This book suggests that the teenager's destructive behavior comes from the same type of emotional disability that prompts so many *adults* to act out their painful feelings through destructive acts toward themselves or others.

If we can discover what causes good kids to turn bad feelings into rage against schoolmates, perhaps we can also unravel the mystery of why there is growing public incivility and violent behavior by average Americans – good people with bad feelings. Using education, we can help parents and their children to understand, develop and exhibit greater emotional honesty. We can prevent new generations from inheriting an insidious disability that causes emotionally insecure adolescents to embrace violence or suicide as the *only* means of resolving their pain. We need more research and education programs that help us understand why emotional distress renders us helpless, impotent and incapable of dealing with our hurt. This book marks a beginning by addressing why we cling to cultural tendencies to blame others or shame ourselves, rather than take responsibility for healing our hurt.

How do we currently deal with our tragic failure to stem the outbreak of school killings in our peaceful communities? Social institutions, educators, and media engage in a flurry of finger-pointing while ignoring the obvious fact that these school murders were committed by good kids unable to deal with their troubling feelings. Too many guns? Too much violence in media? Too little parent involvement with their kids? Maybe. But of the thousands of teens who daily experience painful incidents of peer rejection and put-downs, most *do not* act out their pain in murderous rage. Rather, most *suffer silently* by withdrawing, seeking refuge in depression, or by trying to numb their emotional pain with alcohol or other drugs.

How can we prevent our youth from acting out their pain through destructive behavior toward themselves or their peers? We will need to answer several key questions:

• What *capabilities* do some adolescents possess that allow them to recover from being emotionally wounded by peers without exhibiting destructive behavior or falling into depression?

• What *skills* are needed by teens so that when they *do* suffer emotional pain they can treat each wound openly and honestly? How can we prevent our youth from becoming trapped in the same, self-destructive behavior patterns and violent reactions as their adult role models?

Education is a primary prevention strategy. It is far less costly to society in money and negative impact on kids than many of the repressive measures currently being taken in the aftermath of school violence incidents. In the long run, education is a more effective strategy than the current "bunker mentality" that spends millions of dollars to fortify schools with armed guards, surveillance cameras, and blanket searches of students and their lockers. It does not seem to trouble parents and educators that these repressive measures not only violate students' privacy, but also send a clear message of distrust between school personnel and their students. *With far less funds we could be developing emotional health education programs to help students avoid violence, thereby creating safer schools and a more healthy society.* The FBI and U.S. Secret Service now share with school officials and local police forces "profiling" intelligence they have developed to spot potentially dangerous individuals. Continuing on this misguided course can turn schools into repressive institutions reminiscent of the frightening scenario portrayed in George Orwell's *1984.*

III. Hurt Feelings are no Longer a Private Matter

As I was completing the manuscript for this book, the ABC News popular 20/20 television program broadcast on February 9, 2000 examined a specific case of preventing school violence. This revealing report poignantly illustrates the danger of parents and schools treating feelings as a private matter. This was the story of one troubled high school youngster, Jim Myers of Eastern Senior High School in Voorhees, New Jersey, who is now 18-years-old. The previous year, Myers was close to acting out a plan of retaliation against his school for painful wounds he suffered from taunting classmates. The TV program contained an interview with Myers, who recalled suffering severely from tormenting inner rage, depression, and social isolation. He explained his compelling fantasy of "unfocused hatred" to hurt others for his painful rejection and humiliation at school. On the program, Meyers recalled his need to "cause as much pain and suffering as you possibly can, because that's what you've been through." His secret, smoldering rage was finally divulged to a vice principal, who approached the withdrawn youth after the Columbine High School incident to ask how he felt about it. This was likely the first time anyone, including his father, had ever asked the troubled teenager about his feelings. His disturbing answer, which revealed how he identified with the Colorado killers, prompted the vice principal to recommend that Myers receive psychological counseling before being readmitted to school.

The most sad and revealing moment in the television program occurred during an interview with the teenager's father. The single-parent, elder Myers admitted being "out of touch" with his son and being unable to understand him. When asked by reporter Chris Wallace, "Do you feel you've known what's going on in Jim's head?" his father responded, "Oh, I don't try and guess what's going on in people's heads." Later he offered, "What goes on in your mind is a privacy issue."

Neither the reporter, his father nor school officials identified Jim Meyers as having difficulty dealing with his "hurt feelings," experiencing "emotional pain," or any other direct references to his inability to recover from his wounding encounters. It was the teenager's own words that conveys the humiliation and agony he had silently suffered for so long: He described his inner reaction to the many years of being picked on at school because he was "different." "They're sitting there laughing at you. This pain you're going through is funny to them . . .This is not funny. This is painful. I want you to feel the pain!"

The revealing news program and numerous news accounts of school violence in recent years repeatedly show that kids who commit violence are *unable to safely deal with their hurt feelings,* particularly wounds from being rejected and humiliated by peers. These wounds are often compounded by other normal adolescent losses and betrayals. This particular broadcast, however, underscores the growing need for parents and schools to provide emotional health education for youngsters to help them more responsibly deal with and recover from their hurt feelings. Painful feelings, and the emotional dishonesty used to hide them, are too often seen as " privacy issues" we don't discuss. It's the "don't ask, don't tell" secrecy, which is so commonly seen with taboo subjects.

Learning to be emotionally honest

Emotional dishonesty, the self-deceptive pretense about feelings, is a plague affecting not only emotionally insecure adolescents, but the general population as well. Recent horrifying episodes of teens killing classmates on school campuses across the country send a powerful message about the grave consequences of not providing our children with vital skills that enable them to deal with their inevitable and normal hurt feelings. Yes, there are bullies and insecure kids who need to reject other kids in order to feel secure and strong. But as a society, we can no longer avoid our responsibility to teach basic skills of emotional honesty so that wounded children do not die or kill others in attempting to end their own pain. Parents and teachers need to recognize signs of emotional dishonesty (EDH), which is a preventable emotional disability. By continuing to blame others and thereby ignore EDH as a factor underlying destructive acts, we become accomplices after the fact when adolescents express their pain through violence or suicide. Schools can teach how to recognize and deal with emotional pain in a healthy and safe manner, as part of a broad-based emotional health education program.

Emotional health education can help parents and schools to prepare typically insecure adolescents with specific skills that enable them to safely recover from hurt feelings. *Education is a primary preventive strategy,* for it can end the secrecy that only exacerbates emotional distress when wounds are ignored or denied. Parents and teachers also need to learn how to model the principles of emotional honesty in their own lives, thereby setting examples for children to become more resilient and resistant to deepening emotional distress.

By learning how to honor and accept our hurt feelings, we remove the damaging message and social stigma from having hurt feelings. We can also learn to overcome both the societal influences and family patterns that often perpetuate emotional dishonesty. This change in perspective requires attacking the problem on two fronts:

• Opening a public dialogue about the important relationship between emotional honesty and the prevention of destructive behavior. This dialogue demands a set of principles and a common language to facilitate communication, sharing, and learning about this subject.

• Developing a supportive environment for learning and practicing emotional honesty at home, at school, at work, and in society generally. Not only do adolescents need to arm themselves with healthy techniques for safely dealing with hurt feelings, but their parents also need to see the importance of modeling emotional honesty by the way they deal with their own hurt feelings. Teachers and school counselors can learn techniques for use inside and outside the classroom.

Though it is difficult to consistently practice emotional honesty in everyday life, the basic skills can be taught as part of life education classes in middle and high school, as well as by parents. These lessons can be reinforced by discussions groups, keeping journals and other activities described in this book. At the same time, adult community education programs can help parents learn these same skills, so they can use and discuss them with their children. The essential skills discussed in this book are those which the author believes can help us to *accept our feelings, accept ourselves, and accept others*. Self-acceptance makes us naturally more tolerant persons. Self-accepting people have no need to harm others or themselves. The ability to deal honestly with our feelings is fundamental to our individual and social well-being.

Parents, teachers, adults in relationships, and particularly adolescents can learn how to lead more emotionally healthy and honest lives. Lying about what we feel when we are hurt is not only emotionally dishonest, it is a betrayal of self. It not only leads to dismissing and distrusting what we really feel, but disavows a birthright – the freedom to feel our emotional experiences without censorship!

Those educators who may disagree with the idea that schools should take responsibility for emotional health education to prevent violence must surely recognize that a curriculum for helping adolescents to more effectively deal with their hurt feelings can help to create greater student self-awareness, tolerance and acceptance of others.

Emotional health education can help to restore emotional honesty to our society as a whole. Emotional dishonesty has reached epidemic proportions primarily because we fear and therefore avoid discussing it. It is an issue that affects both our children's emotional *and physical health* and well-being. *The strategy for disarming this virulent disability is public awareness and education.* Schools and parents will need the support of other community and national resources. Mass media, legislatures, community institutions, colleges, foundations, mental health professionals, law enforcement and social service agencies are all potentially key constituents for creating a more open public dialogue. Together they can help to end the secretive practices that have brought such tragic consequences.

IV. Violence-Proof Children to Violence-Proof Schools

We will not prevent violent or self-destructive behavior patterns until we recognize the powerful role that painful feelings play in destructive behavior. *The most effective way to violence-proof our schools is to violence-proof our kids.* The best way to reduce portrayals of violence in our media is to inoculate youngsters with an educational "vaccine" that teaches them how to respond honestly to their own painful feelings without needing to take vengeance against others. As we learn skills for recovering from hurt feelings, we will have less tendency to bury them – only to later use violent means to avenge our suffering. *When our children become better equipped with effective emotional skills for healing their hurt, our entire society will have less thirst for guns, drugs, as well as violence in its entertainment.*

This book begins – as our education system should begin – by discussing why the little understood realm of hurt feelings is such a forbidding mystery, and why we seem so reluctant to delve into it. This book challenges us to focus our energy and intellect to discover what compels distraught teens to desperately try to drive out their inner pain by murdering their peers and themselves.

During the years spent writing this book and searching into the dark secrets of painful feelings, I've become convinced that our cultural tendency to avoid hurt feelings is what *causes* us to engage in pretenses and defenses that deny what we really feel. Moreover, we have come to *expect* that others will lie about their hurt feelings, so why shouldn't we?

EDH is a protective reaction that actually harms us more than the original wounding experience! It is time that we introduce teens and parents to emotional health education so succeeding generations develop greater self-awareness about their wounded feelings. By exploring this forbidden and forbidding subject today, we can help our children and their children to become more resilient and emotionally honest adults – thereby creating a less violent and self-destructive society.

To do this we must acknowledge our society's past failure to emotionally prepare children for adolescence – life's most emotionally challenging period. Children hide their hurt feelings because they see that adults and peers doing it. They arrive at the threshold of adolescence confused not only about what they feel, but lacking an emotional road map to safely navigate through the mine field of wounding experiences they inevitably encounter.

The recent outbreak of school killings is more about the danger of not knowing how to handle bad feelings than being bad kids. These tragic incidents tell us more powerfully than words about the grave danger of hiding hurt feelings in secrecy and shame. It is our children's expression of their unbearable emotional pain in the form of destructive acts toward themselves and others which prompted my search for a truly preventive strategy. It is fitting to begin searching for ways to change our violent society by looking at troubled children who tell us so much about our cultural taboos and fears.

Learning to overcome emotional dishonesty (EDH)

Adolescents are unable to deal openly with their wounded feelings because adults – parents and teachers – are trapped in the same denial as adolescents. Unlike "mature" adults, however, emotionally insecure teens are less skillful and sophisticated in disguising their emotional self-deception and denials. While children are apt students of emotional pretenses that they see around them, they are less capable of controlling their destructive effects. Parents and educators, like teens, are often unable to recognize that the secret realm of hurt feelings is a primary factor in destructive behavior. *They too feel more comfortable dealing with behavior, thoughts and beliefs rather than feelings.*

Being ashamed of hurt feelings – hiding or dismissing them – weakens our natural ability to recover from everyday emotional distress. Children who suffer humiliation by their peers have less experience and skills for recovering from their pain. And so they pretend their wounds don't hurt. They reject what they really feel and substitute a veneer of indifference. However, this denial leads to becoming less self-accepting. *After all, it's hard to accept ourselves when we're rejecting our feelings.*

Confronted by a myriad of challenges to their fragile identity and acceptability, adolescents secretly and shamefully brood over each successive emotional injury. Each hurt seems to reveal a yet deeper flaw, raising a fear that "Something must be fundamentally wrong with me to hurt so much." As wounds accumulate, we ask ourselves, "Why am I so vulnerable to emotional injuries and feel so ashamed when I'm hurt?" The thing insecure teens seem least able to accept is that their vulnerability – which they fear – is a necessary part of being human. Vulnerability is also at the core of their shame when they are hurt. Yet vulnerability is essential for being compassionate and emotionally intimate, precious traits that enable us to be emotionally connected to each other. *Emotional vulnerability is not a weakness.* In our culture, however, it just seems that way.

In their 1986 book, *Being Intimate* (Appendix IV), therapists John Amadeo and Kris Wentworth state, "Being vulnerable is basic to the human condition, however firmly we may resist or struggle to maintain control over our lives and emotions." They believe we have the capability to practice emotional honesty, despite tendencies to avoid our pain: "Honesty is a factor we have a considerable degree of control over; at any given moment, we can choose to conceal or reveal our actual feelings . . ." They see this as an "ongoing process that must be renewed daily."

Taking responsibility *vs.* placing blame

By failing to take responsibility for helping youngsters to understand the underlying *emotional processes that convert hurt feelings into destructive behavior*, we will keep on blaming bullies and bullets, parents, socioeconomic factors, and the entertainment media. Placing blame only serves to keep us from developing parent and adolescent *no-fault* education programs to help our children and ourselves become more emotionally resilient, self-accepting, and resistant to violence.

We need to recognize our personal and collective responsibility to change the prevailing cultural belief that having hurt feelings and being emotionally vulnerable is a *private, shameful matter.* By embracing this responsibility, we can truly begin preventing violence by dealing with its roots that lie deep within us. What a meaningful way to honor all the innocent school shooting victims – from Pearl, Mississippi, to Littleton, Colorado: Creating programs that help teens learn how to deal with their personal pain before it becomes public tragedy.

As a society and as individuals we pay a great price for placing greater emphasis on what we do or say, think or believe, than what we *feel.* The protective, self-betraying response to hurt feelings that I call emotional dishonesty results in needless confusion, insecurity, more distress, and destructive acts. It leads to punishing others and ourselves for our inability to deal with emotional pain.

Being emotionally honest is hard work. It takes courage to honor pain without shaming ourselves or blaming others. These chapters hopefully will make the daunting task more manageable and easy.

CHAPTER 2

What We Don't Know About Hurt Feelings Can Kill Us!

No matter how hard we may try to cover up our true
emotions, they eventually leak out or burst open.
–John Amodeo and Kris Wentworth, *Being Intimate* (1986)

I. How Emotional Pain Triggers Violence

Being ashamed of emotional pain creates a pattern of emotional
dishonesty (EDH) – the dishonoring of feelings that may eventually lead to destructive behavior. Yet some of the most enduring
songs in our culture advise us to "forget all your troubles," "put on
a happy face," and "put all your troubles behind you." Behind this
simplistic optimism lies an unspoken belief that "sad is bad." Beneath this onslaught of cultural messages and urging of well-meaning parents who encourage children to "get over it" and stuff their
pain lies the message that something is wrong with us when our
feelings hurt. No wonder we've become experts at hiding and disguising emotional pain. If we can just keep pretending, have a
positive attitude, get enough love, have enough money; or take
enough drugs, maybe the pain will go away.

Dismissing our hurt as though it didn't occur is disowning what
we feel. *When emotional pain becomes shameful, we're compelled to believe
that we or someone else must be to blame when we are hurt.* This belief
triggers a need to punish ourselves or seek retaliation against others for

what we feel. Not only is such destructive behavior dangerous, but the emotionally dishonest response behind these acts dishonors our hurt feelings. To own and accept troubling feelings without *judgment* requires that we hear the message emotional pain generates. In his 1998 book *Love & Survival,* medical researcher Dr. Dean Ornish says that emotional pain is a messenger; pain is information. He sees danger in taking or doing something to kill the pain without healing its cause. The heart research specialist says "Awareness is the first stage of healing." Ornish explains that by ignoring what really hurts inside, we become confused and distrustful of our feelings as well as the feelings of others.

When we fear revealing our real and painful feelings, we become incapable of healing and recovering from emotional distress. We pretend the genuine pain isn't part of us. I'm reminded of codependence author Robert Burney's (Appendix IV) apt description of alcoholism as the disease that makes you think you don't have it.

The most common way of disowning emotional pain is distancing ourselves from our feelings by blaming others as though *they* are responsible for what *we* feel. When we are hurt, we fear that our secret shame of being vulnerable will be found out. Being ashamed of emotional vulnerability incapacitates us from recovering from normal wounding experiences. Hurt feelings then become signs of our disabling, agonizing sense of unworthiness. Interviewed in the days following the Columbine High School tragedy, a classmate who knew both Eric Harris and Dylan Klebold was asked what he felt triggered their violent outbreak. Was being rejected, humiliated and taunted by classmates enough to cause such murderous rage? The high school student said that the cruelty of teens toward those who don't fit in is too much for some students to take.

Outcast teens are naturally attracted to groups whose rallying cry is blaming others. Since they're typically unable to own their pain, the disowned pain of rejected teens remains buried inside where it is infected and often masked by hate. Insecure and wounded teens have few role models or training for safely recovering from everyday emotional injuries. Many youngsters suffer from an acquired, functional emotional disability shared by their parents. This disability, EDH, prevents them from healing normal, inevitable wounds from life experiences. The accumulation of emotional pain they have learned to avoid causes good teens *and* adults to punish themselves and others for no other reason than being unable to deal with their own buried, hurt feelings.

The emotional hell of adolescence is exacerbated when insecure youngsters taunt their peers. In this manner they deflect their pain from rejection and humiliation toward classmates who also want nothing more than to be accepted. Their unnamed, hidden, and unremitting pain is what is being expressed when they take murderous revenge against peers or commit self-destructive acts. *Shaming ourselves for what we feel and blaming our feelings on others are the twin tragedies of emotional dishonesty.* Unattended hurt feelings that become infected with hate sometimes can find voice only through the punishing acts of murder or suicide. Sadly, these may be the only way some emotionally unaware and insecure teenagers can express their nameless anguish. As one psychologist commented in a television interview following the violent rampage at Columbine High School, since emotionally disabled boys like the Littleton killers cannot cry tears when they're emotionally hurt, they cry bullets!

Once we as parents, educators, and concerned citizens recognize the critical relationship between emotional pain that causes distress, self-deception, and patterns of destructive behavior, we can begin helping adolescents to recognize and avoid the dangers associated with EDH. Feelings contain energy. Held back and hidden, this energy must go somewhere. EDH defenses and pretenses are guardians of our fear. They trap emotional energy and prevent its healthy passage through us. EDH converts angst into anger, and pain into punishment.

Ignoring what we fear

It is human to ignore that which we fear. Painful feelings become dark secrets we dare not disturb. Not only do we ignore them, but we lie about the fact that we ignore them. This is why it is so difficult to be emotionally honest. To become emotionally honest we must first admit that we are fearful of our emotional truth. This self-disclosure is tinged with the shame of admitting that we have been a fake or fraud. We tend to hide painful feelings and then fear acknowledging them, for to do so reveals that we are deceitful. Shakespeare's allusion to life being an act may relate more to EDH *within us* than the way we deceive *others*. Emotional dishonesty is the lie everybody knows, but fears to admit.

When someone says or otherwise conveys that their feelings are hurt by an experience, we may wonder in disbelief how they could be so deeply injured by a passing criticism, rejection or failure. We may react by thinking, "What's the big deal?" Yet when our own feelings are hurt, our experience of emotional pain *is* a big deal, even if we cannot admit it. Why do we tend to trivialize or ignore the significance of hurt feelings others have, and then secretly guard against disclosing our own vulnerability? It is our shame about being self-deceptive. New York psychiatrist and Columbia University medical school professor Willard Gaylin offers a reason in his 1979 book, *Feelings-Our Vital Signs*:

> Given the central importance of feelings in our everyday life, you would think that psychological and psychoanalytical literature would be dominated by them . . .. Perhaps feelings are too close to our vulnerable core to allow for comfortable evaluation. Perhaps it is simply that in a technological society, which values the measurable, the visible, the palpable, and the objectifiable, feelings embarrass us by defying our most respected current tools of investigation.

The subjective, illusive and shameful nature of hurt feelings keeps this topic a mysterious element of human nature. This is one reason why in our search for ways of preventing school violence, the influence of hurt feelings is rarely given importance. As little as we understand how our car works, it is more knowledge than most of us have about our inner reactions to emotional wounding experiences. We can measure and develop standards for behavior, but feelings are seen as a personal, private, mushy concept. For example, millions of high school students are taunted, rejected or ostracized by their peers. Why is it that two such teens in Littleton needed to express their emotional pain with such extreme, violent revenge? Dr. Gaylin explains that feelings have not been analyzed for they are not part of the scientific tradition. He reasons that psychiatrists and medical researchers historically have ignored emotions as a subject for serious study because behavioral research is based on animals, which do not share the same feeling system as humans. His book of 20 years ago concludes with a call to action that has been largely ignored: "We have neglected feelings and have failed to grasp the value of their directives. It is time to change."

II. Can We Die From Hurt Feelings?

The U.S. Department of Justice reports that from 1987 to 1991 the number of teenagers arrested for murder increased 85%. Today, one of every five violent crime victims are 10-17-year-olds. Nearly one million young people aged 12-19 are raped, robbed, or assaulted annually, often by their peers. I would argue that in Littleton Colorado, as well as in hundreds of thousands of violent households, and among the tens of thousands of Americans who annually commit suicide, people *do* die from being overwhelmed by their hurt feelings. It is dangerous to feel helpless and incapable of escaping our emotional pain. The common expression, "I felt I could have died, when he said (or did) . . ." tells us that we consider painful wounded feelings a threat to our survival – physically and emotionally. Writing about her only child's suicide, Karen

Theobald, a mental health and social services worker in Marin County, says "Suicide victims do not wish to end their lives but, rather, *they wish to end their overwhelming pain.*" The suicide prevention authority reports that on average there are 16 attempts for every completed suicide.

The threat posed by having our feelings hurt is that we feel endangered. *Emotional distress is a response to being in danger.* The mechanism for this sense of endangerment is explained in Chapter Five. Dr. Gaylin explains that feelings are a neglected topic in our society because they reveal our *vulnerable core.* The compelling need in our society to try and hide or ignore our emotional wounds indicates that we consider ourselves in danger of being an unacceptable person when we feel hurt. It is as though we have some deep and instinctive anxiety that emotional pain can overwhelm and possibly devastate us.

Given the perilous anxiety that accompanies deep emotional wounds, it is no wonder that these self-deceiving aspects of EDH are so prevalent:

1. We tend to ignore discussing the subject.
2. We tend to lie to ourselves to disguise what we are really feeling.
3. We tend to lie to others to cover up painful and shameful feelings.

EDH is disabling in several ways. We not only lack an understanding of what we are feeling, we lack the social freedom that would allow us to openly discuss with others or truthfully acknowledge the troubling inner effects of being hurt. As a result many people secretly suffer from an inability to heal their painful feelings which they can't acknowledge or accept. As buried pain grows with each additional wound, one way of expressing and temporarily relieving emotional agony is through destructive behavior. We try to deal with our punishing pain *indirectly* by trying to punish others or ourselves for being in pain. Typically this results in harmful acts toward others or ourselves.

Whenever we're emotionally injured and unable to acknowledge and heal our hurt, two types of inner reactions distort our pain. Either may result in destructive behavior:

1. **Self-demeaning shamefulness.** Like a prosecuting attorney we may consider each emotional wound as evidence of our being an unacceptable or unlovable person. We may secretly fear we deserve the punishment and our hurt feelings. Being wounded may lead to outrage that we are powerless to escape from our painful unworthiness. Since we cannot *make* others like or accept us, we silently suffer from the shameful "curse" of being unacceptable and unlovable.

One way we attempt to overcome the paralyzing effects of this curse is to *focus destructive acts upon ourselves to give us a sense of "control" over our pain.* In his 1998 book, *Cutting*, New York psychotherapist Steven Levenkron, who works primarily with women who self-injure, states that:

> The self-mutilator is someone who has found that physical pain can be a cure for emotional pain. It is someone who . . .has absolutely no outlet for her pain and therefore no relief from it. All she has is that short period of time when it is temporarily overpowered, "drowned out," by [self-inflicted] physical pain.

Levenkron says self-injuring behavior patterns usually surface during puberty, when the young person has not yet "acquired the language of emotional expression" to relate to others. Self-destructive people are so "lacking the words with which to express emotional pain, they resort to a destructive physical dialogue with themself." He calls self-mutilation an act of emotional desperation.

When we become incapable of "controlling" our real emotional pain, we act out our sense of powerlessness in ritualistic, disguised behavior patterns. These patterns of emotional deception are most commonly *self-destructive* – chronic depression and withdrawal, victimhood, substance abuse, eating disorders, suicidal thoughts or acts, and a myriad of compulsive disorders. Self-destructive acts seek to disguise or numb the shameful sense of being a weak or flawed person. Levenkron describes the self-injurer and anorexic as characteristically plagued by a fear they are being punished for being deficient, inadequate and a disappointment. In addition they have no one they can trust with these shameful feelings. Tragically, self-destructive behavior patterns only temporarily assuage emotional distress. That's why we must keep on drinking, drugging or abusing ourselves.

Clinical psychologist Michael Nichols in *No Place To Hide* (Appendix IV) explains that "Shame is the inner experience of being looked down upon by others; a painful feeling of unworthiness . . .a deep conviction that one is fundamentally bad, unworthy, inadequate, defective, and, ultimately, unlovable . . .Shame makes us want to hide." Depression is the most common form of this emotional withdrawal to hide shameful, hurt feelings.

2. **Revenge for our pain.** Another way of dealing with emotional pain is to blame others for what we feel. But, by projecting our pain as coming from others we also give others power over our feelings. Vulnerability, our susceptibility to being hurt, is seen as a sign of weakness and a character flaw. Aggressively seeking violent revenge against a "hostile world," is an attempt to disown the vulnerability considered to be a "weakness." The need for revenge takes many forms, ranging from being hypercritical to verbal abuse and physical violence. Since the pain that we blame others for resides within us, no amount of aggressive behavior toward others can stop our suffering. The danger of revenge is intensified particularly today with the easy availability of guns and the entertainment media's glorification of violence as a way to resolve conflict. EDH and defenses are often used in an attempt to relieve us of burdensome painful feelings by transforming our inner shame into outward blame and anger. Rather than continue to suffer agoniz-

ing shame for being "flawed and unworthy" when we're wounded, we seek to punish others for our pain. This sense of "being wronged" means we have a right to angry and hostile behavior ranging from hypercriticism of others to violence.

We use self-deception to transform shameful hurt into blame and then take retribution against those "who make us feel bad." Unhealed pain fuels vengeance, whether by adults seeking revenge against fellow employees or managers who are seen as the direct cause of their pain resulting from being fired or laid off, or by emotionally wounded teens seeking revenge against peers whose taunts and name-calling make them feel rejected and unworthy.

III. Self-Deception Prevents Healing Our Hurt

Feelings are easy to hide because only we know what we truly feel. Hiding our true feelings about being hurt is simple to do and often escapes self-detection. It is also quite easy to be "taken in" and fool ourselves about what we really feel. If we say to ourselves that we don't feel what we really do, or that we feel something we really do not, who is to argue with us about which feeling is true?

Posturing and pretense involves ignoring what we don't want to feel. Hurt feelings signal that we are endangered, and so we protect ourselves from these threats by erecting emotional defenses. We not only develop skill at lying about our feelings as we experience them, we become adept at erecting protective barriers to ensure that future threats to our emotional security and safety do not get through our defense system.

Being emotionally vulnerable is an inevitable part of being human. We all experience hurt feelings and at times feel emotionally overwhelmed. But EDH convinces us that we're not hurt when, in reality, we are deeply threatened by the many, accumulated wounds of loss, rejection, betrayal and humiliation. To support this self-deception, there is an implicit social code of silence that it's okay to deny what really hurts. No one wants to call our bluff because everyone is bluffing. Keeping our real feelings private and secret is such common practice that fooling ourselves about what we feel has become an ingrained cultural trait. *It's so easy to keep our real feelings secret, even to ourselves, that we may not realize the potential harm this practice poses to ourselves and others.*

EDH surrounds us, starting with parents who may have hidden their hurt feelings from themselves and us. Do busy and harried parents really want to know what their children feel inside when they feel bad or hurt? Parents are inclined to encourage children to "get over it," consider their hurt "just a little thing," and try to cheer them up. Adults typically try to help their children cover up sadness and pain rather than teaching them to honor it as a normal part of themselves. Later in life, at work and in social interactions, having learned to disguise real feelings when they vary from socially acceptable norms, we become addicted to emotional deception. By deceiving ourselves about the source and significance of emotional pain, we allow lies to keep us from accepting, owning and healing our hurt. This is how EDH keeps us trapped in distress. Chapter Four explores the widespread cultural influences that shape and reinforce EDH.

Disavowing our emotional rights

When accumulated pain from emotional wounds becomes overwhelming, a common way of seeking relief is to throw an inner switch to disengage our feelings. The Columbine High School killers and other perpetrators of violent crimes appear to disconnect from their own pain by inflicting it upon innocent victims. This same description fits many adults who indiscriminately kill or wound others. Self-injuring persons who seek relief from emotional pain through destructive acts also appear to be cut off from their painful feelings. It's as though an autopilot takes over during intense emotional distress. The problem with disavowing our hurt feelings, however, is that we become fearful of turning back on hurt or any other deep feelings.

In his 1994 book, *Beyond Pain*, Jeffrey Kottler discusses the fear of dropping defenses and confronting our pain: "Pain keeps you in line, stops you from trying anything new. It is like having a bad back that sends out excruciating bolts of fire every time you move . . .It is unlikely that you will voluntarily move from that position unless you absolutely have to." *We lose the recuperative power to bounce back from disappointment and loss once we disavow our emotional right to feel.* EDH, the pretenses and defenses that "protect" us by denying our painful feelings when emotionally wounded, only accumulates hurt. As painful experiences mount, so does our fear of acknowledging and attending to the wounds. We carry the scars of our emotional injuries, but learn to separate the painful feelings associated with them.

There is nothing inherently "wrong" with being emotionally dishonest except that the pain we ignore doesn't go away. Labeling some feelings "bad" can make good people do bad things to themselves and others. It is not the hiding of hurt feelings that perpetuates emotional distress, it's disguising the fact that we've hidden them. The irony of people not being emotionally honest is that their painful feelings won't kill them, but their emotional self-deception may. The emotional *unknown* always seems more threatening than its *reality.* Like the small child afraid of some unexpected noise in a dark room, we are fearful of what we may find if we turn on the lights and reveal feelings we have kept secret. It is less frightening to don the mask of anger, lash out at others, and disguise our pain, rather than illuminate our hurt feelings. This is why we find it difficult to identify and name what truly hurts inside us.

Another danger of living with unacknowledged painful feelings is the possibility that ongoing emotional distress can cause *physical* distress. Not only are psychosomatic illnesses attributed to unhealed emotional pain, but EDH can have serious effects on our physical system. Antoinette Saunders, a child psychologist and former University of Illinois professor, writes in her book, *The Stress Proof Child* (Appendix IV) that "passive emotional states" of unconscious stress can cause chronic secretion of cortisol, which undermines the immune system's ability to resist arthritis, cancer and infectious diseases. Dr. Armand M. Nicholi, Jr., Harvard Medical School researcher of teenage drug use, states that "Childrearing practices [over the last 30-years] have produced angry and depressed children with limited resources and less tolerance to cope with stress." A Johns Hopkins University medical study found that emotionally healthy persons experience the same stress, but have less severe reactions than others, and were therefore able to let go of it sooner.

We become emotionally dishonest as a way of coping with pain and surviving our worst fear – that we suffer *because* we are an unlovable or unacceptable person. To the insecure adolescent, emotional wounds may seem like fatal wounds. EDH can further turns a normal loss into a catastrophe. It's as though we have lost some part of us forever. Indeed, we have lost something important, our freedom to feel.

The U.S. teen suicide rate has tripled since the 1960's. The Befrienders youth suicide prevention web site (www.jaring.my/befrienders/youth1.html) states:

> Tragically, many young people feel they are not able to cope, that there is no one who either cares enough or is able to help them to cope...New overwhelming feelings may seem threatening . . .Many suicidal youths experience family troubles which lead them to doubt their self worth and make them [feel] unwanted and unloved.

In his book, *The Language of Feelings* (Appendix IV), the late David Viscott saw, "The modern world driving many of us crazy" because we have lost our emotional survival skills. He said this results in a perpetual sense of anxiety. We fear we will lose our safety and security by revealing true feelings. Rather than admitting feeling frightened and vulnerable, we deny this anxiety. Viscott believed that we're beginning to lose our sense of ourselves. In his book *Emotional Resilience* (Appendix IV), Viscott views EDH as being perpetuated by a fear of losing control of ourself were we to acknowledge our emotional pain. He sees that "our need to get along in the world" weakens our courage to take responsibility for our feelings. We lose track of what we really feel by substituting how we're supposed to feel. "You can't live your best life telling lies – especially to yourself," he warned.

CHAPTER 3

Seven Important Qualities of Feelings

Our feelings define reality for us more directly and more
completely than anything else.
– David Viscott, *The Language of Feelings* (1976)

The human feeling process defies precise description because emotional states are subjective by nature. Though feelings may be fleeting emotional responses to our experiences, they do leave a deep imprint. This imprint, which can affect our self-acceptance, is easily misread or misinterpreted. We may learn to ascribe values – good or bad – to what we feel. The simple act of identifying what we feel when we feel it is endlessly complicated because we have self-protective reasons for not wanting to know. The denial of our emotional truth occurs most often when our true feelings are clouded by fear or shame. Painful feelings pose a danger or threat to our safety and security. When our feelings are hurt, the pain triggers an instinctive "fight or flight" reflex to danger. Instinctively, what we fear we avoid. We fear being emotionally wounded because the injury reminds us of how vulnerable we are. Something as common as having painful feelings can seem like a threat to our emotional survival. No wonder its so difficult to recognize our emotional truth.

In his 1998 book, *Fear Itself*, Rush Dozier, Jr. states, "Painful emotional memories are much clearer than memories of physical pain. The memory of even a minor humiliating incident decades before may still make you squirm and blush." He points out that feelings play an important role in our ability to remember. He says that we particularly "remember only those things that we feel something about." Despite their illusive and subjective quality, feelings influence us far more than we are willing to acknowledge because they are inner reactions to our most important experiences.

Our feelings tell the truth of who we are, what we love *and* what we fear. Dozier states that "No other species has the enormous breadth of fears as human beings, and no other species goes to such lengths to suppress them."

By examining our responses to wounding experiences, we may be able to disentangle our fears from what we truly feel. Hurt feelings that trigger protective pretenses prevent us from being honest about experiences that cause us pain. Our EDH defends against being vulnerable. Were we able to see beneath the facade of indifference that we have learned to erect when wounded, we would then see our fears or shame. We could also recognize the elaborate, disguised behavior that results from the EDH pretense that painful, emotional wounds don't hurt. Following are key qualities of feelings that adults and parents need to recognize in order to help themselves and their children avoid EDH:

Seven important qualities or attributes of feelings
- Feelings are different from behavior, thoughts or beliefs.
- Feelings are part of who we are.
- We are responsible for our feelings.
- Feelings change, but they are real in the moment we have them.
- Honest feelings are spontaneous and occur without.
- Feelings cannot be removed or replaced.
- Feelings are both/and, not either/or.

I. Feelings Are Different from Behavior, Thoughts or Beliefs.
Feelings are often confused with behavior, thoughts, beliefs or values. In particular, children have difficulty distinguishing between being punished or disciplined for what they feel inside (e.g., hurt)

or for their behavior (e.g., screaming or throwing a tantrum). As we mature, we may associate certain feelings parents considered unacceptable as being "shameful," even though that may not have been what our parents intended.

Parents can learn, teach and model for children the important distinctions between feelings and acts, thoughts and beliefs. Teaching a child right from wrong, good from bad, acceptable from unacceptable *behavior* is a basic parental role. However, intentionally or not, when discipline implies the child's feelings are unacceptable, the *child* may feel also feel unacceptable whenever feeling sad or hurt. This is the double jeopardy of EDH. We feel bad just for feeling hurt. If, for example, the goal is to stop a frustrated child from throwing a tantrum, and not exact punishment for the feeling itself, parents need to acknowledge and honor a child's underlying emotional states even if the resulting behavior is not allowable. "I know you must feel frustrated and upset that you can't go out and play now, but . . ." a savvy parent says to simultaneously reassure their children that their feelings are honored, even though their behavior is not appropriate.

When we make a suggestion at work or school that's rejected by an authority figure or group, we may be incapable of distinguishing between our idea being rejected or our not being good enough. Our behavior or ideas may not be as appropriate or as meritorious as those coming from others, but our *self-acceptability* can be threatened when we or others ignore or dishonor our underlying disappointment. An honoring response would be: "I can understand that you may feel bad about your proposal not being selected, Mary, but you should know how much I value your desire to contribute to our effort." What we think, say or do may not always find favor and acceptance, but underlying *feelings* about our acceptability as a person should not be confused with what we think or do.

The famous *Playboy* magazine interview in which President Jimmy Carter admitted to "lusting in his heart" created a sensation when the world leader and deeply religious Baptist confessed that while he remained faithful to his wife, there were times when he had lustful desires for other women. The publication of President Carter's disclosure was undoubtedly upsetting to some fundamentalists whose beliefs warn against "impure or sinful" feelings or thoughts as well as actions.

An emotionally healthy person can make distinctions between his thoughts, behavior and feelings. While morality in behavior is critical for being a civilized society, judging *feelings* leads to a culture of distrusting and censoring emotional experiences. If we learn to judge and filter our feelings based on whether they're right or wrong, we're destined to become emotionally confused and dishonest.

II. Feelings Are Part of Who We Are

We are our feelings. We can determinedly deny that we aren't feeling hurt, particularly when we've learned from parents or others that it's socially "unacceptable" and embarrassing to show our vulnerability. But these feelings remain part of us. Our feelings are an important way of setting us apart as a unique person. To be self-accepting even our most painful feelings must be owned as part of us. If children observe parents denying their feelings, or if Mom or Dad are unable to express their love or hurt, children will tend to deny and distrust those same feelings within themselves. If parents are unable to acknowledge their hurt, covering their pain with anger or depression, it will be difficult for the children to accept, honor and heal their own hurt. We can't "unfeel" a feeling once we've experienced it, even if we pretend it isn't real. We may wish we weren't wounded by a cutting remark, but the fact is that we are. We may pretend to not be affected by a disappointing athletic performance in front of friends, but we truly feel devastated and humiliated. Since feelings can shift with lightning speed, it's easy to become confused by trying to decide which, in a sequence of feelings, is real. All of our feelings are real. Only our pretense about them is false.

Being uncertain or having difficulty identifying, accepting and owning what we feel is a tip-off that we are engaging in one of the most common emotionally dishonest practices – judging rather than accepting what we feel. I recall a cartoon of a beaming patron smiling up at the bartender. The bartender asked this regular customer why he was so elated. "I just came back from seeing my psychiatrist and he told me I'm happy!" he replied. Only we can know whether the love we feel toward another or hurt from the loss of a friend is real. This is why it's so easy to deceive ourselves about our feelings.

Feelings can be dark secrets held at a distance we dare not tell anyone. Or we can choose to embrace them as an honored part of us. This choice is often the most difficult and courageous part of therapy for those who are habitually emotionally self-deceptive and dishonest. Hurt that remains bound within us, never accepted or healed, will deepen with each new emotionally wounding experiences of losses, rejection, betrayal or humiliation. When we've been conditioned to ignore or pretend that our hurt doesn't exist, we betray ourselves and our feelings.

III. We Are Responsible For Our Feelings

We may try to disown painful feelings by blaming others. Many individuals live as if *their* feelings were *someone else's fault.* Emotions are *our* responses to experience that come from inside us, not from outside. We are not necessarily responsible for having an experience that emotionally injures us, but we are responsible for the resulting inner reaction to that injury, which most often is feeling hurt. When we are emotionally wounded, it is natural to blame others whose words or action resulted in our feeling pain. For many, the only ways for expressing emotional pain are through disrespect, anger, criticism and revenge toward others. *Giving over power and responsibility to others for what we feel, however, means abdicating our responsibility for our own feelings. To achieve self-acceptance, we must recognize that no matter what another person does that may wound us, healing the resulting hurt is our work and responsibility.* If we have the ability to feel and accept our hurt, we can hear its truth and recover from it without distorting its meaning.

Just as we're responsible for our own feelings, others are responsible for their emotional responses, too. When parents blames their child for "making me sad" by what the children do or say, or "not making me happy" because of the children's *failure* to do or say what the parent desires, children are held responsible for the parents' feelings. Children assume a burden of guilt from being given power over their parents' joy or sorrow. This experience may transfer to their parenting style when they become adults. When such guilt-ridden children become parents, they will likely hold their children responsible for the parent's feelings, too. The one hope for breaking this unhealthy chain is for all family members to learn how to take responsibility for their own feelings. We can never be accountable for anyone's feelings other than our own. As adults, we can renounce this practice of holding innocent children responsible for our feelings and break the chain of EDH that otherwise may go on generation after generation.

IV. Feelings Change

In his 1996 book, *The Art of Forgiving*, Lewis Smedes says that because feeling states can change suddenly, emotions are difficult to understand: "Feelings are sometimes hard things to name. Feelings flow in and out of each other like vapors, and they get mixed up and blended even as we feel them. They are mushy, difficult, non-palpable, slippery things. But we need to name our pain in order to forgive someone for it." Feelings are often quixotic, conflicting and evasive. To complicate matters, during a short period we may experience a wide range of opposing feelings. During a good two-hour movie, we may be moved back and forth between tears and laughter many times. Those who habitually censor or question the legitimacy of their feelings are commonly confused by love/hate opposing feelings toward those with whom they have a close relationship. We are often confused by rapidly changing feelings. Children, and particularly adolescents, are frequently perplexed by having loving feelings toward a sibling or parent one day, then the next day becoming upset and lashing out in anger against them.

Yet, each feeling is real and true at the time we feel it. There is no rule that says we must be consistent in what we feel from moment to moment. One morning we may feel the warmth of love toward our parent, and later the same day be hurt by something they did and feel resentment toward them. A student may "ace" a math class test in first period, only to be confronted in the next class with a barely passing grade on an English paper. Emotional responses to our experiences can shift from elation to depression in a matter of seconds. Emotional *dis*honesty involves becoming so protective and guarded about spontaneously revealing our feelings that we may show little difference whether we are happy or sad. This "flat" affect is needed to hide the inner confusion about which of several emotional responses we have had over time is the "real," safe, or appropriate one.

V. Honest Feelings are Spontaneous

Feelings are important to our reality because they're tied to our experiences of the moment. Honest feelings happen spontaneously and without intention, thought or control. But emotionally guarded people, who have a rigid censoring and judging process for what they feel, cannot easily let down their defenses to connect with their spontaneous feelings. When we do not acknowledge and heal our hurt feelings as they occur, we accumulate and bury them with secrecy. Each new loss or rejection, however, is not just a new experience, but also connects with past pain from unhealed wounds. For example, sometimes we emotionally "freeze" in painful reaction to an immediate and apparently minor criticism or rejection. We are responding not only to this particular wounding event intruding into our emotional present, but we connect it to memories of other similar, unhealed painful feelings we have buried in the past.

When we relive emotional wounds of the *past*, every *present* setback or failure becomes magnified by old, unattended wounds. When our emotional responses to apparently insignificant wounding experiences seems exaggerated, our reaction should tell us that we have re-opened past wounds that have not been properly attended to. Compounded wounds can seem so overwhelming that we may become overwhelmed with distress from a simple, social slight or comment.

We all know people who seem to carry grudges over small incidents. For them, often the smallest wounding events open painful self-acceptance issues they are ashamed and fearful to recognize. For example, the tragic murder-suicide in Nashua, New Hampshire, in October 1999 was explained in 21-year-old killer Liam Youens' on-line journal. He recounted one humiliating day in his high school lunchroom when his victim, a former female classmate, ignored and brushed past him. If such individuals were able to openly and honestly deal with each painful rejection or humiliating experience as it happened, they might accumulate less emotional pain which they need to avenge. *Learning to accept, honor and then release our painful feelings as they occur is an essential capability for maintaining resilience and emotional health.*

Anxiety is fear of some future, harmful experience. Anxiety keeps us on edge trying to anticipate what may happen so we can plan how we should react or feel if it does. When our emotional radar is tuned to the far horizon, we are unable to honor and accept our immediate feelings. Blaming others for painful feelings we experience prevents us from taking responsibility for what we feel and honestly dealing with it as it occurs. Living emotionally in the past or future also drains emotional energy from the present. It takes substantial effort to guard against reopening old wounds while also worrying about possible new ones. Lack of insight about what we really feel when we suffer emotional wounds allows them to be combined with past painful experiences, and further intensified with fear of even more hurt. This compounding of fear of past pain with anxiety over future pain severely restricts our emotional spontaneity in the present.

Actors can simulate feelings that are required by the character they are playing. Their skill at pretense allows them to portray what the character *should* be feeling. All of this is calculated role-playing. The same posturing also occurs when we defer emotional responses to wounding events. The delay is needed because we need time and distance from the immediate wounding event to construct a defense and an emotional pretense that denies its impact upon us. Real feelings occur without intention or control. *When we sense our intellect deciding what we should or should not feel, it is a tip-off that our defenses and EDH are engaged.*

In battle, military personnel are known to suffer from delayed, post-traumatic stress syndrome in which they experience their original fear and anxiety long after the actual battle. Without this emotional defense, warriors would be unable to overcome their instinctive fear of injury or dying. By delaying or deferring their response, soldiers are able to take risks and heroic measures required during battles. The problem is that the subsequent, accumulated distress may be severely disabling. Civilians may also delay their deep distress to wounding events by deploying emotional defenses to mask their vulnerability. We commonly use this strategy of self-deception to avoid being crushed by rejection, for example. Our submerged emotional distress, however, may remain long afterwards to haunt us.

Additionally, those who can't respond with emotional honesty in real time, may become dispassionate and removed from all of their spontaneous feelings. *This is how EDH jeopardize s our capability for emotional intimacy.*

VI. Feelings Cannot be Removed or Replaced

Whether we acknowledge them or not, feelings are our real experiences. Though we may try, they cannot be obliterated or replaced. Defenses may *appear* to give us the power to remove a feeling that makes us vulnerable, unacceptable, or embarrassed by obscuring or replacing our initial emotional response with one we have learned to consider more "acceptable." When children's feelings hurt they feel pain. But they may have been conditioned by parents to bravely hold back any spontaneous response (i.e., crying) when experiencing emotional pain. Later, as adults, they come to believe that they can deny any feeling by pretending. The danger is that the dismissed pain of the present is stored in the dungeon of dark denial where all our other unattended painful emotional experiences reside. Children conditioned in this manner stockpile unhealed pain that may later result in behavior that punishes themselves, siblings, playmates and peers, and even pets to relieve their accumulated anguish. Anger or depression often disguise the real pain that we mistakenly believe has been obliterated. *In this manner, the real feelings stay shamefully hidden within us, and continue to haunt us throughout life.*

By the time we have become adults, our self-deception about feelings has reached a highly sophisticated (and often unaware) level. We've honed the skill of behaving one way and feeling another until it becomes automatic. We avoid pain by not only denying when we feel hurt, but by denying feelings of vulnerability altogether. Alcohol, prescription medicine, or other drugs are commonly used to numb those feelings we're incapable of accepting.

VII. Feelings Are Both/And, Not Either/Or

We can both love our children and sometimes dislike their behavior. We can both love our parents or partners but also disapprove of the way they sometimes treat us. Having "mixed feelings" at any one time about someone or some group is normal. Close relationships particularly create this type of emotional confusion. We may mistakenly feel compelled to choose among conflicting feelings to settle on one or the other as being true. When it comes to emotional honesty, for good or ill, we are the judge and jury when it comes to denying or accepting our feelings. *When we sense having conflicting feelings, we routinely feel a need to reject one feeling in order to accept the other.* However, when we can accept each feeling *in the moment we have it*, there is no need to choose between "which feeling is right." It is being emotionally honest to recognize that differing or opposing feelings are *both* right or true because both are our genuine responses.

Teen behavior is often erratic because so are their feelings.

Adolescents, for example, are often distraught by their conflicting feelings about parents. They need and depend upon parents for safety, security and support; yet they also have a rebellious urge to to separate from parents and become independent. Part of the distressing emotional turmoil of adolescence is feeling compelled to "sort out" real feelings from supposedly false ones – an impossible task that leads to uncertainty, EDH and self-deception. Adolescents, being at a particularly emotionally insecure period of life, are often confused and distressed by their "mixed feelings."

Ambivalence is a natural state of emotional confusion we have about our feelings toward any person who is important to us, holds power over us, or has our trust – such as a supervisor, teacher, mentor, lover or parent. When we feel wounded or betrayed by a powerful, loved or trusted person, our mixed or conflicting feelings can be terribly distressing – and because of this remain held in secrecy.

Managerial psychologist and professor Harold Leavitt uses the example of a classic story of ambivalence to help students understand conflicting feelings. The story involves a paralyzed man whose every need must be met by his devoted brother. One day, before going out for a two-hour appointment, his brother seated the paralyzed man in a chair next to the window that was raised to let in the fresh fall air. Soon after his brother left the house, a rapidly developing cold front blew cold wind and rain through the window, chilling the helpless invalid. One hour went by, then another, as the helpless man grew more wet and cold. His brother was late. Finally, an hour-and-a-half after he was expected, the brother arrived, apologizing for being late because of traffic. The question professor Leavitt asks is this: If you were this paralyzed man, what would you feel and how would you behave toward your brother at that moment?

Accepting our feelings is not a true-false test!
One feeling doesn't cancel another. One feeling doesn't have to be wrong for the other to be right. *It just seems that way.* The

rigid valuing (judgmental) habits we probably learned in child-hood do not apply to feelings! Feelings are neither good nor bad. They are just a part of us, our natural response to life experiences. When we are able to accept apparently opposite feelings about the same person and gather the courage to risk being emotionally hon-est about them, we can say after an upsetting incident:

> When you didn't pay any attention or honor how hurt I felt when you ignored me, I got angry at you and stopped loving you. But I also realize how much love I have for you. Despite feeling ignored, misunderstood, and rejected by you, I also realize how much I need and care about you.

When we fully accept our feelings, we can stop blaming others for them. Yes, we feel hurt when a loved one is not there for us, or fails to live up to our expectations of what we need. But these are *our own* feelings. We are *entitled* to them. Emotional honesty is recog-nizing and owning painful feelings, just as we know that we have a loving and caring connection to another person. When we select from our array of feelings, keeping some and discarding others, we betray one feeling for the other. *Betraying any feeling by rejecting or censoring them is rejecting ourself.* It is the price we must pay for EDH. This betrayal of self keeps us from feeling complete and secure. We do have choices: not over which feeling to accept or reject, but rather choosing to risk the courage of being emotion-ally honest or retreating behind the apparent "safety" of our emo-tional defenses and self-deception.

We may feel hurt and wounded by a rejection at work, for example, but have learned that it is not safe, professional or ac-ceptable to express our real pain in the work environment. Playing "office politics" and trying to dismiss feelings creates an undercur-rent of stress that leads to unnecessary tension in the workplace. Parents, in their desire to teach children how to get along in the world, may unwittingly create rules about acceptable and unac-ceptable feelings. Boys are culturally conditioned to not weep when they are hurt, because "big boys don't cry". Later in life when adult males feel emotional pain, they may react in anger for they have learned that anger is their real feeling, and anguish is false. In this manner, the denial and devaluing of one feeling for another leads to ignoring that their real pain *is* painful.

Adolescents always seem to be engaging in some pretense or another because of insecurity about their identity, status, and acceptability. When hurt by the actions of their parents, they become confused by their emotional reactions. Their pain/anger competes with a simultaneous love/dependence need of parents for approval and acceptance. Teens, in particular, may *feel compelled to choose* between opposing feelings and invalidate one or the other, even though it is unnecessary to do so. A student may feel sad about her teammate's illness, for example, yet be excited about the opportunity to take her place in the debate contest. Here she is wracked with conflicted guilt for both feelings: being happy that she has an opportunity to be in the spotlight; and also worrying about not feeling sorry enough for her friend losing her place on the team. Trying to decide which feeling is "true" and which is "false" *is* a false test.

These are the types of conflicts that Shakespeare so brilliantly used to illustrate the inner tension that tests the human spirit. It's not easy to completely trust our feelings because we humans have such elusive and complex emotional reactions to our experiences.

CHAPTER 4

The American Way Of
Denying Hurt Feelings

I. Escape from Emotional Reality

*We have more words to describe the nuances of how we
deceive each other than how we love.*

–Harriet Lerner, *The Dance of Deception* (1993)

We can best understand why there is such avoidance of dealing
with emotional pain in our society by examining our cultural attitudes about physical pain. In her revealing feature article about
American attitudes toward pain, St. Louis *Riverfront Times* feature
writer Jeannette Batz describes a socially-approved pattern to in-
stantly anesthetize pain, which leaves many of us living in a perpetual state of physical and emotional numbness. She reports:

> Americans see no value in pain, flaws, idiosyncrasies or suf-
> fering. We're terrified of pain because we doubt our ability
> to handle it . . . Hence Ivan Ilich's claim that high-tech
> Western medicine "saps the will of people to suffer their
> reality." (*Pacific Sun*, April 7-13, 1999)

We tend to experience emotional pain as not only threatening, but
shameful. This is why we spend so much time, money and effort

trying to escape from our emotional reality. We have become masters at masking our emotional wounds. Why should we acknowledge, own, and try to heal emotional pain when we can fool ourselves that it doesn't exist, blame it on others, or disguise it with a pill, anger or alcohol?

Pretense about what we really feel has been elevated to an art form. "Faking it" is a national pastime. The annual Academy Awards television broadcast is one of the most watched programs in America. We are fascinated with actors and entertainers whom we admire for their skill of pretending to feel differently than they really do. The charade of make-believe feelings has become an established hallmark of our politics, business and advertising. In admiring tones, political commentators spoke somewhat enviously of President Clinton's uncanny ability to "compartmentalize" his involvement in the sex scandal and impeachment proceedings while he coolly went about the business of running the country and directing a multilateral peace-keeping military action in Yugoslavia. Psychologist Harriet Goldhor Lerner, in *The Dance of Deception: Pretending and Truth-Telling in Women's Lives* (see Appendix IV.), appropriately asks: "Does the epidemic of lying, duplicity, and concealment on the part of 'honorable men'– the leaders of our country – make it easier for us to rationalize our own private departures from the truth?"

Emotional dishonesty (EDH) and denying that we are in emotional pain has virtually become a requirement for success in America. Following the ubiquitous office politics skirmishes, wounded employees quickly learn to play the game of hiding their hurt feelings if they want to get ahead.

Emotional play-acting is such a common occurrence in modern relationships that couples learn to co-exist in a make-believe world where being "careful" (i.e., guarding feelings) has replaced emotional honesty and intimacy between partners. Lest we believe this problem lies primarily with men, in *The Dance of Deception* Harriet Lerner focuses on EDH issues confronting her sex:

> Because of the enormous capacity for self-deception, we
> may fail to recognize when we are lying, or when we are not
> living authentically and truly...We can be no more honest
> with others than we are with our self . . .Pretending is so
> closely associated with "femininity" that it is, quite simply,
> what the culture teaches women to do.

Men and women are fearful of opening up and acknowledging feelings they have worked so hard to suppress. And so, honesty in relationships and at work is not only becoming more difficult, as a practical matter it is out of the question.

We learn to escape from emotional reality at an early age. Children love to masquerade and have a natural ability for being convincing actors. Their first stories are fairy tales that feature the wily fox, the cunning villain, and the beguiling heroine. We are raised from childhood with examples of deception and then immersed in television, movies and other entertainment saturated with the art of deception and pretense. *A youngster's first role models outside the family are likely to be actors and other performers.* By the time children reach adolescence, they've observed and admired so much acting that they are experts – masters at fooling themselves about their feelings and particularly accomplished at building defenses to deny their pain. Emotional defenses are pretenses that tell us we don't hurt when we really do, often disguising our pain with depression or other self-destructive behavior.

As previously mentioned, it is easy to be confused and lose the ability to distinguish between real and imagined feelings. Too often we see our emotional wounds not as *our* feelings but as "someone else's fault," or a shameful flaw or weakness too embarrassing to disclose. We may "put on a good face" that we are not hurt or emotionally vulnerable. But in the end, we can't escape from the fact that part of being human is being vulnerable and having hurt feelings.

It is far easier to deceive ourselves than to fool others. Unfortunately, we now routinely expect people to lie about their feelings and reason "so why shouldn't I?" EDH is tolerated and condoned in our society precisely because "everybody does it." We fear being seen as a troublemaker by questioning someone's emotional duplicity. And we carry on this masquerade without recognizing the dangers associated with EDH. A cultural conspiracy of silence has been created – a permissive environment that allows us to *deny our denial* of painful feelings. *The subject of self-deceit and emotional dishonesty is the secret everyone knows, but few of us feel comfortable disclosing.* Being deceitful about feelings in social relationships has become so ordinary that betrayal of trust is one of the most frequently portrayed issues in stage, screen and soap operas. We can look in the mirror our culture reflects without recognizing our own emotional lies.

The game of deceit is no longer about "if we are lying" about our feelings, but how skillful we are at hiding the pretense. Though we worry about being caught in a lie that misrepresents *facts*, self-deception about what we *feel* is a trick we can continually play on ourself. EDH is our own business, so no one bothers trying to call our bluff. All of this would be of no public concern were it not for the fact that our emotional charade is becoming harmful to us personally and as a society. We are losing the ability to be intimate. We are becoming cynical and unable to trust either *our* feelings or those expressed by others. We become unable to tell when we are pretending or what it is we really feel. When we become victims of EDH, we become so confused that we lose our bearings and cannot find our true feelings. And, worst of all, as author Lerner says, "Secrecy ultimately *compounds* the painful feeling it is meant to deflect."

Emotional deception is the dark secret in every relationship, which is why it is so often the theme in popular drama and literature. One of the most memorable and hilarious examples occurs in the 1995 film, "When Harry Met Sally." During lunch in a busy,

New York restaurant Sally questions her friend Harry's contention that he can't be fooled by a woman faking an orgasm. While seated at the lunch table, Sally publicly demonstrates for her friend, and other startled restaurant patrons, just how easy it is for women to convincingly simulate a climax.

In "The Emperor's New Clothes", 19th-century Danish writer Hans Christian Andersen created a classic folk tale of vanity and self-deception. The fable portrayed how even monarchs and entire communities can become trapped in the web of self-deception. In the tale, swindlers convince the emperor to give them gold, which they promise to weave into the world's finest clothing. They claimed to create material with strands of gold so thin that only the most refined and competent persons could see it. The swindlers hid the gold for themselves and pretended to weave the emperor's magnificent outfit. Court officials, though perplexed by seeing nothing being woven, dutifully made glowing progress reports to the emperor about his emerging gossamer garments. Finally, the weaving was "completed." The duped emperor announced that a town procession would take place to show off his fine garments. Although he paraded naked through the village streets, townsfolk dared not speak for fear of admitting that they were *unable* to see the fine-woven cloth. The deception went unchallenged until one innocent boy viewing the procession came forward shouting, "Look, the emperor has no clothes!"

II. The Unacceptable Self of the Rich and Famous

I hate feeling like I'm unacceptable because of who I really am.
I don't tell anyone the total truth.
–Actor Jack Nicholson during an interview

A celebrity admired by millions may have an abundance of riches, be honored by peers, be surrounded by adoring friends, and yet deep inside remain haunted by an inexpressible fear that somehow he is unacceptable or unlovable. What stains his fame and celebrity status is an inner struggle between his enormous need for love and acceptance and the sense that his past, current, and future emotional pain is a deserved punishment for being unworthy. The unacceptable self does not feel entitled to love and success. Emotional defenses and pretenses are how we avoid confronting our painful wounds. We dare not examine why we hurt, for we fear that we will find we are a flawed and unworthy person who deserves to suffer.

The following examples demonstrate how the pain that the rich and famous avoid acknowledging, like our own, becomes twisted into a shameful undertone of suffering. This suffering is often what fuels the drive and creative energy of highly successful people in the fields of acting and music. Unfortunately, most of us do not have the ability to achieve fame and success through creative efforts that help to compensate for our unacceptable self.

Despite her stardom and status as the world's most sexy woman, Marilyn Monroe failed at successive marriages. Alone and lonely, she killed herself without ever recovering from losses in her early life: She was abandoned by an unknown father; her mother was emotionally disturbed; and she spent much of her childhood in foster homes. Children endure painful losses such as these usually by adopting a veneer of emotional pretense and self-deception. Professional actors and performers often draw talent from years of pretending not to be in torturous emotional pain.

A recent penetrating television biographical tribute to world famous conductor and composer Leonard Bernstein revealed that the influential American composer and musician died under a cloud of self-doubt and despair. Bernstein suffered from painful depression, brought on by feeling he was not good enough to take a place among the world's great *composers*. Beneath his ebullience as a conductor of the world's great symphony orchestras, he was plagued by a sense of unworthiness that no amount of acclaim could undo.

Bernstein was enthralled with the music of Gustav Mahler,

the 19th Century Viennese composer and symphony conductor. He believed it was his destiny to become a composer equal to the stature of Mahler. His final years were filled with despair for never achieving what he most wanted. He died in deep sorrow for never being recognized as a classical *composer*, even though he was recognized as one of the world's most popular conductors. During most of his life, this widely admired musician battled an inner sense of unworthiness by adopting an exuberant conducting style. But inside lurked a sense that all of his success was a sham. He was unable to reveal the hidden emotional pain lying beneath his monumental musical achievements.

Successful actors and public figures are often driven to succeed by a desire to prove their acceptability and lovability by their *performances*. Their act, however, cannot heal the troubling, hidden wounds that are shielded by EDH. *We all tend to guard secret feelings of not being "good enough" for fear of being devastated by acknowledging our emotional pain.* If successful people are plagued by doubt about their acceptability or lovability, imagine the kind of deceptive defenses everyday, average people carry around to protect their inner sense of vulnerability!

This may explain why some actors, athletes, and other public performers feel driven to continue their public roles long after their popularity wanes. Emotional defenses – which seductively lure us into taking on roles that may bring success and acclaim – often stem from an underlying fear of being unacceptable or unlovable. Rather than acknowledge our hurt, it is human nature to protect ourselves from emotional vulnerability. The celebrity's unquenchable thirst for fame typically masks their deepest fear of revealing unspeakable, unhealed inner pain.

> As a writer, I tend to be very analytical. I rationalize things. Or it could just be that when I was growing up I was ridiculed for crying. It was hard for me to contact the sadness.

The above revealing statement comes from best-selling author John Gray, whose most popular book is the relationship guide, *Men are From Mars; Women are From Venus*. Gray's 1984 books, *What You Feel, You Can Heal* (Appendix IV), addresses the topic of healing hurt feelings, and its importance in achieving good relationships.

It's no accident that people whose defenses lead them to be trapped in pretense about their feelings often achieve high levels of public success as accomplished performers or creators of music, literature or theater. The unhealed painful feelings and fear of vulnerability are often given voice through their characters.

Consider the childhood of Stephen Sondheim, acclaimed world renowned musical theater composer and lyricist. His father left the household when Stephen was a child. Such a devastating loss, as we will see in the next chapter, is a form of abandonment which is one of the most painful emotional wounds we can suffer. In a probing biography of the musical genius, *Stephen Sondheim: A Life* (1998), Meryl Secrest interviewed Sondheim's family and childhood friends. They uniformly reported that he acted like any happy child and seemed to lack deep concern nor appear distressed over being abandoned at such a young age. Thinking of himself as a happy child may have been a grand self-deception that enabled him to deny underlying pain that must have haunted him throughout his life. The loss of a parent, through divorce or death is a core wounding experience which threatens a child's inner sense of safety, acceptability and lovability. Denying that wounding experiences such as this are painful tends to disconnect one's other feelings, including the ability to express or accept emotional intimacy. In Secrest's biography, Sondheim's friend, actress Mary Rogers, reveals that he is terrified, not of giving love, but of receiving it.

Sondheim, whose precocious talents were rewarded by skipping 7th and 8th grades, certainly had the creative ability to construct the facade which denied the deep emotional pain from loss of his father. He excelled both in school, and later as an extraordinarily successful Broadway song writer and lyricist. His world-acclaimed musicals include lyrics for *West Side Story* (interestingly, a collaboration with composer Leonard Bernstein), *Gypsy*, *A Funny Thing Happened on the Way to the Forum*, and *Sweeney Todd*.

The most poignant commentary in Meryle Secrest's biography is how the musician and lyricist uses his genius to express his haunting emotional fears and doubts in memorable songs for stage and screen. Secrest writes, "His ability to create a world of his own imaginings saved him when life was at its bleakest. If his themes were somber – the essential loneliness of the human condition and the death of illusion – in the end it was his ability to metamorphose his private anguish into something outside of himself that saved him."

One of his collaborators, composer Arthur Laurents, commented that Sondheim's lyric for *Anyone Can Whistle* (from the 1964 musical of the same name) is a fitting epitaph for the composer. The beautiful and poignant lyric speaks eloquently of his yearning for freedom from pretense. This beautiful and moving song, set in a mental hospital, describes a woman patient *unable to express her inner feelings*.

> Anyone can whistle, that's what they say, easy
> Anyone can whistle, any old day, easy,
> It's all so simple: Relax, let go, let fly!
> So someone tell me why can't I?
> I can dance a tango, I can read Greek, easy
> I can slay a dragon any old week, easy
> What's hard is simple, what's natural comes hard,
> Maybe you could show me how to let go, lower my guard,
>   learn to be free
> Maybe if you whistle, whistle for me.

In his book, *Why Am I Afraid to Tell You Who I Am?* (1969), author John Powell, a Jesuit priest, describes the dilemma of EDH: People "don't want to be a fake – a sham, but fear risking honest self-revelation and thus hide their feelings from themselves and others until it is difficult to tell who is the real self, and which 'me' is a fake".

III. Defenses as Illusions

Hurt by its nature is difficult to deny. Hurt, hurts.

–David Viscott, *The Language of Feelings* (1976)

In the above book, psychiatrist David Viscott (appendix IV.) observed that while "*It hurts to lose something important; it hurts worse to pretend otherwise.*" The most self-damaging aspect of EDH is that to counter an emotional assault we launch a counter-offensive by *pretending our experience of loss has not deeply wounded us.* Rather than acknowledge and accept this pain, the defended person denies it and pretends that the loss is really not painful.

In their 1990 book, *Forgiveness: How to Make Peace With Your Past and Get on With Your Life* (Appendix IV.), Dr. Sidney Simon and Suzanne Simon state that defenses are an attempt to stop the pain when we're hurt. They say that defenses seem "to help you cope with circumstances that you are not prepared to handle, and to protect you from feelings that you fear will overwhelm or destroy you." They explain that defenses are diversionary actions we take when we believe we are not equipped to acknowledge, understand, or do anything constructive about a painful experience. We create diversions in the form of anger or other destructive acts that disguise our pain. If we've been hurt before in same or similar ways, we vow to never again leave ourself open and vulnerable. Defenses become "security forces" needed to ensure the next time we are emotionally wounded it won't hurt as much as before.

The more unbearable and threatening our emotional pain, the more rigid our defenses must be to disguise our suffering. We may be able to overlook physical pain by distraction or denial. But these techniques fail to erase the emotional pain of feeling unacceptable or lovable. There are various ways our society models how to "shrug off" physical pain. These are revealing allegories for how we're conditioned to deny emotional pain. Take the following case:

> This is a scene many of us have seen in professional baseball. A hitter is struck squarely on the arm by a pitcher's 95 mph fast ball. Obviously in pain, the hitter is given first base. Being a professional, the hit batter is conditioned to never show the opposing team the severity of his pain. He stands on the base, suppressing every instinct to hold or rub his injured arm. No matter how deep his agony, he will not cry out or "give in to his pain." This convention in baseball EDH also sends a signal to the hit batsman's team that "he can take it." This is part of the game.
>
> Yet everyone on both teams, the stadium crowd, as well as the television audience and announcers, know the batter must be in severe pain, judging by the velocity of the pitch. But we all respect the batter's "self-control" for not showing his pain. Since the player doesn't want us to know it hurts, as observers we respect his denial of pain. We collude with the player's self-delusion that it doesn't hurt. This denial seems essential for the baseball player to go on and play effectively – even heroically. The literally battered player gains our respect for his ability to deny and pretend his hurt doesn't bother him.

The heroic denial of feeling hurt is more honored in our society than is emotional honesty and admission of being vulnerable. This heroic, stoic indifference to emotional pain is considered a sign of strength in our culture. But, as psychotherapist Susan Forward says in her 1989 book, *Toxic Parents*, "Denial is the lid on our emotional pressure cooker." It can also make us professional victims whose silent suffering shuts off intimacy and destroys relationships. Is it any wonder that so many battered women are afraid to leave their abuser? They live in denial, fearing to acknowledge their pain. Denial of painful feelings, as we will see in the next chapter, is part of our fear of facing the self-message that when we are hurt we consider our suffering a shameful sense of weakness. This is why so many people play the role of "victims," stoically enduring physically or emotionally abusive relationships. David Viscott calls denial a "self-administered emotional sedative."

Life is filled with many types of wounds that indeed should threaten our vulnerable sense of self. We may temporarily feel devastated by the loss of a close family member, lover, or friend. Our sense of self is assaulted when a partner in a close relationship walks out on us, or when a confidant betrays us. We are also vulnerable to being hurt whenever we trust others and risk being emotionally honest. When we lose a valued possession through theft or fire, there is insurance to cover the physical loss. But how do we emotionally recover from such losses when we can't accept that we even have these painful feelings? The masquerade of EDH is, at best, a holding action that sets aside our feelings and prevents our recovery from painful emotional experiences. Defenses often prolong and deepen normal emotional distress.

IV. Confusing Causes and Effects of Feelings

Emotional honesty is a self-deception that keeps us from dealing with our emotional pain. Pain is our ability (sense) of feeling hurt. When we're emotionally wounded, one way of denying that our hurt feelings are ours is to blame others as the source of the pain we have. This confuses causes and effects. Once the pattern of giving others power over what we feel is established, authorship of our feelings becomes difficult to take back. One of the hallmarks of becoming an adult is taking responsibility for owning our hurt feelings, accepting and healing them. We may feel wounded by an interaction with another person, but we are responsible for what we feel. Only we truly know how deeply we are hurt. We may deny it, but the pain is ours.

Blaming others for our own feelings seems logical. The error is understandable because part of self-deception is confusing the causes and effects of our feelings.

For example, someone upon whom we depend for a sense of acceptance – a boss, mate, or teacher – makes a casual comment not intended to be a criticism or rejection. When we are suffering from previously experienced, denied and unhealed emotional wounds, we need very little suggestion from a person who has power in our life to become the source of our pain. It is not that we are "too sensitive" when we interpret an innocent remark or physical gesture as rejection, for example. It is that by habitually disowning the real pain we have denied, we experience other people as having control over what we feel. We become hurt, but it's easier to believe that our pain is due to others "being at fault." In her 1937 biography, *This is My Story*, Eleanor Roosevelt wisely declared, "No one can make you feel inferior without your consent."

We have the power to deny and store our hurt, or accept and heal it. When we deny and store our hurt feelings, it's usually because we consider emotional pain and vulnerability shameful or frightening. Many of us learned to devalue our feelings in childhood (see Chapter Eight). For "self-protection" against these denied feelings, we learned to hide hurt feelings in a dark dungeon of denial. We construct a prison surrounded by a powerful defense system to prevent us from acknowledging our frightening vulnerability. We feel being overwhelmed and devastated by the threatening sense that something must be wrong with us to hurt so much. But emotional dishonesty never truly allows us to feel safe since the more pain we have imprisoned, the greater our fear of "letting it out." When we are controlled by EDH, the fear of uncontrollable, devastating pain is our worst nightmare! We may resist to our death taking responsibility for our feelings.

Emotional distress confuses us because we believe that we have our feelings "under control." We are so fearful of being vulnerable that the denied painful feelings take on a mystical, menacing quality. Putting denied feelings into a cage appears to protect us from our secret fear. But, alas, this is only an illusion.

Can you recognize the common theme in the following two stories?

The job applicant

A young man applying for a job in a corporation that requires psychological screening was sent to a consulting psychologist's office. The psychologist's first exercise was the classic Rorschach test designed to evoke associations to a series of abstract ink blots on paper. So the psychologist asked the applicant to say the first thing that came to his mind as he saw each image.

The first ink blot shown the applicant looked somewhat like a butterfly. "What does this one seem like to you?" the psychologist asked. "Oh, it is very erotic," the applicant replied, "and reminds me of sex." The applicant was shown a second ink blot that was even more abstract. "This one is even more sensual than the last, and is quite sexy," replied the applicant. The psychologist went through three more increasingly abstract ink blots, and each time the applicant said they were more and more erotic and sensual.

Finally the psychologist stopped the test, took off his glasses and said, "As you know, my evaluation is used to determine the psychological fitness of applicants for employment by the company. I must say that your responses to these ink blots force me to conclude that you have a deep sexual obsession. Based on this, I could not recommend you for the job."

The applicant replied with disbelief and bewilderment. "What? But, you're the one who's showing me the dirty pictures!"

Wild elephants

An eccentric man goes to his first visit with a psychiatrist, sits down, and crosses his legs. The doctor notices his patient is wearing a yellow sock on one foot and a red sock on the other. Struck by the strange choice of apparel, the doctor asks his patient if he realizes that he is wearing totally different colored socks. The eccentric nonchalantly offers the explanation that he always wears one yellow and one red sock "to keep the wild elephants away."

The psychiatrist reacts to this absurd explanation by commenting, "But this is New York. There are no wild elephants here." To which the patient exclaims, "See, it works!"

Both stories, beyond their obvious humor (at least to the author), carry a deeper meaning. They remind us how we sometimes make false conclusions about the causes and effects of our feelings.

Humans can never be fully aware of their self-deception. Over time, EDH becomes an automatic response whenever we feel vulnerable. It seems that we have an infinite capacity to fool ourselves and distort the meaning of fearful or shameful hurt feelings. EDH invites this confusion about what we feel when we feel it. We become unclear if we truly feel love or compassion, for example, or are we just being nice. We confuse *thinking* about a feeling with having (owning) the feeling. We believe we *should* feel something, and therefore pretend we do. We are confused by having concurrent opposing feelings, such as love and hate for a parent, or both caring for and being angry at our mate – and so we believe we must choose one or the other.

Where we have the most confusion, however, is identifying what is so painful and frightening about being hurt. Pain may trigger our anger or depression, for example, without our ever acknowledging why we are in pain. Hurt feelings are often disguised by what we do to avoid dealing with them. Errors are also made by assuming that feelings follow actions, rather than the reverse. We confuse thoughts or behavior with feelings. There is a conventional way that expresses this confusion when someone does something foolish. We ask "What were you *thinking* of when you did that?", not "What were you *feeling* . . .?"

The ultimate confusion: feeling we deserve our misfortune

Inherent in our defense system is a confusion about deserving wounds we suffer when our feelings are hurt. *Secretly embedded in every wounding experience is a a message that something must be wrong with us to hurt so much.* The unacceptability we feel deep within our inner sense of self may also spur a belief that we deserve the loss, rejection, betrayal or humiliation we encounter. This defective emotional reasoning confuses causes with effects. We reason that when something bad happens – being rejected in a social situation, or being "abandoned" by a divorcing parent – we are somehow to blame for our misfortune. In the case of children of divorced parents, these children may secretly agonize that they are the cause of their parents' divorce and thus are the reason the family has broken up. Dramas are written about children whose lives are destroyed by guilt over an accident in which they were unable to save a parent or best friend from being killed. The innocent child may feel responsible for loved ones dying, particularly if they had ever previously harbored anger toward them.

EDH is a double whammy: We may not only have normal wounding experiences such as hurt, loss, rejection, betrayal, and humiliation,, but we also believe we deserve the misfortune. Feeling ashamed and fearful of being hurt are why we deny that our pain comes from within us. EDH involves harboring unhealed, unattended and nameless wounds within us. We continue to hide them for by recognizing them we fear revealing our unacceptability or unlovability. Each successive hurt, loss, rejection, betrayal, humiliation, or other misfortune can appear as mounting "evidence" that we feel hurt because we deserve it.

When Bad Things Happen to Good People, Rabbi Harold Kushner's 1981 National Book Award-winning work, offers a spiritual and psychological explanation of how confusion about the causes and effects of our hurt feelings compound emotional distress: "We don't feel we deserve to be helped, so we let guilt, anger, jealousy and self-imposed loneliness make a bad situation even worse." He offered the suggestion that Job's suffering from God's testing his faith might have been lessened if friends would have said to Job about his misfortune, "Yes, what happened to you is terrible and makes no sense" rather than Job's comforters saying "Cheer up, Job, it's not all that bad." Kushner is advocating emotional honesty. He suggests that when we attempt to comfort those in emotional distress, we make things worse when we try to talk them out of their hurt feelings, rather than help them to own, acknowledge, and accept their hurt. Used in this way, emotional honesty helps us to recover "guilt-free" from our pain.

When we have a deeply wounding experience, we may say or think, "Someone must be to blame for me to hurt so much." We never make a distinction between the wounding event and the resulting feeling. If we feel there is something so undeserving or flawed about ourselves that we are at fault for every misfortune we endure, we in effect say that we deserve the pain. Something must be intrinsically wrong with us. If we accept our hurt feelings when we suffer an emotional injury – by acknowledging our vulnerability and capacity to have these feelings – we take responsibility for our pain and its healing. This capability is vital to our emotional health. When we secretly feel "we deserve the pain," our guilt and self-blame prevent us from recovering from our emotional wounds.

Kushner offers an explanation for our readiness to feel guilt about events we didn't cause. "[We have a] strenuous need to believe that the world makes sense, that there is a cause for every effect and a reason for everything that happens." Humans are reasoning beings who seek meaning from troubling events, even when there is none. We tend to place blame and fault for what we feel, when there is no need to do so. Our ability to sense we are hurt by an experience means we have a "sense of self" that registers feelings, similar to our sense of sight, smell or touch. Humans are unique, in part, because they are capable of feeling hurt. To deny this human sense makes no sense!

EDH and defenses are needed because we are too fearful and ashamed to own our hurt. This endlessly confuses us. How perplexing to secretly take responsibility for deserving a misfortunate event, but deny the resulting hurt feelings. We end up feeling defective, unacceptable and unlovable in the world. We become marred by a harsh, inescapable sense of being "wrong" just for what we feel! By allowing ourselves to dishonor our true feelings, EDH also spoils our sense of accomplishment and can undermine loving relationships. We become victims of our emotional confusion.

Encountering emotionally wounding experiences is inevitable. Recovering from them is not. What stands in the way, most often, is emotional dishonesty. I believe EDH must be understood for us to become more safe, secure and healthy as individuals and as a society. Due to the difficulty of overcoming EDH, learning about it is essential for these reasons:

• Emotional honesty is far more simple to understand than to practice, for we live in a culture that glorifies the ability to deceive ourselves and each other by dismissing or disavowing our real and particularly painful feelings.

• Unfortunately, feeling emotionally vulnerable and acknowledging our true fears when we're hurt are not considered a virtue in our society.

• Emotional health education involves learning to honor our feelings, no matter how upsetting, shameful or terrifying they may seem. This is the only way to break the chain of EDH that can rule families for generations. It is no easy task. But it is well worth the risk and effort.

CHAPTER 5

Our Vulnerable Sense of Self

I. Emotional Survival Needs

Emotions are powerful influences on our behavior because they are linked to our survival. We humans are unique in the animal kingdom, in part, because we are born with instinctive *emotional* survival needs, as well as *physical* survival needs. Our physical survival needs are quite clear and obvious. We need food, water, air, warmth, shelter, etc. Our emotional survival needs are less self-evident. As helpless infants, totally vulnerable and dependent upon parents for our needs, we are born with few survival capabilities other than crying when hungry, afraid or uncomfortable. In his 1979 book, *Feelings* (Appendix IV), Psychiatrist and professor Willard Gaylin notes that humans, unlike other animals, have few instinctive capabilities for survival. Humans are born at an incredible disadvantage vis a vis other animals. We are both physically and emotionally vulnerable and helpless, explains Dr. Gaylin:

> The abiding lesson of the first year of life is that he who is loved is safe . . . If that is so, then the first fear experienced by the individual in relationship to his environment must be separation anxiety. The most dangerous thing is not to be weak, but to be unloved."

Humans come equipped with an emotional survival system which monitors emotional security. This system, which is primarily designed to protect the helpless infant from emotional devastation begins operating at birth and continues to function throughout life. The greatest emotional and physical threat to the vulnerable infant is the danger of being abandoned. To feel emotionally safe, infants need reassurance that Mother is there to care for them.

There is a subjective means by which infants interpret how safe they are from the threat of abandonment – their deepest, instinctive survival fear. This inner, self-protective system tells us, "How lovable and acceptable do I feel?" This survival monitoring system, which initially protects the helpless infant, continues throughout life. It tells adolescents and adults just how lovable, acceptable and emotionally secure they are, too.

As we develop and mature into adults, this emotional need to feel acceptable and lovable remains a core survival need, although it takes on new interpretations. The infant's instinctive emotional survival need to feel acceptable and lovable is forever bonded to the individual's general sense of safety and security. Gaylin explains how the abandonment fear from infancy continues to evoke terror in adults. "If separation from those who love us produces insecurity, it is compounded if we fear there is no one who loves us." The intolerable pain of feeling unworthy – unacceptable and unlovable – is the emotional corollary to being threatened by physical death. We talk of feeling devastated by a painful experience such as the loss of a loved one, because emotionally it seems as though we can't survive.

Our inner sense of self

What monitors our sense of being lovable and acceptable might best be described as our inner sense of self (ISS). The sense of self is like other senses such as touch, feel, taste, sight and hearing which also have a vital function to warn us of danger. This inner sense issues internal warnings when wounding experiences threaten our emotional security. Because it monitors how emotionally vulnerable and secure we feel, we experience these warnings as emotional distress signals.

Emotional distress is often experienced as a general sense of dis-ease, a vague feeling that "something is wrong with me." This discomfort is our protective ISS telling us that we are in danger. It is our individual job to interpret precisely what is the cause of our inner turmoil or distress. However, we are not always willing and able to inquire as to the specific cause of our distress. For example, when we experience pain from betrayal by a friend, we may sense being uncomfortable, irritable or angry. But we often use anger or depression to cover up the fact that we are in pain. When this occurs, we may even try to rid ourselves of the painful distress without ever acknowledging that it comes from within us. We try to end the distress that began as our ISS signaling we are in danger. By ignoring or trying to "disown" our painful feelings, we may seek to eliminate our distress through an elaborate pretense I call emotional dishonesty (EDH).

Emotional pain, exacerbated by the distress signal from our ISS, may seem so terrifying at times that we need to "turn off" or distort our feelings. This is the guardian role that defenses play when we are emotionally dishonest. The following diagram and description show the *Anatomy of Inner Reactions to Wounded Feelings*. This conceptual model relates the central role of our inner sense to our emotional experiences, behavior, thoughts, beliefs and defenses when we are hurt.

The diagram shows emotional defenses surrounding the inner sense of self, as guardians of our vulnerability. Our defenses against painful feelings are activated when the inner sense of self, alerted by a threatening or wounding experience, sends a danger signal to protect ourself. The ISS is primarily an instinctive, self-protective, alarm system that signals defenses to guard against threatening, painful feelings. The job of defenses is to try and quell the fear that we are too vulnerable to emotionally "survive." This becomes a self-deception, a ploy to fool ourselves that we are not in pain, when our ISS says we are in danger of being devastated. EDH confuses the interpretation of our feelings. By contrast, emotional honesty is a clarification of what we feel

Rather than experience our pain as a natural reaction to being emotionally wounded, our defenses deny, dismiss, devalue, or pretend that the hurt feelings don't really hurt. *Defenses are triggered by fear of what our pain means: That we may be unacceptable or unlovable.* This is how we deceive and experience ourselves when we are in emotional pain. In contrast, emotional honesty allows us to focus on dealing with the specific incident that causes our pain so that we accept our feelings. When EDH defenses are triggered in response to a wounding experience, they actually perpetuate emotional distress through a confusing array of pretenses and disguised acts. Emotional honesty recognizes that our pain is real and specific. EDH covers up the pain out of general fear. The fear is based on interpreting emotional pain as though it is an indictment of our character: "There must be something wrong with me to hurt so much." EDH is our instinctive, survival fear keeping us in denial, living a lie about what we feel. All of this confusion occurs when we experience deep emotional pain.

Emotional honesty is the process whereby we become aware of our inner reactions to painful feelings. It uses our ability to recognize and counteract the survival danger being signaled by our inner sense of self. By acknowledging the pain from each wounding event, we honor and accept it for what it is – our own experience. Emotional honesty allows us to override the panic signal from our inner sense of self. It provides us with the ability to experience and accept hurt feelings without a sense of being in danger of emotional devastation. On the other hand, defenses – and the pretenses and self-deception that go with them – can have the effect of disabling our normal feeling system by disguising the fear associated with being vulnerable, unacceptable or unlovable. The reactions to our wounding experiences are more critical to our well-being than the event itself. We give the meaning and power to our pain. David Viscott, in *The Language of Feelings* (Appendix IV), says "It hurts to lose something important; it hurts worse to pretend otherwise."

We instinctively hide our faces when we cry. This is meant to protect us from exposing our vulnerability. Whenever we have painful emotional experiences we also have some degree of shame. To the extent we recognize this secret shame and deal with it honestly and openly, we prevent ourselves from succumbing to the belief that we are unlovable or unacceptable. We then have less need to hide our hurt or wear a mask.

Totally helpless infants have one main survival fear: Their life is always in danger because at any time they might be abandoned. To admit being vulnerable to emotional pain is always risky, because it requires exposing ourselves to a punishing fear that "I am a flawed and defective person." Such a person secretly fears that they may deserve the emotional distress and pain they suffer. We deserve to be abandoned; to lose a loved one; to be rejected; to be taken advantage of; or to be unhappy. This is unnecessary emotional torture we must endure if we do not know why being hurt, *and denying it*, makes us secretly feel unlovable and unacceptable.

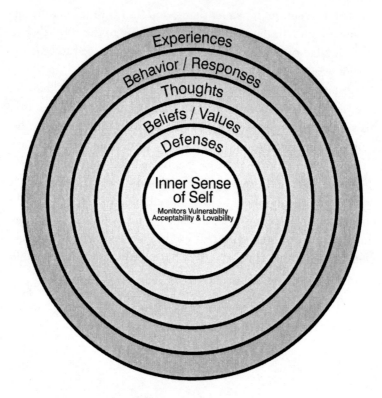

Experiences
Behavior / Responses
Thoughts
Beliefs / Values
Defenses

**Inner Sense
of Self**

Monitors Vulnerability
Acceptability & Lovability

Anatomy of Inner Reactions
to Wounded Feelings

© 1998, Ronald R. Brill

Anatomy of Inner Reactions to Wounded Feelings

Level 1: Experiences
- Both physical and emotional experiences
- Our perception of reality
- Our experience of our environment

Level #2: Behavior Responses
- How we respond/react to experiences
- Expression of feelings (including indifference, anger, disappointment, etc.)

Level #3: Thoughts
- Thinking, cognition and awareness
- Considered and planned physical and emotional responses
- Our problem-solving process

Level #4: Beliefs and Values
- Choosing criteria
- Judgments of experiences, feelings, people and things as being good or bad
- "Our rules" for behavior and preferences
- Determine our "likes" and "dislikes" in ourselves and others
- Basis for accepting or rejecting people, behavior, thoughts, feelings and ideas

Level #5: Defenses
- Defense mechanisms, distortions and pretenses
- Protection against physical/emotional dangers to our well being and survival
- "Countermeasures" which deflect/shield us from acknowledging wounded feelings
- Lies we tell ourselves about our feelings to prevent us from feeling vulnerable
- Barriers that screen our wounding experiences to protect us from unbearable pain

Level #6: Our Inner Sense of Self (ISS)
- The control center for our emotional security system
- Monitors our vulnerability, acceptability and lovability
- Determines our sense of "worthiness" to be accepted or loved
- The core repository for our self-acceptance and negative self-beliefs
- Our sense of being "good enough" to deserve what we want or have
- Thermostat for measuring how emotionally safe we feel to risk being vulnerable

The higher numbered levels are more instinctive, reside deeper within us, and thereby have greater impact on all other levels. Defenses, being closer to our inner sense of self, are easily triggered by the ISS. Levels 5 and 6 tend to shape our values (level 4), thoughts (3), and behavior responses (2) to our experiences.

II. Our Sixth Sense: Core of Vulnerability

What is the mechanism by which the ISS measures our vulnerability to emotional pain and devastation? Aaron Beck, M.D., the father of cognitive therapy, speculates in *Love is Never Enough* (1988): "Perhaps we have a specialized circuit in the brain attuned to picking up psychological threats . . .This apparatus could alert us to threats to our well-being or safety." Dr. Beck emphasizes that "Psychological pain . . .is just as real as – and often more unpleasant than – physical pain."

The ISS, control center for our emotional security, functions like a sixth sense. It has a critical function to alert us when our emotional pain and vulnerability reach dangerous levels. Our instinctive emotional need equates being lovable and acceptable with being safe and secure. This explains why, when we experience deep emotional wounds, the inner sense recognizes a vulnerable state as dangerous and alerts us to take defensive action *as though our life depended upon it.*

Hiding shameful feelings

Psychiatrist and Massachusetts Institute for Psychoanalysis professor Andrew Morrison's 1996 book, *The Culture of Shame* (Appendix IV), reports on research that shows how original shame forms:

> Studies based on observations of interaction between infants and their mothers strongly suggest that an inborn, biological form of shame exists . . . .. Infants reacted with slumping posture and lowered eyes and face when their mothers failed to respond to their attempts to engage their attention. Were the infants experiencing shame? Although we can't be certain that the infant experiences shame as we know it, the physical expressions that we correlate with shame are convincing testimony.

Morrison explains the steps: The mother fails to respond to the infant. The physiological letdown is experienced by the infant as being the infant's own "fault" – that something the baby did caused the mother's lack of responsiveness.

Albany Medical College Professor of Psychiatry Michael Nichols in his 1991 book, *No Place to Hide* (Appendix IV), states: "Shame is the pain of feeling unlovable. The infant's instinctive anxiety about separation/abandonment continues in later life. While an infant uses defenses for emotional survival, it is an instinctive response rather than a cognitive process." Dr. Gaylin suggests that the human infant is so vulnerable and helpless that he is incapable of avoiding danger. This explains the terrifying anxiety children and adults experience when they are emotionally wounded. *Emotional pain and vulnerability seem as though they are life-threatening.*

Later in childhood and during adolescence and adulthood, we feel ashamed of this instinctive fear. In her book, *Shame and Guilt* (Appendix IV), Jane Middleton-Moz observes, "When we experience shame we fear abandonment, and vise versa." Shame causes us to hide our fears and pain. Middleton-Moz describes the double bind created by hidden feelings: "If we let ourselves and others see and hear our shameful secrets, we fear abandonment. If we don't, our shame increases and we can never feel fully accepted or loved by others. Of even greater importance, we cannot fully love and honor ourselves." Fearing the "shameful message" our wounded feelings convey results in transforming every rejection into another dagger that rips open our "not-okayness." Our inner sense of self continues its emotional safety monitoring activity throughout life, long after the frightening dependency of infancy.

In the 1996 book, *Heal the Hurt That Runs Your Life*, Bill Ferguson notes that:

> As a little child, the only way you could explain the painful loss of love was to blame yourself. In a moment of hurt, you bought the notion that you were worthless, not good enough, a failure, not worth loving, or in some other way, not okay. This wasn't the truth, but to a little child, this was the only explanation that made any sense at the time. You then hated the very notion that you created. "No one can ever love me if I'm worthless" . . .. The moment you bought the notion that you were not okay, . . .you created a mechanism that would then sabotage the rest of your life. From that moment on, the underlying focus of your life would be to avoid this hurt.

III. Abandonment Fear Throughout Life

The innate sixth sense initially serves as a survival protection system in early infancy when infants are completely dependent upon parents. Infants literally feel endangered by the temporary disappearance of parents or caretakers upon whom they continuously rely for their very survival. This self-protective system, which began as an instinctive need for survival, continues to function throughout life. It warns us of emotional danger despite the fact that we are no longer in danger physically. The emotional dangers and fears of older childhood, adolescence and adulthood have more to do with symbolic, emotional abandonment than physical abandonment. However, our ISS treats traumatic emotional wounds *as if they are life-threatening.*

The experience of emotional pain from loss, rejection, betrayal or humiliation can create an unbearable terror and a sense of helplessness characteristic of the primal, abandonment anxiety.

We feel threatened and traumatized by everyday wounding experiences because our inner sense of self warns us that if we are in pain we are endangered. We again become the helpless and powerless child who feels overwhelmed by a menacing threat to emotional survival.

The late psychiatrist David Viscott described the carry over of the infant's instinctive fears into later childhood and adult life. He describes how children's fear and sense of helplessness comes forward and threatens to overwhelm them as they mature. This reminds them of the weakness and insecurity that prevailed during their dependent infancy. In his 1992 book, *Emotionally Free*, Dr. Viscott wrote that no matter how secure one's childhood may have been, as adults we encounter "Moments of sheer terror, overwhelming loss, profound abandonment and spirit-crushing defeat," a traumatic state similar to "childlike helplessness." He explains that children in their relatively helpless period needed defenses and denial to shut out unbearable discomfort and threats to their emotional safety. We might liken our emotional sensory system to the "flight or fight" instinctive response mechanism triggered by threats to our *physical* security and survival.

Throughout childhood and adult life protective instincts operate in distinctly different ways. Infants sense emotional attachment as well as physical closeness and nurturing. Before they can talk, infants communicate their delight by cooing, smiling and laughing. The infant's state of delight comes from reassurance that they are safe because parents attend to them, particularly when they are distressed. Mothers instinctively react to a baby's cry of panic after an accidental fall, for example, by holding the infant and offering comfort, "Don't worry, Mommy is here."

After infancy the child continues to please parents since parental praise and acceptance reduce the child's abandonment fears and anxiety. Parental confirmation that children are acceptable and lovable is critical for their self-acceptance in the years before they reach school age. The emotional safety and survival needs of young children is fairly direct and simple. Parents are usually eager to oblige by being attentive to children, particularly since young children have such openly joyfully responses to attention they receive.

Self-acceptance during school years

In *The Resilient Child* (1994), Joanne Joseph writes that the inner sense of self is fully formed by the age of eight. Therefore, we can surmise that by this age defense systems are also in place. During early school years their social acceptance by peers, comparisons with other students, grades and the need for teacher acceptance, all can create a new threat of insecurity and vulnerability that reaches its peak during adolescence. With the early school years comes the trials and tribulations of social acceptability and status within peer groups, setting the stage for the more pronounced acceptance needs during adolescence.

Social acceptance is, of course, different from self-acceptance. When we feel lovable and acceptable – less fearful of emotional devastation when we are hurt – we can accept painful feelings as part of us without blame or guilt. Accepting our feelings, including our pain is a requirement for accepting ourselves. The issue is not that we are *actually* loved and accepted by others, but whether we *feel* we are an acceptable and lovable person. This is a purely subjective measurement. As the child enters adolescence filled with doubt and insecurity, every rejection is taken as evidence of unacceptability. Peer and social acceptance needs reach their peak. Adolescents tend to interpret every wound as a dangerously vulnerable condition. They become the frightened infant again, just as they are nearing the time of becoming independent from parents. They become filled with doubts and anxiety about their lovability and acceptability outside the home.

Throughout life, whether during adolescence or in adulthood, a major loss, rejection, betrayal or humiliation tends to result in emotional insecurity and vulnerability. When we are deeply or repeatedly emotionally wounded, our inner sense warns that we are in danger. We again feel helpless, just like the defenseless infant.

Being acceptable and lovable is more fundamental to our sense of security than having self-esteem, confidence, or even caring parents. Throughout life, it is also more important to our sense of self than just being respected, publicly recognized, or having social "approval." Sociologist David Riesman, author of *The Lonely Crowd* (1973), suggests that the need for social approval is stronger in "outer-directed" persons than those who are "inner-directed." But, for all of us, self-acceptance is far more critical to our well-being than social approval. Without self-acceptance, when we hurt we become a rudderless ship, buffeted and tormented by a sea of shameful fear that we are a flawed, worthless person. In *Pudd'nhead Wilson's New Calendar*, Mark Twain recognized: "We can secure other people's approval . . .but our own is worth a hundred of it, and no way has been found out of securing that."

IV. Surviving without Being Controlled by Defenses

As adults, we rationally know that our feelings can't kill us. But overwhelming emotional pain from accumulated losses, rejection, betrayal or humiliation can make us feel as though we are being devastated. Whenever we are wounded and sense that we are unacceptable or unlovable, a combination of panic and shame makes us feel mortally threatened. Our inner sense of self recalls the infant's helplessness and inability to escape from the fear of emotional devastation by being abandoned. The gripping nightmare that we are unworthy is so tormenting that even our defenses cannot help us escape this frightening message. Chapter Six examines the defensive armor used to shield us from our vulnerability. Defenses may disguise our fear in order to help us temporarily escape the unbearable emotional agony of feeling helpless and powerless. But when we habitually rely upon EDH to avoid our pain, we feel utterly helpless when these security measures fail. When defenses are not sufficient to protect us from a sense of emotional devastation, we may feel there is no way to escape from our pain. It is then that we are at risk of committing the ultimate destructive acts of murder or suicide.

We can learn to reinterpret the warning signs from our inner sense of self that tell us our emotional survival is endangered. Emotional honesty enables us to recognize that our need for defenses and emotional protection is triggered by an instinctive fear of being emotionally devastated. It is this ability to acknowledge our core fear of being vulnerable when we experience painful emotional wounds that releases the pain and prevents the panic over being unlovable and unacceptable. Being honest about having painful experiences includes identifying the inner warning signals that put our defenses on alert. This keeps us from shutting down or disguising our real fears.

Emotionally healthy persons know they cannot escape having hurt feelings. So they develop the ability to acknowledge the pain from each of these normal wounds as they happen. By removing the stigma of having emotional pain, we can recover from wounding experiences more rapidly and completely. We then have less need to blame others and seek retaliation for our painful feelings. Recovering from emotional injuries with emotional honesty takes practice. With experience we can counteract entrenched EDH habits, our misguided defenses and pretenses. Emotional resilience is developed over time as we become more confident that by acknowledging wounds without over-reacting to them, we can recover from painful experiences. As individuals beyond the stage of dependent infancy, hurt feelings are not life threatening, unless we treat them that way. We can learn to be selectively vulnerable without feeling helpless and threatened. *Being emotionally honest requires having the courage to listen to and learn from our emotional pain and distress, for they tell us what we most fear.*

When defenses go up, emotional honesty goes down. Unless we learn the reason behind emotional defenses and dishonesty, we may become controlled by them. Defenses, initially deployed to protect us from experiencing our pain and vulnerability, eventually make us feel guilty for what we feel. Defenses both shame and dishonor our feelings, all in the name of avoiding our fear of being vulnerable. Highly defended people, unable to accept their feelings, often compensate for their sense of being powerless by adopting a self-centered, inflated attitude of themselves. They diminish the importance of others, and overstate their own influence and accomplishments. This facade covers their hidden sense of unacceptability. Overblown defenses come into play when we feel the least acceptable or lovable.

With practice, we can learn to detect and re-evaluate our instinctive, inner panic signals that tell us that something must be wrong with us to feel hurt. Emotional honesty is the quiet courage that enables us to confront our fear of vulnerability and risk dealing with each hurt openly and truthfully.

PART TWO

Emotional Dishonesty

(EDH) as a Disability

CHAPTER 6

The Danger of Hiding Hurt Feelings

A man in armor is his armor's slave
– Robert Browning, *Herakles* (1871)

I. The High Cost of Self-Deception

In his 1985 book *Vital Lies, Simple Truths: The Psychology of Self-Deception* (Appendix IV), Daniel Goleman, author of the 1995 best seller, *Emotional Intelligence*, refers to the high personal cost of emotional defenses. In his chapter, "Forgetting We Have Forgotten," Goleman states that defenses cauterize emotional pain. Defenses are part of an instinctive self-deceptive process that protects us from emotional devastation. It is easy to become an expert at hiding our pain. It is difficult to reverse the process. A tragic consequence of emotional dishonesty (EDH) is being caught in the trap of "I want to change, but can't." Denials become so strong, we deny our denying. Goleman refers to Wilhelm Reich's concept of "character armor" (*Character Analysis*, 1972). Reich says character armor is the face the wounded self turns to the world. "Defense mechanisms," says Goleman, "are in essence, tricks we play on ourselves to avoid pain."

In *Self-Defeating Behaviors* (Appendix IV), professor Milton Cudney and consulting psychologist Robert Hardy see defenses as acts of desperation that protect us against "a mythical fear." We fear what will happen if a particular defense mechanism is not used. Incredibly, people tend to become dependent upon defenses even if they recognize them for what they are. Fear of lowering defenses and dealing with hurt feelings traps us in a self-fulfilling prophecy. The scenario goes like this: *See, I was vulnerable and exposed my hurt, and sure enough I got wounded even more!* Cudney and Hardy believe, "We are not to blame for having defenses, but are responsible for perpetuating their use." They warn that "Disowning . . .allows us to lie to ourselves. It creates a sort of psychic chaos where cause and effect are confused." When we disown feelings, we may exhibit "feigned remorse" for our EDH defenses but keep on infecting ourselves with the disease.

Defenses are emotional Novocain to kill pain arising from emotional injuries. Defenses are not selective. When defenses are operating, they tend to block or nullify all deep feelings, from love to pain. We may become so invested in our self-defenses and protective of our vulnerability that our self-deception is too embarrassing to acknowledge. Deep down inside our defenses we feel like a fake.

Over time, emotional defenses become automatic. We may feel our hurt as a fleeting pain but deny its impact. When EDH traps us in chronic emotional distress, we cling to denying our real pain because we fear if we lower our defenses, a flood of anguish will be unleashed.

Defenses that protect our wounded self appear to keep us from feeling hurt, but they have unintended, serious side effects. Once defenses become automatic and habitual, our emotional responses become calculated and rigid. We lose our emotional honesty and spontaneity. We become distrusting and skeptical about the loving and caring feelings expressed by others. *Because we sense our own deceitfulness, we assume that other people are also not genuine about their feelings.* This inability to trust feelings sabotages intimacy and trusting relationships. We lose the emotional resilience and adaptability needed to recover from wounding experiences. We lose the ability to experience our feelings in the present moment. We calculate what we *should* feel, rather than what we *really* feel.

Babies are emotionally honest. What you see is what you get. They are devoid of guile and pretense about what they feel. You know when they are happy or sad, frightened or secure. But as we mature, we develop defenses and learn to disguise, deny or devalue our feelings. However skillful our self-deception, defenses are never perfect. Defenses delude us into thinking that painful feelings are safely hidden. But when a single event or series of wounding rejections, losses, misfortunes or betrayals overwhelms our defenses, our core vulnerability is exposed. Accumulated, unhealed wounds cannot be contained by defenses forever. The emotional lies keep us stuck in anger, depression or other destructive modes of behavior.

Avoiding the subject of emotional pain

Why should we care if people are emotionally dishonest? Should parents, educators, adolescents, mental health professionals, law enforcement and other public officials, and the news media be concerned if people deceive themselves about their feelings? After all, if some people suffer from emotional distress because they lie about their feelings and can't handle rejection, loss, betrayal or humiliation, isn't that their problem?

Unfortunately, this head-in-the-sand attitude has sentenced generation after generation to be trapped in EDH because having hurt feelings is not anyone else's business. As we mature, we learn that being emotionally wounded is itself a sign of weakness, and it just isn't safe to acknowledge hurt feelings.

A cultural myth prevails that the best way to handle emotional wounds is to simply be tough. This tendency of denying emotional vulnerability prevents us from being a more humane and caring society. One of America's leading radio psychologists, Laura Schlessinger, has risen in popularity by dispensing a brand of advice appealing to the idea that being emotionally vulnerable and experiencing pain is a sign of weakness. Rather than focus on honoring and accepting their hurt, callers are advised to stop "whining" and get tough with those who take advantage of them. This "get tough" school of mental health particularly appeals to a population inclined to blame others or themselves when their feelings are hurt.

Blame feeds anger and a desire for revenge. When we are wronged and feel emotional pain, it seems only proper to exercise "our right to get even." Some politicians proudly proclaim in response to being publicly betrayed by a colleague, "I don't get mad, I get even." Rather than take responsibility for dealing with our pain, we want to get even by punishing those whose actions or words hurt us. Retaliation only escalates hostility. Painful feelings become a shameful flaw or weakness that we are persuaded must be disowned. Being emotionally guarded then becomes a virtue.

The widespread practice of disowning or invalidating painful feelings drains emotional energy and desensitizes us to the feelings of others. In her 1997 book, *Don't Take it Personally*, therapist Elayne Savage writes about the art of dealing with our fear of emotional pain. "With repeated experiences of rejection, abandonment, or betrayal all of our energy goes into avoiding this excruciating pain at any cost."

Typical teenagers struggle to deny being wounded for to do so exposes their embarrassing sense of vulnerability and emotional insecurity. Being emotionally desensitized by EDH they find it hard to understand and tolerate their emotional distress, let alone have non-harmful ways of recovering from it. Nor do they find it easy to empathize with peers or understand how a cutting remark wounds a classmate. Teens often feel isolated and alone since they have a fearful sense of shame whenever they experience pain from normal wounding experiences. This is particularly true when adolescents are emotionally wounded by peers who wield the mighty sword of rejection or acceptance.

The game of EDH is dangerous for emotionally insecure teens since their defenses often can't protect them from overwhelming, painful feelings arising from wounds of peer rejection, harassment, and discrimination. They feel devastated when ostracized for being different, being talked about behind their back, being given the silent treatment, or being left out. Teens who have not learned how to name, accept and deal honestly with painful emotional wounds may express their suffering through self-destructive means or violent revenge against classmates. For teens, alcohol, drugs and compulsive behavior become ways to dull their pain. When their suffering becomes intolerable, violent rage against peers may seem the only way to silence them and their own emotional agony.

Teens who kill classmates at school can't recover from their emotional pain. Everyday emotional distress resulting from hurt feelings just keeps building up, and they can't prevent its devastating impact upon their sense of self. If they have not learned the fundamentals of emotional anatomy and know why their hurt triggers EDH responses, they become caught in their masquerade of indifference. They can't safely recover from nor prevent the devastating effects of being emotionally hurt.

An advanced society like ours is certainly capable of teaching young people the dangers of EDH, and how to deal with painful feelings in a healthy and responsible way. We could do this, of course, were it not for our reluctance to discuss the subject of upset feelings. Sadly, if the Columbine High killers had "only" committed suicide, Littleton, Colorado would not have been considered a shameful, national tragedy. Grieving families of murdered school children across America attest to the fact that the private pain of those teenage killers can no longer be considered a private matter. The shameful lack of emotional education that could help adolescents deal with their inevitable hurt feelings has become a stain on our national character. We now see the tragic results of neglecting emotional education in middle and high schools. *Since these are places where adolescents experience so many emotional wounds, schools should be the first line of defense against violence.* This is where all adolescents need to learn facts about feelings and how to deal honestly with their hidden, inner pain that may otherwise find voice in tragic, destructive acts.

In the 1993 report of their Commission on Violence and Youth (Volume I Summary), The American Psychological Association states that "There is overwhelming evidence that we can intervene effectively in the lives of young people to reduce or prevent their involvement in violence." Yet, conspicuously absent from their recommendations, is any reference to helping youth through improved emotional health education so they can better understand their emotional processes and develop their capability to overcome painful experiences.

II. "If Everyone Else Ignores my Feelings, Why Shouldn't I?"

Both our culture and human nature cause us to avoid dealing with unpleasant and painful issues. It is natural to avoid what is painful. It is also no surprise that we have learned "If everyone else ignores my feelings, why shouldn't I?" Indeed, if no one cares about our feelings, it is easy to believe that "My feelings are not worth caring about." Marshall Rosenberg, a leader in the Nonviolent Communication educational movement, states that in all his schooling never once was he asked about his feelings. In a society that diminishes the importance of feelings and sees emotional wounds as shameful, why would we want to examine our emotional pain? After all, our parents, successful athletes, politicians, business leaders, and entertainers routinely ignore being in emotional pain.

In our society, pretending not to hurt is so highly prized that we value being "thick skinned," "compartmentalizing," "holding back tears," "letting it slide," "forgetting about it," "shaking it off," and other determined denials like "Hey, it's nothing. I'll get over it." Americans loves "a professional," someone who successfully hides not only their pain and disappointment, but any deep feelings that "interfere" with their life or work.

During the 1972 democratic presidential primary campaign in New Hampshire, leading democratic candidate Senator Edmund Muskie was confronted during a television news interview with disturbing allegations about his wife. Reports had been circulating that she had exhibited drunken behavior and made ethnic slurs that were insulting to French Canadians, many of whom live in New Hampshire. During the emotional interview Muskie appeared to cry while refuting what was later learned to be unfounded allegations planted by Republican dirty tricksters. News reports of the interview, of course, focused on the candidate's emotional response. Muskie denied that he had cried, claiming snowflakes had blown into his eyes. Within months, however, Muskie withdrew from the campaign. Years later he described how the "crying" incident "changed people's minds about me . . .They were looking for a strong, steady man, and there I was, weak." Like so many politicians, he was more fearful of being seen as vulnerable than emotionally honest and capable of acknowledging the pain from his wife's character being publicly attacked.

III. EDH Syndrome in Emotional Distress

EDH is often an elaborate protective reaction to having our feelings hurt. The EDH syndrome involves five characteristics that together weave a deceptive fabric that cloaks true feelings and often deepens, lengthens and distorts episodes of emotional distress. These elements of EDH Syndrome are:

1. Judging Feelings.

Experiences of rejection, losses, betrayal, or humiliation are the most deeply wounding sources of hurt feelings. Many children are conditioned to judge their feelings as either good or bad, acceptable or unacceptable. Children, first of all, learn by examples their parents set in their reaction to experiencing emotional pain. Additionally, parents, teachers or other adult authority figures often unintentionally use a style of discipline and training that devalues children's hurt feelings or belittles their emotional distress. "Now come on, Johnny. Stop crying. It didn't hurt that much, did it?" When our wounded feelings are ignored or dismissed, we equate feeling bad with being a bad person. When painful feelings are interpreted as not being okay to display, there must be something wrong with us for having them. We think, "Since we're not supposed to hurt, maybe there's something terribly wrong with me because I do feel hurt?" "Maybe I deserve to suffer because I'm not an acceptable or lovable person." Each successive wounding experience seems to validate our worst fears. We must hide our hurt feelings for they are shameful. We judge ourselves guilty merely for having painful feelings.

Judging feelings literally puts our emotions on trial. Once painful feelings are "charged" as unacceptable (typically starting with parents), we need a "defense counsel" to rescue us from our sense of shame when we hurt. The job of our defense system is to convince us we can't be guilty if we deny that our pain exists. Being "charged with the offense" of having unacceptable hurt feelings requires that we employ a defense team to "prove our innocence." This defense team comes at a very high cost. Since we cannot afford to be caught off guard and reveal our real feelings and vulnerability, we must maintain constant vigilance to stifle any emotional spontaneity.

2. Developing Defenses.

As explained in Chapter Five, when we are deeply wounded emotionally, our inner sense of self sends a warning that our emotional survival is endangered. We instinctively "check out" our pain, fearing that it may be punishment for our being an unlovable or unacceptable person. We then develop protective defenses – lies and rationales to cover this forbidding fear and shame. Defenses become necessary as we need them to maintain our emotional safety and security. *Defenses may cover up our hurt, but they do not allow us to heal or overcome our pain.* Each time we experience deep emotional distress, a familiar, shameful fear reappears to remind us how undeserving we are. Every time we experience a new emotional injury, more defenses are deployed to keep past, unhealed wounds from surfacing. Our defenses against emotional pain are not impenetrable. Denying, dismissing, devaluing and disguising feelings may be overwhelmed by an accumulation or escalation of wounding experiences. When this armored wall is pierced or caves in, a storehouse of pain comes to the surface. We generally call this an "emotional breakdown," but it might be more accurate to describe it as a *defense system breakdown.*

The 14 Emotional D-fences

The following alphabetical listing includes the most common defenses used to keep us from acknowledging our wounded feelings from loss, rejection, betrayal or humiliation. These defenses are an attempt to protect ourselves from the devastating fear that we are an unworthy person. Visualize these planks of EDH by viewing them as boards in a fence surrounding our inner sense of self. These "D-Fences" are part of our protective arsenal of self-deception that helps us to pretend that our feelings really don't hurt when they do. At any one time we may use a combination of these planks in our efforts to hide our hurt feelings, rather than acknowledge, honor, and accept them as part of us:

Deceive (self)
Deflect
Defer
Degrade
Delay
Deny
Devalue
Discount
Disguise
Dismiss
Disown
Displace
Distort
Divert

The term "displace" in regard to feelings means redirecting our emotional responses from the original wounding source to substitute targets. For example, after dealing with complaints, criticism, and rejection at work all day, the harried employee returns home filled with emotional pain and starts yelling at family members "for no reason."

3. Disowning Feelings.
When children were "talked out of our feelings" by parents, they may have never learned to accept their own pain from emotionally wounding experiences without shame or blame. EDH

becomes a shield that distances us from our feelings to keep us from acknowledging emotional pain. But it has a more broad disabling effect. EDH tends to disconnect, distance and devalue all of our deep feelings. When we cannot accept our feelings as genuine, our distrust leads us to question the sincerity of even loving or caring feelings expressed to us by others.

Being confused about our own feelings and suspicious about others' feelings is a recipe for sabotaging relationships. Unacceptable feelings and guarded vulnerability destroy intimacy in relationships. We pretend we don't care when we really do, and do care when we really don't. Judith Viorst, author of *Necessary Losses* (1986), explains how pretending not to care protects us against our worst fears. She says, "We cannot lose someone we care for if we don't care." It is common to blame others for the pain we feel, giving away ownership by denying normal, human feelings. The blaming process gives others "control" over our feelings so we can never heal our own pain.

When we begin to experience good feelings (joy, love or a sense of achievement), we spoil them by questioning whether we are "deserving" enough to have them. EDH can render us incapable of emotional spontaneity, love and intimacy. The quick-witted comedian Groucho Marx once explained why he was quitting the Friar's Club Hollywood Chapter: "I just don't want to belong to any club that would have a person like me as a member." This famous Groucho Marx paradox is a humorous example of one tragic consequence of EDH, which is so damaging to our self-acceptance: EDH leads us to devalue or question the motives of anyone who offers us acceptance and love. Emotional pain that is denied remains a persistent reminder, despite our pretenses to the contrary, that we are an unlovable and unacceptable person. Therefore, "Something must be wrong with anyone who would love or want me."

4. Emotional Confusion.
Adopting pretenses about what we feel confuses us about which of our feelings are real and which are "faked." People suffering from

EDH find it difficult to respond truthfully to the question, "What are you feeling?," because real feelings often seem unclear, threatening, shameful and unsafe to reveal. With EDH, *we mistakenly believe our emotional disguises and defenses are a strength and our true feelings of vulnerability are a weakness.* We suffer from cause-and-effect confusion, blaming others for controlling how we feel. We lose authorship of our own emotional experiences. Conflict resolution trainer Marshall Rosenberg, in his 1999 book *Nonviolent Communication*, notes that "what other people do is never the cause of how we feel. What others say or do may be a stimulus, but never the cause of our feelings." Dr. Rosenberg's powerful conclusion is that "All violence is the result of people tricking themselves . . .into believing that their pain derives from other people, and that other people deserve to be punished." When we feel hurt, each new wound seems to confirm a secret, underlying fear at our core that we are an undeserving and unworthy person. We feel guilty just for being hurt. We feel embarrassed for being so easily upset by a simple rejection or loss. Then we become angry and resentful of those who we believe have the power to control how we feel. EDH so disables our normal feeling capabilities that we also become confused and uncertain as to what emotional effect we actually have upon others.

5. Disguised, Destructive Behavior.
When we blame others for the pain we feel inside, we're likely to feel angry at the world for fact that we hurt. Because EDH causes us to believe that others have power over our feelings, we often feel overwhelmed and powerlessness to heal our emotional wounds. Each new emotional injury further deepens our distress and inability to recover from it. Underneath its veneer of protection, EDH leaves us hopeless and helpless to deal with our ignored pain. EDH causes us to suffer in shameful secrecy and silence.

This is why it's so difficult to predict when people who are emotionally defended and overwhelmed by pain are likely to harm others or themselves. When we blame others for our pain, the inner pressure or seething resentment may erupt at any time in anger and self-destructive behavior. Turning blame on ourselves for suffering when we are emotionally wounded can lead to a broad range of self-destructive behavior, including depression and suicide. EDH can also lead otherwise "normal" people to avenge their suffering through indiscriminate violent acts – "blind" rage toward a hostile world – punishing others for the pain they cannot heal. We seem perplexed why disgruntled employees "go postal" killing work colleagues, or gun-toting teens "come unglued" and attack their peers "for no apparent reason." So many violent acts of this type are unexplainable because perpetrators are those who are ashamed to reveal any sign that they are hurt and devastated by what they consider to be their shameful, painful feelings.

EDH is based upon being too ashamed of our pain to deal with it openly and honestly. This causes hurt feelings to be disguised and unrecognizable. It follows that destructive acts that arise from the denied pain will also be a disguised response. Whether it is depression or violence, behavioral responses are deceptively masked expressions of unhealed wounds that are too shameful to be openly and honestly acknowledged and accepted.

Each wounding experience seems to validate the fear that something must be wrong with us to suffer so much emotional pain. In her book, *Shame and Guilt* (Appendix IV), Jane Middleton-Moz distinguishes between guilt and shame: "When we experience guilt we blame our behavior. When we experience shame, we blame our character and being." If we secretly fear that we deserve the pain we feel, we will do anything to relieve our shame and suffering. This is why pain is distorted and disguised in the form of violent acts toward others, or as self-destructive behavior – suicide or self-injury, abuse of alcohol or other drugs, compulsivity, and eating disorders.

There is varying speculation about the precise underlying reasons for the Columbine High School tragedy. One reason for failing to identify the elusive "triggering" factors is that anger and violence are disguised behavioral responses to unbearable, shameful, emotional pain. In their final videotaped "confessions" about the violent acts they were about to commit, Harris and Klebold said their rage was put inside them by others. Since they apparently could not own and therefore take responsibility for their feelings, the Columbine students killed 13 innocent people who paid the price for the troubled teens' emotional pain.

These tortured teenagers could reveal their shameful, hurt feelings in the videotape, because it was to be their final message. One wonders if they had felt free to share these secretly held feelings with parents or others perhaps they could have been helped to deal with their pain more honestly and safely. Perhaps the tragedy of Littleton could have been averted.

At high schools across America each day, perhaps tens of thousands of other teens experience rejection and humiliation. They are tortured by painful feelings similar to those felt by the Columbine killers. How can anyone know precisely when secret, inner pain is about to reach the boiling point? EDH specifically prevents us from acknowledging and truly knowing how much we hurt. The more we hide our shameful sense of powerlessness when we are hurt, the stronger our need to take some retaliatory action to avenge our pain. When we feel trapped, helpless, and incapable of ridding ourselves of unrelenting emotional agony, we may have nothing more to lose by unleashing rage against those "responsible" for our feelings; or we may destroy ourselves and thereby end our suffering.

6. Disowning happiness and our hurt

EDH involves not only disowning painful feelings. It may also disown and devalue self-affirming feelings that we would normally be free to experience such as happiness, love and accomplishment. Our defenses may be powerful but they are not always precise. They can over-protect by cutting off emotional capabilities we need to enjoy life. Consider EDH as a powerful drug. It is initially taken to dull the painful effects from emotionally wounding experiences. But this potent potion has unanticipated side effects. One such side effect is disabling other feelings. After a stunning achievement, for example, we may fleetingly experience a sense of pride, only to have it quickly dissolve. The price we pay for dulling our pain may include dulling our delight. EDH is a powerful but non-selective sedative that allows us to block feelings. Overdosing on it means deadening our feelings. Too little, and we risk being devastated by our pain. By allowing us to dull our pain, it may also dull our joy. EDH is a two-edged sword. We run a high risk when protecting ourself with a weapon capable of wielding such indiscriminate and destructive power.

IV. The Emotional Protection Racket

Using defenses to deny that we are hurt and vulnerable leads to self-deception that blinds us to the fact that we even use them. After all, the reason for not recognizing pain from wounding experiences is based on the fear and shame of being hurt. As long as we remain unaware of this emotional protection racket, we will also be blind to the high cost we pay for our defenses.

EDH is a protection racket and an extortion scheme that punishes us more than our original wounding experiences. We often pay a terrible price for disowning our feelings. We live in terror of our denied painful feelings from the past, and have paralyzing anxiety that we can be devastated by more wounding events. In his 1994 book, *Beyond Pain*, Jeffrey Kottler says that through past hurts we learn to protect ourself from future harm. Emotional defenses freeze our normally spontaneous feelings of hurt and happiness. Relying upon dishonesty and denial of feelings our "self-preservation" means we may continue the damaging game *no matter what the cost – even if it means loss of our life or happiness.*

Medical researcher Dr. Dean Ornish explores the relationship between emotional defenses and physical distress. He has written that defenses require physically harmful expenditures of energy to protect against past painful feelings and guard against experiencing new ones. In *Love & Survival*, Ornish admonishes that "With constant vigilance comes chronic stress and often enormous suffering." Patricia Evans, in her book, *The Verbally Abusive Relationship* (1992), describes the sense of imminent danger that requires maintaining rigid defenses: "If I let my guard down for one second, I get zapped!" Not only do we fear hurt feelings, she notes, but we also feel anxious when we're successful. With EDH comes a fear that someone will find out we're a fraud. Psychiatrist Willard Gaylin, author of *Feelings* (Appendix IV), says that we cling to our defense mechanisms even when they don't work. He emphasizes the danger: "You pay a bigger price for the defense than for that which is defended against."

Throughout life we use many code words to substitute for the fear associated with feeling unacceptable or unlovable. Being flawed, wrong, dumb, incompetent, or selfish are just a few. We are fearful and ashamed that there is something defective or missing in our very being that makes us unacceptable. Anyone who has the power to reject us – parents, lovers, bosses and peers – becomes "the enemy" who can destroy our self-acceptance. We learn not to show our real feelings to potential "enemies," which becomes just about everyone.

Evans lists some of the damaging self-beliefs that are associated with EDH:

> My good feelings depend upon approval from others.
> I feel angry, unappreciated, and used a great deal of the time.
> Happiness and good feelings easily dissolve like cotton candy.
> I pretend that everything is fine when it isn't.

Denying that we are deeply wounded by a painful loss by pretending it " doesn't bother me" also allows our defenses to deprive us of our true grief. EDH may remove both the *opportunity and the will* necessary for us to acknowledge and heal our hurt.

David Viscott perhaps has written the most extensively about dangers of EDH and emotional defenses. In *Emotional Resilience* (Appendix IV), he warns that "The same defenses that block feelings also block people from knowing or telling the truth about their feelings." He describes the denial: "You can still see reality clearly, but cannot relate to it emotionally. You almost sound like you are talking about another person when you talk about yourself." He says that emotional defenses are "A lie that becomes built into your character." He sees self-deception leading us to become "prisoners of feelings we cannot accept; stuck on replay and repeat." Social psychologist William Swann (*Self-Traps*, 1996), describes the tendency of EDH to perpetuate one's emotional distress. The most self-damaging aspect of EDH is that to counter every emotional assault we launch a counter-offensive by pretending that neither past or present experiences of loss have deeply wounded us. Rather than accept and get "in touch" with this pain, defended people live in denial that the loss was even painful. Defenses create an illusion that since we are cannot experience vulnerability, our emotional pain must not be real. Yet our anger and rage over being hurt *does feel genuine*, and thereby tends become a substitute for denied pain.

Letting go of emotional defenses is hard to do

Humans have an incredibly creative capacity for erecting emotional defenses for their self-protection. While we all need emotional protection to some degree to cope with life's traumas, this sophisticated armament – like any country's "national defense" – carries a very high cost. When we become addicted to EDH as a means of coping, not only does it rob us of emotional and physical energy (depression is a type of emotional fatigue), it destroys our capacity for intimacy and self-acceptance. Again, like a nation's defense system, no amount of defenses are ever enough. Pain from wounding experiences continues to assault our emotional security system, pounding away – loss after rejection after betrayal or humiliation. Thus maintaining our defenses against life's normal assaults places a heavy strain on our emotional (and physical) health and well-being.

Despite having a strong defense system, some slings and arrows manage to slip through. Every now and then they penetrate that guarded place within us that houses our vulnerable feelings – that not-okay part of ourselves we are fearful and ashamed to claim.

It is then that we are in danger of having our elaborate defense system break apart and all of our vulnerability and sense of help-lessness surface. Being heavily defended involves a dangerous risk that when EDH fails to protect us we may become emotionally disabled. We may be incapable of emotional honesty even when it is important for the survival of our marriage or emotional intimacy with our children or loved ones. EDH is a high risk emotional protection racket for the more we depend upon it, the less we can risk "lowering our shield" to share deep and vulnerable feelings even in our most close relationships.

Learning to unmask our self-deception
One of life's most challenging tasks – one that is central to successful healing during therapy – is identifying hidden feelings we secretly hold deep inside that make us believe we are unaccept-able or unlovable.

In commenting upon a 1998 national survey of 10,000 10th through 12th grade high schools students about self-confessed widespread lying by today's teenagers, the Rev. Jesse Jackson ob-served: "Lying is one of those human foibles that seems more seri-ous when someone else is doing it. No one likes to admit to lying." (*USA Weekend* magazine, October 16, 1998).

English writer Edward F. Benson (1867-1940) reflected upon the ease with which we lie to ourselves: "How desperately difficult it is to be honest with oneself. It is much easier to be honest with other people."

Discovering the dark secrets of EDH is difficult because the purpose of self-deception is to keep us unaware that we are being emotionally dishonest by hiding our pain. The difficult pursuit of emotional truth first requires admitting that we practice self-de-ception about our feelings. To be unaware of the process by which we hide painful feelings in everyday life keeps us ignorant of how much we fool ourselves about our true feelings. Being aware of the barriers to emotional honesty is essential for overcoming them.

Ignorance or denial may seem protective, but only hides from ourselves the source of our pain, anger and disappointment.

In *Emotional Resilience*, David Viscott explains that "No wonder we feel confused by emotional dishonesty. Its purpose is to confuse us about our own feelings. We are driven to act as if something didn't upset us when it was devastating." EDH is an instinctive, self-protecting human process that must be controlled, or we will live in fear of feeling our pain. We typically over-react to the painful feelings that we deny which brings on unnecessary, additional distress.

Educational materials and programs about the EDH process need to be developed so that adolescents and adults learn to deal more honestly with normal, but recurrent, emotional pain before it becomes disguised and distorted by self-deceptive defenses. Education that includes discussion of emotional honesty gives us access to ways of practicing emotional honesty – insights and skills that allow us to safely recover from our hurt feelings. It is critical that we learn how defenses and pretenses prevent us from accepting our feelings and thereby keep us from harming and accepting ourselves and others.

V. Strategic vs. Chronic Uses of EDH

No one can be emotionally honest all the time. Sometimes we are simply incapable of dealing with one more painful experience. Emotional distress is distracting to our self-awareness. It's therefore impossible to recognize the real meaning in every emotional wound we experience. But, to the extent we can identify our own EDH patterns and tendencies, we can resist relying upon this subterfuge to shut out or shut down our feelings. We can keep ourselves from becoming the unwitting prisoner of our pain.

Emotional dishonesty may be harmless pretenses we use *strategically and selectively* by design in situations where we need to overcome anxiety or embarrassment. This is different than giving in to compulsive, habitual defenses that keep us from experiencing our true feelings and render us incapable of emotional spontaneity or intimacy.

We may choose to use emotional dishonesty in temporary, strategic ways that aren't harmful. In my professional life I have experimented with consciously using the "not-caring" pretense in an attempt to reduce my anxiety and dread that a major educational program I was producing might fail. Knowing my own anxiety about failure and being seen as an incompetent person, I tried convincing myself that "It really didn't matter if the program failed." The pretense worked and my anxiety lessened. I turned my apprehension, fear and vulnerability into a win-win situation. If the event failed (I pretended) it didn't matter anyway. If it succeeded, I would be pleasantly surprised! Rather than subject myself to normal, stomach-churning anxiety anticipating possible failure, in that particular instance, I intentionally used EDH to deny my fear and insulate myself from my real feelings.

We sometimes protect ourselves by hiding our upset when a work colleague makes an insulting remark to us, for example. Rather than responding to our hurt and creating public embarrassment for ourselves and our colleague by expressing the pain, we choose to remain silent or make some comment to "smooth over" the situation. *But to ourself we recognize that we were and are wounded,* so that we can deal with hurt in private where it is more safe. This example of "benign" emotional dishonesty may also help spare work colleagues unnecessary embarrassment were their cutting remark unintentional. This is one of the most common, strategic uses of EDH. However, in these instances it is important to remind ourselves that do have hurt feelings to heal, even if we choose not to express them publicly. In *Emotional Resilience*, psychiatrist David Viscott answers the question, "How emotionally honest should you be with another?" He says that in each instance we have to assess, "How much truth can the other person stand?"

Used in the context of this book, emotional honesty refers to being truthful with ourselves about our feelings. This is far more critical to our emotional health than withholding or not expressing our real feelings to others.

Dr. Viscott recognized that society cannot tolerate totally free expressions of whatever one feels, when one feels it. However, the danger of living emotionally dishonest lives, is believing the lies that we tell ourselves about our feelings. Even if we choose to not express our hurt to others, we need to acknowledge to ourselves that we're experiencing emotional pain. Chapter 11 describes the Emotional Honesty Journal process which is a useful tool for developing self-awareness of and overcoming our deceptive inner reactions to emotional wounds.

VI. The Signs of EDH

You may find it helpful to complete the Emotional Honesty Self-Evaluation included at the end of this chapter. This series of statements is useful for determining if you may have been or are currently inclined toward EDH. This self-evaluation is one of several awareness resources adolescents and adults can use as a basis for discussing, assessing and overcoming EDH influences in their lives.

A telling characteristic of heavily defended people, caught in their web of emotional deceit, is that underneath their pretense they feel like a fake. They can never truly trust either their feelings or their judgment of them. They are embarrassed by feelings and substitute objective and analytical explanations rather than risk disclosing a shameful, inner secret. In *Love & Survival* (1997) Dean Ornish, notes there are telling signs in our language that indicate when our defenses are engaged. When people respond to our question, "How do you feel?" by saying "I feel that . . .", what follows "that" is usually not their real feeling but their *thought* about a feeling.

Prolonged emotional distress is often a sign that we are caught in some emotional lie or conflict. When we are overly tense and irritable, filled with unexplained anger, or "on edge," we may be dealing with the added distress of maintaining defenses to deny that we are hurt

We have six typical reactions when we are wounded by painful experiences:

1. We deny or devalue the feeling ("I don't really care" or "It's no big deal.")
2. We are unaware of or pretend to ignore the hurt.
3. We deepen the hurt by judging our painful feeling as shameful, "wrong," or unacceptable.
4. We project the hurt by acting out in anger or criticizing others.
5. We accept the hurt and own it as part of us without judgment, blame or shame.
6. We express the hurt and risk exposing our vulnerability to the person who hurt us.

The first four responses are typical EDH defenses that tend to perpetuate the original distress from our wounding experience. The last two responses require emotional honesty.

We have many ways of denying our hurt, including masking our feelings with feigned indifference, numbing our emotional pain with alcohol, stuffing our anger with food, engaging in compulsive acts, or escaping by over-work, depression and fantasy.

When wounded feelings are reopened by new experiences of rejection, the deepened hurt requires even stronger defenses. The response of emotional dishonesty and self-deceit becomes more deeply ingrained. As emotional distress continues, despite (and because of) our defenses, we become trapped in prolonged suffering. We become increasingly fearful of removing defenses for to do so would invite emotional devastation. The longer we depend upon defenses and pretenses, the more courage it takes to risk changing directions and reclaiming our emotional honesty.

Emotional Honesty Self-Evaluation
© 1999, Ronald Brill

This series of statements can serve as a self-evaluation exercise to help readers identify some personal factors associated with emotional dishonesty. Check each statement that applies to you. When you are finished, review your response to each question and double-check those which you feel are major factors in your present emotional makeup. You may also recognize some statements which were true in some earlier period of your life. Next to these write "pre" to indicate a previous influence that may no longer exist.

_____1. I tend to be critical and judgmental of others, and intolerant of their mistakes.

_____2. I feel uncomfortable discussing my faults or weaknesses with others.

_____3. When someone makes me angry, I have difficulty telling them so.

_____4. When I hurt inside, I hide it and behave differently from how I feel.

_____5. Other people consider me distant and not disclosing of my emotions.

_____6. My parents rarely talk(ed) openly about feeling hurt or afraid.

_____7. My parents rarely ask(ed) what I feel (felt) about my experiences.

_____8. My innermost feelings, fears or desires have been betrayed by parents, friends, partners.

_____9. I believe that showing your emotions is a sign of weak–ness or being unprofessional.

_____10. I sometimes feel that nobody really understands me and my feelings.

_____11. Others don't know when I hurt inside since I'm good at not showing my pain..

_____12. I feel uneasy and afraid of asking people what their true feelings are about me.

_____13. I believe that if a person finds out how I really feel, they won't like me.

_____14. I get embarrassed when someone finds out what I'm really feeling.

_____15. I find it difficult to say "I love you" to those close to me.

_____16. I usually have a difficult time saying "no" when asked to do something.

_____17. I usually recognize my feelings after, rather than during, an experience.

_____18. In stressful situations I'm sometimes confused and wonder, "How am I supposed to feel?"

_____19. People generally can't read my feelings or know whether I like them or not.

_____20. It is difficult for me to give myself praise or compliments.

_____21. I tend to relive painful emotional experiences and hold onto my anger.

_____22. I usually get disturbed, defensive, or angry when I am criticized.

_____23. I am generally in control of my feelings.

_____24. It is difficult for me to forget disappointments and failures.

_____25. I tend to censor my feelings and wonder if I'm entitled to feel a particular way or not.

_____26. What I'm feeling really doesn't matter to others, so my feelings are unimportant.

As you read about terms and principles of emotional honesty in this book, use this self-evaluation to identify how your personal emotional experiences and characteristics relate to these general concepts. The more items checked, the greater the tendency of EDH.

CHAPTER 7

Core Emotionally Wounding Experiences

Sticks and stones may break my bones, but words will
never hurt me.
–Childhood proverb of unspecified origin

Humans are unique in being vulnerable to suffering hurt not only
from actions and events, but also from words. The above aphorism
which many have learned at their parents' knee is not only false in
terms of human feelings, it might serve as a mantra for emotional
dishonesty. Of course we are wounded by words. Only we are
taught to pretend that we aren't hurt. In advanced societies words
more than physical acts are used to hurt people. School children
are routinely called "dirty" and humiliating names. Words convict
us in courts of law. Reputations are ruined by words. Words can
be so deeply wounding that we have libel and slander laws to
protect us from their vicious use. Despite what the well-inten-
tioned saying suggests, most advanced cultures engage in wars of
words – from epithets shouted in sports arenas against opposing
teams, to propaganda and diplomatic salvos exchanged by disput-
ing countries.

Whether by words or actions, human feelings are particularly
vulnerable to four core emotionally wounding experiences: *loss,
rejection, betrayal* and *humiliation*. The last three types of injuries
occur as often through words as actions. These four are the most

common sources of disabling emotional distress and inner turmoil. These wounding experiences tend to leave deep scars for they
threaten our inner sense of self safety and security. But it is our
reaction to these wounds that can lead to even greater distress! As
we have seen, Emotional dishonesty (EDH) is a protective reaction to having painful experiences which are shameful, frightening
and uncomfortable.

Consider how many, and how often, these common types of
wounding experiences occur in your life, as well as the lives of your
children, parents, partner or friends:

- Being rejected in social situations
- Being humiliated in front of peers
- Being publicly criticized or told we're "wrong"
- Being divorced by a spouse
- Being left by a loved one
- Being fired from a job
- Being "passed over" for a work promotion
- Being ignored or ostracized
- Being abandoned, neglected, or uncared for
- Loss (death, injury or moving away) of a family member, loved one or friend
- Loss of our own health, physical, or mental capability
- Loss of innocence and security by childhood incest, emotional abuse, or rape
- Childhood loss of a parent through divorce, separation, or abandonment
- Betrayal by a trusted person

Which of these typical wounding experiences you have encountered
recently? If you look carefully, you will see that these events occur
more often than you think, but you may not admit to yourself how
upset you were by them. These common emotional experiences con-
stitute threats to our vulnerable inner sense of self. They tend to make
us feel not only hurt but uneasy. They create a gnawing sense within

us that in some vague way, we feel endangered by our wounds. As discussed in Chapter Five, these core wounding experiences raise a fear that we may not survive particularly painful wounds. Feeling one's emotional survival is in jeopardy triggers EDH and the deployment of defenses used to fend off these painful feelings. This can lead to extreme reactions to our fear and pain. These inner reactions may include destructive acts toward ourselves or others.

Experiencing these core wounds repeatedly over time is known to create high levels of emotional distress. While each individual wounding experience may not seem (or be) significant at the time, by not attending to each hurt as it happens, we allow wounds to grow and fuse together much like a cancer that multiplies out of control. As this distress accumulates it takes on more threatening proportions. The more overwhelming it becomes, the more shameful we feel about our "secret" suffering from unacknowledged, unattended wounds. Unless addressed, painful feelings build up until even our defenses can no longer contain them. The accumulated pain may then detonate as self-destructive or violent behavior.

To understand the process – from wounding experience to emotional dishonesty reaction in everyday circumstances – take the common example of being rejected. You are not selected to participate with some of your work colleagues chosen to be on a new project team in an area for which we are unquestionably qualified. The pain from this rejection initially wounds and confuses you. You ask yourself: "Why was I not included on the project team? Since I have the ability and experience, why would I be excluded? What is my boss's motive for leaving me out? Is there some problem with me I'm not being told about?" Notice how quickly we shift from the initial experience of the pain to the self-message behind it. Part of our inner reaction to any emotional wound is questioning ourselves or blaming those whose actions have left us with hurt feelings. We may then combine individual rejections or other wounds into a larger and more painful injury, then wonder "Is there something wrong with me to hurt so much?"

As we continue to react to painful experiences, we conduct a "damage control" assessment to determine how badly we hurt and what action, if any, we should take. This assessment includes adopting a reactive strategy for responding to the wounding event. Let's say you experienced several similar incidents of rejection over the past several years. To cover your shame and pain that this rejecting incident proves that you are an unacceptable or unworthy person, you put a "spin" on the incidents that is protective. You may deny that you really wanted to be on the project team to begin with. "Sure, it's a disappointment, but its nothing I can't handle." "Hey, the whole thing didn't matter and wasn't at all important to me," you rationalize. This is how EDH works, by defending yourself against an unspeakable fear by denying that a wounding experience is truly painful. Without going into further description of what follows, we can see by this brief example that the way we deal with pain from wounding experiences is both complex and often self-deceptive. The inner reaction to having hurt feelings is far more critical to our well-being than the precipitating emotional injury.

As stated before: Having hurt feelings is a natural, common experience. Recovering from them is not. The four core wounding events discussed in this chapter are universal and inevitable experiences encountered throughout our lives. Unless the pain of each new wound is acknowledged as ours and dealt with as it occurs, our level of emotional distress is likely to rise. This may result in harmful acts toward ourselves and others to express – or relieve – the tension from our mounting pain.

Hurt feelings are real even when there is no intent to hurt us

Is our pain truly our own responsibility whether or not someone says or does something with the intention of hurting us? The answer is yes. The first principle of emotional honesty is that *any* hurt we have is real and part of our feelings. Accepting hurt feelings as our own is essential whether or not they result from another's intention to harm us. Despite another person's innocent actions that happen to hurt us, if we feel rejected, our pain is no less real than were another's actions calculated to inflict pain.

Psychiatrist and author Dr. Willard Gaylin (Appendix IV) reasons that even if you are rejected for a reason unrelated to yourself, it is the judgment you make about your hurt feelings that threatens your survival and deepens your distress.

Certain distressing experiences will trigger the alarm from our inner sense of self that we are in danger of being annihilated. Let me repeat: *When we are emotionally upset, it is not so much the wounding event, but the inner reaction we have to our hurt, that keeps us in emotional distress.* Our emotional survival need demands that we respond to any instinctive warning about a "life-threatening" emotional injury that our inner sense of self issues. One such response is the use of pretenses of emotional dishonesty to diminish or mask our most terrifying and disabling fear: Our pain is deserved because we are an unlovable or unacceptable person. In our culture, being able to take painful abuse (verbal or physical) really means avoiding feeling our pain. Unfortunately, this self-deception is what blocks our recovery from emotionally distressing experiences.

The following four core wounding experiences are those that cause the most troubling pain, most often trigger defenses, and cause emotionally dishonest reactions.

I. Loss

Any man's death diminishes me, because I am involved in
mankind; and therefore never send to know for whom the
bell tolls; it tolls for thee.
– John Donne, *Devotions* (1623)

Experiences of loss come to us in many forms. The emotional injuries from physical losses are the most devastating and therefore the most difficult to recover from. Loss is also the most difficult source of pain to acknowledge. Experiencing loss makes us feel we have lost something of ourselves. If we cannot acknowledge the losses as painful, we cannot grieve and recover from them. As we examine the four sources of hurt feelings, all involve some form of loss.

Whenever we are hurt, we are diminished in some way. We have lost something that is important to our being. In the above famous lines, English poet and clergyman John Donne expressed in philosophical terms what we know to be true in our emotional experience of losing people who are important to us.

In *The Language of Feelings* (Appendix IV), David Viscott suggests that whenever we feel hurt, the first question to ask ourselves is "What have I lost?" Judith Viorst, in her 1986 book, *Necessary Losses*, claims "The lives that we lead are determined, for better and worse, by our loss experiences." These painful experiences encompass an extensive array of upsetting events including death of a family member or loved one, as well as loss of one's physical or mental abilities due to injury, disease or aging. It is also painful to lose valued possessions, such as occurs when our home is destroyed by fire, or our life's savings are lost in a stock market crash. Personal loss not only occurs from death, but also when a mate, child, sibling or close friend moves away. Any form of parental or spousal abandonment is a crushing loss, evoking the infant's primal, instinctive survival fear discussed in Chapter Five and below.

Children feel various losses if their family moves frequently. Each relocation means the loss of friends, schoolmates and familiar places that are important to the young child's sense of security and identity. In the aftermath of the Littleton tragedy, a videotape previously recorded by the teenagers who killed themselves was made public. The videotape by Air Force "brat" Eric Harris revealed his anger and distress at he and his family being forced to move when the government closed down air bases where his father worked. He lamented that after each move he was socially demoted: "I am at the bottom of the ladder again." (*San Francisco Chronicle*, December 14, 1999.)

Unlike the three other core wounding events, loss is experienced not only from social interactions, but from changes in ourself such as losing one's health, physical or mental capability. It is far easier to recover from having lost a game or being defeated in a competitive situation than losing a loved one or someone upon whom our safety and security depends. Even "minor" losses, which on the surface seem insignificant, can add up and deepen into painful suffering.

Losing one's job can be traumatic because it involves multiple losses: One's status in the workplace, the loss of income, and the loss of one's work colleagues. Without question, the most traumatic experience for a child is losing a parent through death, divorce or desertion. As previously mentioned, the fear of abandonment appears to be our most primitive and strong survival and self-preservation instinct. Abandonment is more than a simple loss. Whether it is actual or symbolic, abandonment is devastating. This "mega-hurt" is further addressed later in this chapter.

Reactions to loss include denial, sadness, helplessness, loneliness, feeling like a victim, guilt and anger. Grief, the normal and natural response to loss, is the natural way of healing our loss. However, EDH, the pretense that our loss doesn't hurt, takes away our opportunity to grieve and therefore recover from our losses. Experiencing and accepting painful feelings is fundamental to our recovery. Because loss can threaten our very sense of safety and security, it is the emotional wound that most often triggers protective defenses and emotional dishonesty. Losses cause sustained pain because they are often irreversible. These losses include diminished physical or mental capacity, unfulfilled aspirations and unrealized dreams as we age. The devastating wounds of unbearable loss are a major factor in the high suicide rate among the elderly.

Failure, frustration, and disappointment are milder forms of loss. Being called "a loser" is punishing for it strikes at a secret fear that we may be fundamentally flawed and therefore unworthy of "winning," achieving happiness or success.

II. Rejection

In its many forms, rejection is life's most prevalent, wounding, social experience. Being rejected as a suitor or lover; a teenager's rejection by peers; not making a sports team; not getting the job promotion, performance recognition or salary raise; or being rejected because of one's race, religion, sex or sexual preference, or ethnicity – are all common causes of emotional distress. These forms of rejection are also at the core of social discord. Prejudice and being excluded from peer groups are common types of social rejection.

Elie Wiesel, whose writings and advocacy focus on preventing recurrence of the horrors of the Holocaust, says (in the chapter, "The Anatomy of Hate," from his memoir, *And the Sea Is Never Full*, 1999): "The opposite of love is not hate but indifference," which is the ultimate rejection.

Subtle forms of rejection may hurt as much or more than direct, overt ones. Being ignored, discounted or criticized are not outright rejections, but a succession of these wounds can have damaging effects, particularly upon children. For example, children suffer *silent rejection* if their emotional pain from distressing experiences are ignored or dismissed by parents. Children whose hurt feelings are treated as unimportant, or considered exaggerated feel not only their pain, but also the guilt and debilitating shame for being wounded. Even devaluing a child's emotional pain unknowingly, such as parents' comforting a child with "Oh, it's nothing. You'll get over it" is a subtle but damaging form of having one's feelings diminished and rejected.

Since our greatest fear is not being an acceptable or lovable person, everyone is sensitive to the pain of social rejection, even if they don't admit it. The fear of being rejected is so strong among teens that they put great effort into acting "cool"– pretending not to care – while smarting inside from peer put-downs, for example. Defended persons often become hypercritical toward others to alleviate anxiety about their own acceptability. Teens in particular can become brutally rejecting and sarcastic toward peers and adults. This behavior often expresses their disguised wounds of rejection.

III. Betrayal

Betrayal involves being hurt by someone we trust who lies, takes advantage of, cheats, or turns against us. Infidelity by a spouse, a close friend who reveals secrets or confidences, or a work colleague's treachery are common wounding experiences. Child sexual abuse by a parent or trusted family member is among the most painful of betrayals. When we are injured by betrayal, we may not only lose the ability to trust our own feelings, but also become excessively wary of any feelings we encounter from others. The pain arising from betrayal by a significant person in our life, if not owned and accepted with emotional honesty, remains to poison our trust of anyone with whom we become close. When someone we have valued and trusted has intentionally wounded us we may lose the ability to trust and jeopardize our future happiness. John Amodeo, in *Love & Betrayal* (Appendix IV), cautions that if we do not heal the pain of betrayal, we surely will carry the wound into our next relationship.

Rabbi Harold Kushner, in *How Good Do We Have to Be?* (Appendix IV), speaks of the "sense of unworthiness we feel about ourselves when someone we care about has mistreated us or let us down . . .These offenses bother us so deeply not only because they are wrong. . .but because they hit us where we are most vulnerable. *They touch our fear that we may really not be lovable after all.* [my emphasis]"

One of the first questions I ask of participants in emotional honesty groups is "Which types of experiences cause your feelings to hurt the most?" While there is no common pattern in men's responses, many women report that *being lied to, being deceived or betrayed* by someone they have trusted is their most upsetting experience. In discussing this response with therapists and women acquaintances, women generally consider betrayal a particularly painful emotional injury. Why does betrayal cause women such deep pain? One explanation is that trust and intimacy are priority issues for women. Linguistics professor Deborah Tannen in her popular book, *You Just Don't Understand* (1990), refers to her research on differences in communication patterns by men and women. She concludes that from early childhood, girls use language to reinforce intimacy. Boys' conversations are more about protecting their independence and status. She calls women's conversations rapport-talk; men's, report-talk.

There is a double jeopardy when betrayal is exacerbated by EDH. When we are deceived by someone we trust, we may further deceive ourselves by denying the pain that's trapped inside us. We may still feel love toward our betrayer, but fear to acknowledge it, since this would make us even more vulnerable to their harmful acts. Betrayal wounds are difficult to forgive. Extensive effort is needed to overcome emotional defenses and dishonesty that guard against admitting we are hurt. Betrayal often evokes a response of anger. I call anger one of our "disguised emotional responses" to hurt feelings because it *conceals pain* while blocking our ability to forgive others and accept ourselves.

In business and national affairs, betrayal is serious. Espionage and treason are crimes of betrayal punishable by death. Betrayal at work includes employees engaging in industrial espionage, insider trading, and breaking business agreements.

IV. Humiliation

Humiliation is public embarrassment. Humiliation is typically more painful than private shame because it exposes to the world our inner shame of being vulnerable, flawed, incompetent or socially undesirable. Being humiliated is being disgraced. Humiliation, of course, may occur by accident or be intentional. Often it is brought on by our own fear of it. One of the greatest social fears is speaking before a group. This anxiety stems from fear that some unacceptable part of ourselves will be publicly exposed leading to our being humiliated.

One of the most brutal images of humiliation in recent history was the famous Vietnam War photo of a hysterical, young, South Vietnamese girl running naked down the road to escape from her burning village. More common forms of humiliation are having our secret indiscretions revealed in public. President Clinton risked impeachment and lied to his friends, the nation and world because, as he explained, he feared the public embarrassment if details of his affair with Monica Lewinsky were disclosed. The pain of humiliation was a primary factor in the 1999 killing of University of Wyoming gay student Matthew Shepherd. One of the convicted killers who brutally pistol-whipped Shepherd and left him dying on a fence, revealed that his violent act was prompted by being embarrassed when homosexual Shepherd flirting with him in front of friends. (The judge in this case rejected the attorney's "gay panic" defense.)

V. Abandonment: The Mega-Hurt

I call abandonment a mega-hurt because it can simultaneously assault us with multiple core wounds involving loss, rejection, betrayal and humiliation. This painful experience leaves deep scars that strike at our survival fear of not being a lovable or acceptable person. This type of wound is difficult to heal since abandonment, or even apprehension that it may occur, elicits an instinctive abandonment fear we carry from once being a dependent infant. Abandonment, in its many forms, is deeply wounding not only because it attacks us on so many vulnerable fronts; it also threatens our emotional survival. The pain from abandonment triggers powerful, instinctive, and often intractable emotional defenses and denial.

Nearly 50% of American children in many communities now live in single-parent households. This shocking reality means that half the nation's children are growing up in homes where children likely suffer from feeling "abandoned" by one or the other parent. Many of these children are unable to identify the distress they feel as originating from fear of further abandonment. As we have seen earlier (Chapter Five), the dependent infant grows up with an innate survival fear of abandonment. Thus the infant's primary emotional need is to feel lovable and acceptable. The helpless infant's emotional survival appears to depend upon this inner sense of safety and security.

Both children of divorce and their parents may suffer painful wounds of "abandonment" that they are incapable of admitting.

Their fear is not necessarily "abandonment" in the legal sense, but in emotional terms. Even when separating adults believe they are "free" from a painful relationship, they may carry unacknowledged, painful wounds of betrayal, abandonment and loss. It is important to recognize that one's underlying shameful and distressing feelings from family break ups are both complex and often denied. Adults, like children, may disguise these secret or denied feelings as anger, which keeps them from confronting the true pain they can't admit to themselves, their ex-spouse or family.

Multiple impacts of abandonment on family members

Real or feared "abandonment" traumatizes both adults and children with a combination of one or more of the four core wounding events – loss, rejection, betrayal and humiliation.

1. There is the obvious **loss** of a loved one, even if that person does visit, has joint custody, or maintains some contact. The main loss for all family members is the shattering of the family unit! Children of divorce are likely to be tormented by fear that the remaining parent will also abandon them. In their 1986 book, *Guilt*, Lucy Freeman and Herbert Strean write:

> The main fear of a child is that his parents will abandon
> him, which means the death of the child . . .He also expects
> death if a parent rejects him.. He has the additional fear
> death will be meted out to him for his anger at the violent,
> rejecting or abandoning parent.

2. Both the remaining adult and child(ren) experience painful **rejection** by the parent who leaves. Children often feel responsible when their parents break up. A child may be tortured with guilt: "Maybe I should have done something to keep them together. Maybe I deserve to be abandoned because I am not lovable or acceptable." Parental neglect is also a devastating, silent form of rejection to the child who is left to wonder "What is wrong with me that my parents won't accept my hurt feelings?"

3. When parents break up, there is often an implied if not overt issue of **betrayal** of trust. Breaking a loving partnership or marriage vow usually involves at least one person's betrayal, such as an extramarital affair. Further, there may be other promises broken, such as financial, visitation, or other custody agreements. Children whose mother or father leaves the family also experience a deep sense of betrayal: "How could my mom (or dad) who loved me so much no longer want me?"

4. Despite modern mores and the growing incidence of divorce, there remains an acute sense of public embarrassment and **humiliation** when either an adult or child is left or abandoned by a mate or parent. Being left by our mate or parent causes painful loss, rejection and betrayal wounds. It is also the source of intense shame and humiliation that we are reluctant to admit. So-called "rebound" relationships are a common way of dealing with the unbearable pain from feeling unlovable or unacceptable, particularly following (symbolic or literal) abandonment. Humiliated adults tend to rush into new liaisons to "prove" their lovability and acceptability to themselves as well as others.

VI. Emotional Wounds of Adolescence

Why are core wounding experiences particularly troublesome for adolescents? Adolescence is the most emotionally insecure time of life. In *The Heart of Parenting* (1997) psychology professor John Gottman describes pre-adolescence (ages 8-12) as the period when a child's primary fear is to "avoid embarrassment at all costs." And this is only the warm-up for when they become a teenager. If teens could tell us their most troubling fears and what really hurts their feelings, we would likely discover that they live in terror of the four core wounding experiences – particularly rejection and humiliation.

Adolescents, insecure in their attempt to be independent from parents, and unsure of their identity, often suffer their emotional wounds in painful loneliness. Too embarrassed to share hurt feelings with peers, they commonly believe "Adults don't know what

I'm feeling." I would argue that neither do adolescents truly understand the nature of their troubling pain from emotional injuries. Only a few years before, they began to express their inner feelings verbally. Now, as they hesitantly stand before their peers and adults – vulnerable and desperately searching for identity and acceptance – they must deal with a hailstorm of stinging emotional injuries. At no other time of life is emotional dishonesty so prevalent and so disabling as during adolescence. Adolescents rely heavily upon emotional defenses as a protective shell to prevent parents, teachers, peers and others from seeing the troubling pain from emotional wounds that lurks inside themselves.

In his book, *No Place to Hide* (Appendix IV), Michael Nichols reviews the litany of emotional injuries caused and endured during adolescent years:

> Most of us associate painful public memories of humiliation with childhood and adolescence. All we wanted was to just be loved and included; all we got was laughed at and left behind. Parents and playmates mortified us with criticism and mockery. Some of this was a deliberate attempt to mold our behavior, some of it was just plain cruel. Unfortunately we do unto others as was done unto us.

Many adolescents who are hurt by wounding experiences are quick to take the offensive by first denying their pain, and then trying to vent it by ridiculing, mocking, scorning, teasing, taunting and humiliating their vulnerable peers. For good measure they also hurl insults and criticism at their parents. Teens quickly become masters of emotional deceit and experts at humiliating others, all the while feeling overwhelmed by their own vulnerability and emotional pain.

Adolescence is "prime time" for exposure to wounding experiences. The typical adolescent's response to loss, rejection, betrayal and humiliation is to disguise or cover up their hurt, just as they have observed adults doing. Adolescence is a frightening time filled with

---

emotional self-deception and protective use of an arsenal of defenses learned at home and from peers. For all these reasons, emotional health education in middle and high schools is essential if we are to prepare teens for their perilous emotional journey from childhood to adulthood.

Adolescents feel hurt much of the time because they are particularly vulnerable to the four core wounding experiences:

1. **Losses** abound during adolescence. The primary loss is caused by teens separating from parents and striving for independence. Teens are filled with ambivalent feelings toward parents arising from their desire to be a unique and distinct person different from their primary role models. On one hand, they are driven to individuate and disassociate from parents, while also feeling a complicated sadness about their "loss" of parental approval, safety and security. They are in double jeopardy because, as a matter of fact, they are not yet self-sufficient and independent. And they secretly fear losing the nurturing their parents have provided during their childhood. *Teens might be said to suffer, in part, from mourning the loss of their childhood.* At the same time they are losing their innocence and beginning to see parents as the imperfect humans they are, adolescents are also becoming more sensitive and aware of their own imperfections. Every one of their physical, behavioral or emotional flaws is magnified. In addition to loss of their childhood and distancing from parents, teens may "lose" older siblings who move out of the home or go away to college.

2. **Rejection** is THE big issue for teens. Adolescents have a burning need for social acceptance from peers. Teens place such great value on being liked and identifying with peer groups that any type of social rejection can be crushing. To complicate their lives, teens face a litany of potential rejecting social experiences in the form of cliques, rituals of exclusion, put-downs, name-calling, brutal criticism by peers, taunting and being shunned. School, for teens, is a theater of pain where acceptance or rejection can take on

life or death importance. During this period, romantic and sexual relationships develop and the possibility of devastating rejection and betrayal increases. Some teens who experience accumulated incidents of rejection and humiliation by peers adopt the role of "outcasts," flagrantly dressing or adorning themselves in the most outrageous manner imaginable. In effect, the outcast behavior says "I'll reject myself before others reject me." This protective behavior is similar to the pattern commonly used in adult relationships wherein one rejects partners "before they can reject me." Adolescents are consumed with hypercritical behavior directed toward others and themselves. As they grow into adolescence, youngsters rail against the hypocrisy of adults, and revel in taunting peers with critical, demeaning and rejecting remarks.

3. Teens are vulnerable to **betrayals** in many forms. As they have more social interactions outside the home, they experiment with trusting adults and peers with personal secrets and vulnerable feelings. Adolescents are particularly vulnerable to having their new found confidences breached. Embarrassing feelings are exposed by fickle friends or jealous enemies. The first forays into intimate, romantic attachments result in betrayal of trust that is often inevitable. Adolescent girls are primarily focused on forming trusting relationships, and therefore tend to experience even more betrayals than boys. A girl's trusted teacher, neighbor or even a family member may inappropriately seek to exploit their role as a valued friend or advisor.

4. **Humiliation** is a common theme in adolescents' nightmares. Insecure teens fear that some private or embarrassing aspect of themselves may be publicly exposed at any time. Blushing is commonplace. The teen's fragile, emerging identity is frequently shattered by humiliating experiences including pervasive incidents of peer ridicule. Because adolescents are at the peak of emotional vulnerability, their hurt feelings often lead to emotionally dishonest cover-ups of their secret pain. Teens want to be treated as adults, but their insecurity and need for acceptance leaves them highly vulnerable to betrayal.

Adolescents who experiment with new identities run the risk that their differences in personal appearance or behavior may further lead to their humiliation by equally insecure peers. To avoid the risk of being excluded or humiliated, adolescents feel compelled to slavishly dress and act in conformance to accepted peer norms. Adolescence is both a time of "pack mentality" and a risky period when being unique verges on the dangerous edge of being publicly embarrassed. EDH leads to even more pretenses, particularly about what they feel. Acting and saying what is "cool" and acceptable – even if it is against their principles, values or emotional truth – goes along with attempting to protect themselves from being excluded for being "different." To reveal their "real self" means exposing their vulnerability, being ridiculed or humiliated.

Teens are adults in the making. They are always trying on new identities, experimenting with whom they can trust, exploring who they are and what they feel. By definition, adolescence is a time of inner turmoil and insecurity. Teenagers live in secret fear of humiliation were their frailties or flaws to be discovered and publicly exposed.

Modeling emotional honesty in dealing with hurt feelings

Youngsters, who are in danger of practicing unhealthy self-destructive or violent ways of dealing with inexpressible emotional pain, need to know there are alternative, healthy ways for dealing with it. It is important for parents, teachers and others who deal with teens to understand, acknowledge and honor their own emotional pain, discomfort, insecurity and shame. By doing this openly, they not only provide adolescents with an example of how teens, too, can handle their painful wounds with emotional honesty; they also give them "permission" to do it. Teachers and parents can destigmatize having hurt feelings by demonstrating safe and effective ways of using emotional honesty to recover from wounding experiences. They can demonstrate as well as teach the "no fault" way of dealing with wounding experiences that avoids blame and shame. Adults who do this will naturally develop more genuine communication and deeper trust with adolescents.

Adolescents need adult role models to risk becoming more emotionally honest. By the time youngsters reach adolescents many will have learned that emotional pain and vulnerability are shameful signs of weakness. They need the example of emotionally honest, supportive parents and teachers – people who recognize but don't judge the teenager's naturally acquired EDH responses when they are hurt.

CHAPTER 8

The Family Tradition of Emotional Dishonesty (EDH)

We aren't born with the ability to understand our feelings,
we just have them.
– David Viscott, *Emotional Resilience* (1996)

I. If Infants Could Describe Their Feelings

Were it possible for infants to explain their anxieties, fears and needs, we would probably hear something like this:

Okay parents, listen up.

Since babies don't come with operating instructions, here are some simple rules you need to know about me:

1. I felt pretty safe and secure inside the womb, but being outside of mommy can be pretty frightening. So when I cry, the first rule is I want some reassurance that I am safe and secure.

2. The most frightening part of being so completely dependent on you is that you might abandon me and I'll die. You've got to realize that I interpret experiences a lot differently than you adults. Since I can't take care of my own needs, you need to be on 24-hour alert in case I get frightened.

3. Not only do I want to be fed when I'm hungry, my diaper changed when it gets wet or messy, and reassured when I hear a loud noise, I need constant attention to my feelings. When I'm scared, it seems like life and death. So don't ignore me. Sometimes I don't even

know why I'm frightened, so when in doubt assume my crying means I'm either physically or emotionally in pain.

4. About this abandonment thing: Now, as adults you might never even think of going away and leaving me to die. However, there are lots of ways it seems to me this could happen. Mommy or Daddy may go on a long trip, become ill, and stay in a hospital. I'm frightened when you get sick because you might die and I'd have no one to care for me. And, of course, there's this worry whenever you argue or fight that one or both of you will leave me. Maybe you're mad about something I've done or didn't do. I'm frightened when I cry a long time and you don't come and hold me and attend to my needs.

5. I don't deal with losses real well. You know, when my favorite plaything, my "bankie," my "binkie" (pacifier) and other reassuring things disappear, I do feel a loss and deep hurt inside. Infants don't reason real well, so to understand me you've got to think like a kid. Anything that provides me with a sense of safety, security and reassurance is vitally, I mean critically, important. Remember, here I am thrust into a new and frightening world. Yes, I am pretty easy to please, but I really get scared easily too. That's why I cry so darn much. When I get older I'll continue to have losses. At some point you'll teach me not to cry every time I'm upset and my feelings get hurt. You're then going to have to teach me what to do with my hurt feelings. *If you don't, I'll start to hide them (maybe like you, Mom and Dad).* I may learn to defend myself from hurting to the point that I'll deny that my feelings hurt even when they really do. I'll learn not to talk about my hurt. I'll feel ashamed and wrong every time I sense my feelings are hurt. I'll carry all this hurt within me the rest of my life not knowing how to accept, heal, and recover from my emotional wounds.

6. When I start to walk, you know, get my wheels and experience myself as a separate person, you're going to give me lots of rules about not touching hot stoves, hugging strange dogs, and playing in the street. I'll try to learn the rules. But remember, once I become a "real person," I'll be discovering my sense of self

with feelings separate from you, Mom and Dad. I won't want you to get angry with me. I know sometimes you can't help but get angry when I become defiant (saying "no" to every command you give). But I don't like it when you're angry at me because it makes me feel like I'm a bad person inside. And when I cry if you scold or spank me, not only my bottom but my feelings hurt. Even when I do something you don't like, I don't like feeling that I'm wrong or a bad person. If my feelings get hurt, I'll probably either throw a temper tantrum or go off and sulk somewhere. If you don't want me to act this way the rest of my life, teach me to accept my hurt feelings without feeling shame or not being OK.

7. I guess the bottom line for understanding me is that kids feel terribly vulnerable. We haven't learned to be "cool" and let rejection, abandonment, loss, betrayal, failure and criticism roll off our backs like you adults can do. The big deal here is that if you can somehow help me accept my vulnerability, a normal part of being myself, I'll feel better about me. I know doing this may not be easy for you because you may be afraid of your own emotional vulnerability. Maybe your parents didn't teach you to honor and accept your own hurt feelings. So, if I'm going to grow up emotionally healthy and honest about what I'm feeling, even if it's scary, accepting my hurt feelings and vulnerability, I'm going to need some help.

Thanks for understanding how I feel. Like you, I primarily want to feel acceptable and lovable. I was born with emotional honesty. My feelings are very much part of me. Help me honor and keep them that way.

II. The Chain of Emotional Dishonesty

> In the child's open and vulnerable pain, parents confront
> feelings they were forced to deaden in themselves long ago
> . . .and now reject in their children.
> – Arno Guren, *The Betrayal of Self* (1988)

Parental inability to deal with painful feelings

In **Love & Survival** (1998), Dr. Dean Ornish states "Each generation takes on the uncompleted emotional work of previous ones." Families tend to create their own style of emotional defenses. Dr. David Viscott, in *Emotional Resilience*, describes the legacy of emotional honesty passed from generation to generation:

> Understanding how your family shaped your defensive style helps you grasp your capacity for distortion . . .The way your family encouraged you to misrepresent the truth [about your feelings] becomes your emotional legacy . . .Until you recognize the patterns of emotional concealment that corrupted your honesty, you are just like them, doing the same thing to your children without understanding why . . .Everyone wonders what it would have been like to have been brought up in another family, to have grown up [emotionally] free and natural, without restriction.

Children are avid learners who instinctively pick up what their parents really feel, even though adults have developed great skill in attempting to hide their hurt. Consequently children tend to reflect to some degree their parents' emotional deceit by hiding or disguising their pain. In her 1978 book, *The Sorrow and the Fury*, about overcoming hurt and loss, Lucy Freeman writes that "How a mother accepts her losses influences how the child accepts his losses." Antoinette Sanders, in *The Stress-Proof Child* (Appendix IV), says that even though parents feel they have to cover up their hurt feelings in the family, "Children know just what is going on . . .Something is wrong in the family when their parents try to protect them [children] from the truth. The discrepancy between what they experience going on and what they are told frightens them."

Harold Kushner (Appendix IV) states, "Very few parents are brave enough to take off the armor of parental expertise and reveal their vulnerability . . .to their children." In his 1995 book *Family Secrets*, John Bradshaw tells how "It can be crazy-making for family members when other members, especially mom and dad, act as if they are not feeling what they are really feeling...When parents keep their feelings a secret, their children often become confused and anxious."

Parents who honor and acknowledge their child's hurt feelings provide a mirror of acceptance that reflects into the child's self-belief system. When parents are unable to validate their children's emotional pain, the children will likely grow up suffering from an inability to honor and accept their feelings. Parents who are unable to acknowledge and express their own hurt feelings without shame or blame, will model EDH before their impressionable children. Parents who are used to dismissing their own emotional pain may literally avoid their children's feelings also. Often those parents who are unable to acknowledge and accept their own hurt feelings, cannot tolerate their child's emotional distress, and so diminish its importance. They ignore what the child feels, just as they hide their own pain. They focus more on behavior, thoughts or values. Children conditioned in this manner, who do not have emotionally honest role models or appropriate emotional education programs at school, will tend to carry on the tradition of dishonoring feelings with their children when they become parents.

This chain of family emotional deception and dishonesty will continue, generation after generation, unless one or more family members can find the courage to stop the self-deception. Blaming parents for the way we handle our feelings isn't true emotional honesty, for as long as we blame *somebody else* for the way we feel, we are being dishonest and disrespectful of our feelings. *Emotional honesty is a no-fault process that starts with taking responsibility for our feelings at this very moment.* I have long been aware of my late parents' many weaknesses in child-rearing. But amazingly, only in the last several years, in my 60's, have I begun to recognize that my parents were unknowing, tragic captives of EDH, undoubtedly modeled by their parents. I now realize how emotional defenses and pretenses ruled their lives and, therefore, how they have ruled mine.

While the pattern of family EDH reflected in children may appear to be a genetically acquired trait, I see it as something acquired quite easily and innocently. Children learn their coping styles by observing parents. Unrecognized EDH is dangerous because it devalues the feelings of all family members without them being aware of the loss. In his 1973 book, *Emotional Common Sense: How to Avoid Self-Destructiveness*, Rolland Parker argues that an emotionally distressed child whose feelings are devalued "First experiences personal devaluation and then is self-destructive since he believes that his feelings have no influence on others. Furthermore, he never learns to evaluate the feelings of others, since his parents did not express feelings to accompany their actions."

Parents may hold children to a rigorous standard of not lying in general, and particularly not lying to them. But these same parents may have no idea how much they and their children's engage in *emotional* dishonesty. EDH is not telling a lie in the general sense that it is purposely telling a falsehood. It is pretending to feel something other than what you really feel.

When families devalue or invalidate feelings

In his book, *No Place to Hide* (Appendix IV), family therapist Michael Nichols notes that parents are often unable to tolerate a child's upset. Parents become upset at their children's distress and thereby try to convince children to not feel what they feel. Nichols explains that children learn from the way their parents react to their own distress – that having hurt feelings is shameful. This is how children learn how to hide their own shameful pain with defenses.

Evans, and other family therapists, often speak of problems created when a child's feelings are not validated. When parents react to the children's distress by trying to minimize their pain, a powerful message is conveyed that there is something wrong with having hurt feelings. Because feelings are a major aspect of our true selves, we lose an important part of our being when emotional responses are invalidated by parents. This devaluing occurs whether

or not it is intentional. When emotional pain is treated as something unacceptable, we believe we must avoid acknowledging it at
all costs.

Professor John Gottman, in his 1997 book, *The Heart of
Parenting*, describes how children who are "told time and time
again that their feelings are inappropriate or not valid, grow up
believing there is something inherently wrong inside themselves
because of the way they feel."

In her 1992 book, *The Verbally Abusive Relationship*, Patricia
Evans describes how emotionally neglected children begin "to feel
invisible" when they and their feelings don't count. Children "need
their parents to validate their needs and feelings," she observes,
"and this is difficult when the parent's own feelings and emotional
needs are overwhelming." In her 1993 book, *The Dance of Deception*, which addresses women's emotional honesty problems, clinical psychologist Harriet Lerner states that it isn't easy even for
mothers to share their personal feelings with children when they
cannot name them and have been taught so many fictions about
what they *should* feel.

Codependence recovery author Robert Burney (Appendix IV)
writes that "The emotionally dishonest environments we were raised
in taught us that it was not okay to feel our emotions . . .so we had
to learn ways to control our emotions in order to survive."

Defenses and pretenses are easy for children to use. Playing the
game of EDH is playing hide and seek with one's hurt feelings. In his
1988 book, *Betrayal of Self*, Arno Gruen examines how children respond when their real feelings are invalidated by parents:

> By repressing their spontaneous reactions which are too threat-
> ening [to parents] children are able to live 'in harmony' with
> their parents . . .They then deny their own suffering and
> gradually forget how to listen to their inner voice.

John Gottman (1997) explains how children feel overwhelmed
when parents are unable to deal with their own hurt feelings:

Children raised in violent households are afraid to raise issues about parents' problems or question how they are feeling for fear of inflaming the adults' anger. And, when these children become parents, they will be reluctant to raise issues about feelings with their own children. "Parents may begin to see all their kid's expressions of sadness and anger as impossible demands which they are unable to fix," writes Gottman. Thus they disregard or minimize the child's distress. When children's hurt feelings are ignored or dismissed, they react by taking the cue from parents, "If this [painful experience] is no big deal, why am I feeling so lousy? I guess I'm nothing but a big baby."

III. The Five Emotional Sins of Parents
The key role of parental discipline
    The complex relationship between our inner sense of self, our emotional safety and security fears, and our behavior are obviously beyond most youngsters' comprehension. However, parents who do understand these interrelationships can discipline children in ways that do not increase the young child's instinctive fear of feeling unworthy when they are hurt. *Young children cannot understand the distinction between being punished for something they do or say, and their acceptability as a person.* When children are punished, they naturally tend to assume that not only is their behavior unacceptable, but something is fundamentally wrong with them that causes their parents to reject and abandon them. Early in life, children interpret discipline as a loss of love and acceptance. They feel rejected, betrayed, and humiliated by punishment from parents upon whom they depend for their sense of security.
    Parental discipline, rewards and punishment, may be intended to mold children's behavior, but it may inadvertently stimulate protective defenses that make children fearful of their emotional pain and anxiety. When children translate discipline as punishment for their unacceptability as a person, *they learn to associate every painful experience as a form of deserved punishment for being unworthy, unacceptable, and unlovable.* Painful feelings become

twisted into a sign that "there is something wrong with me. My feelings hurt because I am a flawed or bad person." In *Emotional Resilience* (Appendix IV), David Viscott explains how an innocent criticism unlocks the mind's filing cabinet of evidence, proving we are bad. This fearful reaction is primarily why we lie to ourself about having painful feelings. Early in childhood, we learn to switch off feelings by denial, pretending we "don't care" when we're hurt. Disabling our feelings is one way defenses try to protect us. EDH can have dangerous side effects when the denied emotional pain accumulates and reaches an unbearable level. Children, and adults, who do not know how to deal with their hurt feelings may keep burying them until they explode as violent behavior or lead to withdrawal into depression.

Children who become dependent upon EDH for their safety and security may appear to function well on a day-to-day basis, but their emotional equilibrium depends upon continually de-ceiving themselves about the meaning of every rejection and loss. Defenses attempt to fool us into believing that our "hurt" really doesn't hurt or that the way we feel is our own or someone else's fault. The more we rely on self-deception to deny emotional pain, the more rigid and automatic our defenses become. It is not that we don't know we're wounded when our feelings hurt. It is that we have learned to disconnect from the pain through blaming others or shaming ourselves for feeling it.

As Chapter Five explained, children have instinctive defenses that deploy when their emotional survival is threatened. Infants protect themselves from life-threatening danger when their needs are not being met. They do this by crying out in panic. Their inner sense of self, which monitors how safe and secure they feel, issues an alarm that causes the infant to fear for its very life. In later life, intense emotional wounds are capable of reawakening this primal, childhood fear. Older children and adolescents, whose emotional safety and security is often threatened by painful emo-tional wounds – particularly loss, rejection, betrayal and humilia-tion – experience that same terror as when they were helpless infants totally dependent upon parents for survival. For them, the danger sign they feel internally is emotional distress. When emotionally insecure children and adolescents experience emotionally painful injuries, they often seem life-threatening.

The crying infant may be frightened, hurt, or hungry, but most of all it is fearful of not having its distress attended to. Nothing is so alarming to a parent as a small child's crying. This is nature's way of evoking a response so that helpless infants can have their survival needs met. Parents typically respond with a soothing touch, loving sounds and gestures to reassure the hysterically crying infant that it is not in danger of being abandoned.

As we progress through childhood, however, crying out becomes less acceptable and tolerable to parents. Parents soon lose patience with children's crying and begin teaching them that they do not approve of certain types of behavior. Parents see the crying out of an older child as a sign of "immaturity" and something to correct. Later in life children learn that expressing their distress by crying is not always acceptable. Parents may unknowingly condition their children by their manner of discipline – offering or withholding love and affection from children to control the *expression of their fearful or painful feelings*. Children naturally adopt their parents' responses and begin censoring painful feelings using the parents' guide for which emotional expressions are acceptable those feelings that are not okay. This early emotional censoring may then become a lifelong pattern.

Even under the best of circumstances, parenting is a daunting responsibility. Parents realize that infants are virtually dependent upon them for their survival. Yet, in addition to being protectors of a new human life, parents are also the source of their children's response patterns to painful feelings. If parents have not learned to accept their own hurt feelings and don't take responsibility for owning their own pain, no matter how much they love and nurture their their children, they may unintentionally become the child's EDH model. Instead of overcoming emotional distress, children conditioned in this manner tend to be disabled by pain and emotional vulnerability – feelings they are unable to acknowledge or express.

Adults who have not learned to distinguish between thoughts, behavior and feelings will also tend to confuse these characteristics in dealing with their children. Too often children are unable to identify what they are actually feeling because there is so much emphasis on how they are behaving or thinking. By denying and devaluing painful feelings, in particular, children take their cue from the clever, self-deceptive way parents often appear to be unmoved by obviously painful experiences that would be devastating to youngsters. Sadly, neither parent nor child may realize that they are holding their hurt feelings prisoners deep inside themselves, treating them as too dangerous and shameful to even recognize and reveal.

As parents struggle to overcome their own emotionally dishonest tendencies, they need to be alert to particular interactions with their children that reinforce EDH. Theses five emotional sins of parenting are critical errors for they tend to weaken and disable the child's ability to be emotionally honest and recover from painful experiences:

• **Ignoring or not attending to a child's feelings**

When parents don't ask or pay attention to what a child *feels* about an experience – or if there is no time for sharing feelings – children fail to learn the importance of owning their feelings. Ignoring a child's feelings is a silent form of rejection. Children whose feelings are ignored, experience a form of punishment that leaves them with a sense of guilt and shame. The believe that what they feel doesn't matter. Their feelings are not only unimportant, they are embarrassing. The parent's oversight leads to the child's disability. By not acknowledging children's sad feelings from a loss or rejection, for example, parents reinforce the defensive tendency to fool themselves by pretending they are not feeling pain. Defenses deprive us of our ability to accept, grieve for, and recover from our hurt feelings. Children caught in this denial process may also question and suppress spontaneous feelings of love, affection or joy.

Children conditioned in this manner may conclude that "Since my feelings are not important or worthwhile, I'm not important or worthwhile."

Emotional neglect can even affect the physiological basis for children's feelings. Dr. Bruce Perry of Baylor College of Medicine has examined how parental emotional neglect impairs the development of the brain's cortex, which controls feelings of belonging and attachment. Prolonged emotional distress from neglect of one's feelings can have powerful physiological impact. We have long known that our physical health affects our emotional health. Now medical research is discovering the significant *physical* effects from the way we deal with our emotional experiences. Medical research may soon be able to quantify the extent to which emotional distress perpetuates and exacerbates physical illness and incapacity.

- **Being unaware of a child's feelings as distinct from behavior or thoughts**

  If parents do not distinguish between children's behavior as being unacceptable and their feelings being "bad," children may interpret any discipline as punishment for not only what they did, but what they felt. What they think or how they behave become more important as feelings are devalued. Parents may not take into account the misbehaving or withdrawn children's hidden hurt or fearful feelings which sometimes lie behind their conduct. Focusing on correcting their behavior, for example, may send a message that devalues the importance of their feelings. Parents upset by a child's inappropriate behavior often issue a broad reprimand which carries far beyond the act itself. By disapproving behavior and not recognizing the feelings that may lie and have precede the act, parents fail to teach youngsters to deal with their hurt in more responsible ways. By learning to ask questions that allow children to talk about their hurt feelings, parents can help their children (and themselves) "get underneath" thoughts or actions to clarify the specific nature of their pain. This help focus children's awareness on their emotional responses to wounding experiences.

• **Judging or diminishing the importance of feelings**

To adults, a child's emotional responses to pain, loss or rejection may appear ridiculous and exaggerated. Or parents may tell their child, "You are just being too sensitive." Well-meaning parents who react to children's emotional distress with belittling terms may ridicule their feelings as inappropriate for the children's age or sex (e.g., "Big boys/girls don't cry"). Or parents may try to set examples for correct emotional responses by comparing their children's feelings to those of another person or some social "standard." All of these parental actions condition children to judge their feelings as being inappropriate or wrong. If their feelings are wrong, then they must be wrong. *There is no such thing as right or wrong feelings, nor good or bad emotional responses.* Feelings are part of who we are. Once negatively judged by parents, children's "bad," "childish," silly, or negative associations with these feelings may remain long afterward. Children then establish defenses to avoid feeling childish or pretend the unacceptable feelings don't exist or don't bother them. In later life, these children will have difficulty being spontaneous and open with their feelings.

• **Being responsible for others' feelings**

To hold children responsible for their parents' feelings is emotional incest. In his 1986 book, *Emotional Child Abuse*, clinical psychologist Joel Covitz says that emotional child abuse often occurs because there is a lack of respect for the "authentic feelings of some family members – especially the children." Covitz refers to this as a "family curse" that is mostly unintentional and often beneath the parent's awareness. When young children see their mother crying, they are naturally frightened and perhaps think that Mommy is dying. To try and comfort her, children put their arms around their mother and say, "Don't cry; I love you." The incest occurs when the mother responds, "Oh, that makes Mommy feel so much better when you do that." In this way, children learn that they hold the power to keep Mommy from hurting, and that they are somehow responsible for her good feelings. Perversely, when she is sad or hurt, they are guilty of not doing enough or being good enough. When parents tell children that their happiness or sadness depends on how children behave, feel or obey their wishes, parents cause children to feel responsible or guilty for the parents' own feelings.

Children are not responsible for their parents or anyone else's feelings. Children conditioned to believe they are responsible for parents' feelings will learn to be "people pleasers." They will lose the capability to know and trust their own emotional needs and feelings. Parents can acknowledge their children's compassion or concern over their welfare, but as adults they set an example of healthy emotional responsibility for children by showing they know that their pain is their own responsibility to heal. By knowing what hurts and accepting it, we become more capable of healing our own emotional wounds.

- **Trying to talk children out of their hurt feelings**

When parents try to assuage children's emotional pain arising from wounding experiences such as social rejection, loss of a pet, a close friend, or loss of a parent, they can actually cheat the child out of respecting their own feelings. Well-meaning parents may instinctively try to comfort a child by saying, "Don't feel sad; you'll get over it" or "Lots of children lose a playmate, and they don't cry about it." These parental responses to a child's painful experience conveys a hidden message that "You shouldn't have or show hurt feelings." Rather than coax, reward, or encourage children to dismiss hurt feelings, parents should take the opportunity to help them own these feelings and accept them as an important part of themselves. Rather than imply that they must get over it quickly, they encourage children to dismiss their hurt feelings as shameful. By talking about their own hurt, parents set an example of not being afraid of learning why they hurt. This is important information about who we are. Bribing children to stop them from being worried, frightened or sad actually devalues their feelings. Similarly, trying to coerce or talk children out of their hurt feelings sends a message that something must be wrong with having them.

IV. Why Love Is Not Enough

It is not enough for parents to love their children, or even
say that they love them.
They must also be attuned to the child's emotional experience.
– Michael P. Nichols, *No Place to Hide* (1991)

"I don't see why I need to know about emotional honesty when what's important is telling your kids you love them and building their sense of self-esteem." This common belief ignores the critical negative impact of emotional honesty that shapes a child's self-acceptance. I am still haunted by the public statement issued by Dylan Klebold's parents following the violent killings at Columbine High and the suicide of their son: "We could not have loved him more."

Loving children has nothing to do with helping them to safely deal with terrifying, painful feelings that result from emotional wounding experiences. Emotional honesty is modeled by the way parents deal with their own hurt feelings. Parents primarily help children learn to become emotionally honest with themselves by being honest with their own feelings. Parents want to be accepted, just as their children do. *But it's hard to be self-accepting when we're reject our feelings!* The denials and defenses used to protect us from owning and accepting painful feelings actually devalue ourselves as well as our emotional experiences.

Parents, inevitably and often unknowingly will model EDH by the way they hide their own hurt feelings. When parents are upset and angry at how their children act – which makes parents feel embarrassed, ashamed, or a failure – they need to deal with their own feelings as well as their children's misbehavior. By withholding and not honoring their own hurt feelings in the moment, parents demonstrate that denying pain is more effective than dealing with it honestly. Parents who are unable to express their own hurt, convey the idea that: "There must be something so bad or terrible about having emotional pain that I dare not reveal it."

In his 1988 book, *A Good Enough Parent*, child psychologist Bruno Bettelheim states that there are times when a parent does not feel loving toward a misbehaving child. At other times the parent may feel deep love for the child. But parents may be reluctant to acknowledge or express these opposing feelings to their child, even though each is true for that moment. With emotional honesty comes the prerogative for one's feelings to change, and to have ambivalent feelings about oneself or others. We do not always feel the same way all the time about anyone. Children have the innate capability to "see through" emotional pretenses, particularly when parents hide their distressing feelings. After all, as infants, their emotional survival depended upon sensing if their parents were in danger of being incapacitated and therefore be unable to attend to the helpless baby.

Parents may be reluctant to be emotionally honest and freely express what they feel in the moment. Were they able to do this, parents could give their children the same freedom. By withholding and thereby not honoring their own pain from a wounding experience, parents show children how to deceive themselves with they are hurt. Hidden feelings may convey an even more terrible message to the child than were they revealed. For example, the child who senses the silent tension between parents may think: "Something is wrong with Mommy or Daddy that is so bad they can't tell me. Maybe I have done something wrong. Maybe something is wrong with me." Left to their own devices, children see themselves as the center of their universe and may conclude that they are the cause of the family's problems. Children who do not hear parents express their painful feelings may get a sense that painful feelings are shameful feelings.

The trauma of family conflict

The parents' belief system of "Isn't it enough to love my child?" fails to recognize that to be emotionally healthy, children need to learn honest and effective ways of handling their hurt feelings. Otherwise, painful losses and rejection become twisted into destructive behavior. With so many children today growing up in single-parent families, we are seeing significantly more childhood emotional conflict and distress than at any other time in recent history! Family research recognizes that children from broken homes often secretly fear that they are the cause of their parents' divorce. These children also feel powerless since they cannot help reunite the family. They may feel like an unlovable and unacceptable person to have been left by someone who is supposed to have cared for them. This trauma is the legacy of shame and guilt from parents and children who are unable to deal with their painful results of abandonment issues that involve experiencing rejection, betrayal, loss and humiliation.

Parents who engage in frequent conflicts but never divorce or separate may unknowingly display their distress in an unspoken way that is particularly frightening to children. Parents' arguments, their emotional distancing and the wounding experiences trigger instinctive fears in children that they too may be unacceptable to one or both parents. A child listening to parents argue may feel compelled to take sides by judging which parent is right and which is wrong. Children, from early years through adolescence, may have been conditioned to attach judgments to certain painful feelings as "bad" or "wrong." Parents who neither honor nor accept their own nor their spouse's hurt feelings teach a powerful lesson about how children should handle their own painful experiences. Children become confused why people who once loved each other can treat each other with such anger and disrespect. This charged atmosphere leaves children both confused and anxious. Wounded feelings become fearful, painful experiences they are ashamed to openly acknowledge.

The confusion and anxiety about what they feel is a great burden for these children to bear. For their self protection, they develop emotional defenses. They hide and then distort their frightening feelings of insecurity and unworthiness. Denials of their fearful vulnerability and emotional pain seem the only way of saving themselves from emotional annihilation.

Lessons in emotional dishonesty from parents

Parents who act angry or depressed when they are rejected, fail, or experience a loss, demonstrate to children how to cover up their hurt feelings. Parents who have not learned to acknowledge and accept their painful feelings directly and honestly, may lash out at others, withdraw into depression or overly criticize family members.

Parents whose emotional dishonesty (EDH) deprives them of self-acceptance are less likely to be accepting of others, *including their children.* Children may be held to unachievable standards or pressured to excel by parents whose own self-acceptance is lacking. Parents who need constant reassurance of their own lovability and acceptability may fail to adequately set boundaries of behavior. They may "show their love" by being overly permissive with their children because they fear that disciplining them means losing their love. Parents whose EDH hides their fear of being unlovable and unacceptable must eventually confront a rebellious adolescent whose judgment and criticism of the parent can be devastating.

Parents who fear their own emotional vulnerability may be incapable of true emotional intimacy with each other. Children who grow up in families where vulnerability is frightening or a sign of weakness among parents, will have difficulty honoring and accepting their own vulnerability.

Parents who are heavily defended and unable to take responsibility for their feelings, will find it difficult to teach their children how to be emotionally honest. Parents who feel uncomfortable talking about their own painful feelings are usually too embarrassed to help children recognize and accept their hurt feelings. It is possible to be loving without being self-accepting. But children growing up in emotionally dishonest families, as they mature, become aware of differences between what parents say or do and what they are probably feeling. They become confused about which aspect of their parents is real, and which is a pretense.

Children who grow up in environments where feelings are not trusted, may later in life receive love, but will be unable to truly feel they deserve it. When children observe parents' EDH and pretenses, they may come to believe that *none* of their experienced feelings count. *They may grow up suspecting they are loved under false pretenses.*

Radio celebrity and author Garrison Keillor is a master at portraying the psychologically wounding effects of parenting in the emotionally repressive Minnesota Lutheran culture. In his mythical Lake Wobegon, discipline is honored far more than feelings. His descriptions of fictitious characters in this make-believe town are witty and profound parables that dramatically help us to understand the effects of being raised in emotionally dishonest families. The following two excerpts from Keillor's 1985 best selling book, *Lake Wobegon Days*, show how families and social institutions can turn lessons of humility into a humiliating sense of unworthiness. These two excerpts are part of a list of "95 Theses," a fictional series of complaints about parental and church influences printed in the Lake Wobegon newspaper.

#29:
You taught me not to go overboard, lose my head, or make a big deal out of it, but to keep a happy medium . . .Hold your horses. Keep a lid on it. Save it for later. Be careful. Weigh the alternatives. Wear navy blue. Years later I am constantly adjusting my feelings downward to achieve that fine balance of caution and melancholy.
#34:
For fear of what it might do to me, you never paid a compliment, and when other people did, you beat it away from me with a stick. "He certainly is looking nice and grown up." He'd look a lot nicer if he did something about his skin. "That's wonderful that he got that job." Yeah, well, we'll see how long it lasts. You trained me so well, I now perform this service for myself. I deflect every kind word directed to me, and my denials are much more extravagant than the praise. "Good speech." Oh, it was way too long, I didn't know

> what I was talking about, I was just blathering on and on, I was glad when it was over. I do this under the impression that it is humility, a becoming quality in a person. Actually, I am starved for a good word, but after the long drought of my youth, no word is quite good enough. "Good" isn't enough. Under this thin veneer of modesty lies a monster of greed. I drive away faint praise, beating my little chest, waiting to be named Sun-God, King of America, Idol of Millions, Bringer of Fire, The Great Haji, Thun-Dar The Boy Giant. I don't want to say, "Thanks, glad you liked it." I want to say, "Rise, my people. Remove your faces from the carpet, stand, look me in the face."

Children whose hurt feelings and inner conflicts are unacknowledged, dishonored, or ignored by parents will likely come to believe their feelings don't matter. If parents discount their children's feelings, children learn to disregard them too.

Peer and social acceptance influences outside the home

Even those children who receive love and encouragement from parents can develop EDH and defenses from experiences with peers and adults outside the home. Once children enter the formal school setting, their social interactions become a major influence upon unformed self-acceptability.

Even five-and six-year-old children can behave brutally toward playmates at school. Parents who are aware of principles of emotional honesty in disciplining, and who model how to acknowledge hurt feelings, give their children a good foundation for self-acceptance. But even these children must learn to "get along in the world" and particularly within their school and immediate social environment. They learn "new rules" and social norms that can undo their emotionally honest family conditioning. The new rules of EDH that children learn during their early school years, are similar to those most of us learn when starting out in the world of work.

Unfortunately, the world outside the home can be a hostile environment for young, impressionable, and insecure children. The pressure to belong, "do the right thing" and be accepted by peers, has a powerful impact not only on children's self-acceptance, but on their tendencies to hide their real feelings. Children, even those from loving homes where feelings are honored by parents, must adjust to new settings where other children may be jealous, critical, and not so accepting. Bullying, rejection, taunting and put downs from other children, as well as insensitive discipline by teachers unaware of the dangers of EDH, can create additional challenges affecting the school-age child's emotional health and resilience. Parents should not underestimate this influence. Once their children enter school and spend increasing time in social situations outside the home, children need all the emotional honesty and self-acceptance coaching that parents and teachers can provide. They will be continually challenged by new influences bringing into question the emotional honesty influences from parents.

CHAPTER 9

Punishing Ourself or Others
for our Pain

I imagine one of the reasons people cling to their hate so
stubbornly is because they sense once hate is gone, they
will be forced to deal with the pain.
–James Baldwin, *Notes of a Native Son* (1955)

I. Punishment for the "Crime" of Being Hurt
When there are no words to express our pain

What we cannot name has power over us since it remains a mystery. Destructive behavior is often the disguised expression or "vocalizing" the pain we have not named, acknowledged or accepted. The disabling effects of emotional dishonesty (EDH) – the self-deception and confusion about what we feel and whether we should feel it – prevent us from limiting our pain from common wounding experiences. When the unnamed and unhealed hurt boils over it may take form as destructive behavior toward ourselves and others. Even our defenses and denials of pain may be unable to prevent its harmful effects. People who suffer from addiction to EDH are emotionally disabled in the sense that they have limited means of expressing their accumulating, unattended pain. Were they able to acknowledge and name their pain and limit its corrosive effects upon themselves after each injury, they could more likely recover from and release it without harm to themselves or others.

Shame and fear of our pain keep it hidden inside. Being ashamed and fearful of our hurt means we give it greater power. Emotional honesty is taking responsibility for it, naming and owning pain, giving it boundaries and reality. We are frightened and tormented by ghosts, particularly, for they are formless, ethereal and difficult to detect. The same is true of feelings that are filtered through the distorted lens of EDH.

When we cannot identify, name and isolate the pain from each wounding experience, hurt coalesces and is intensified. The general alarm from our inner sense of self (see Chapter Five) then warns us we are in danger of being devastated. We worry that something must be wrong with us to suffer so much pain. This inner confusion about our hurt is often the legacy of childhood lessons of parents imploring their children to not cry or otherwise express their pain when they were frightened or wounded – in other words disregarding their hurt feelings. *This creates a mistaken belief that something must be wrong with us when we're in pain.*

Each new wound we cannot own or name causes added distress and pain. Secret shame about the pain intensifies. We hurt, but we can't acknowledge the shameful pain since doing so confirms our unworthiness. This is the dilemma confronting those who have not learned or can't practice emotional honesty. The deepening cycle of EDH intensifies the pain we feel when we are wounded by loss, rejection, betrayal and humiliation. As our unattended pain escalates, we feel more helpless and powerless to escape from it. Depression – the withdrawal from our feelings – or acts to punish others for our tormenting pain, seem to be the only way to keep from being annihilated by hurt feelings we can't even name let alone accept. Destructive behavior that injures ourselves or punishes others appears to relieve our pain. But it is only one more illusion of EDH. For this disability prevents us from knowing why we hurt. EDH prevents us from safely recovering from our emotional pain.

In his 1985 book *Vital Lies, Simple Truths: The Psychology of Self-Deception* (Appendix IV), Daniel Goleman alludes to the self-destructiveness of dishonored, hurt feelings. "The anger does not evaporate, but it can be made to seem to. It is disguised by turning it against oneself: that way lies a lifelong conviction of worthlessness."

Emotional honesty involves learning to use the language of feelings to own and honor our pain when we are wounded. In this manner we limit destructive effects of our painful experiences.

Anger, a feeling or behavior?

In terms of EDH, anger is an action masquerading as a feeling. When we say we "feel angry," we are substituting "anger" for "pain." Since we can't admit we're feeling pain, we say we're feeling angry. Feeling angry in our culture is acceptable (within limits), but feeling pain is often shameful and unacceptable. When we "admit" to being angry, we literally substitute a behavior for a feeling (pain) that is too frightening and stigmatizing to be called by its name. When we are angry at someone for what they did to us, or angry at ourselves for a stupid mistake, "anger" is more safe to acknowledge than the fact that we are in pain. Pain remains hidden while anger becomes overt. The pain that triggers anger remains unnamed and unacknowledged. This pain most often arises from experiences of loss, rejection, betrayal and humiliation. By not naming "pain" we give it even more power. We also dishonor our real feelings. EDH dishonors pain and ourselves, for it is human to be hurt and feel pain.

When killers murder in anger, or we "feel depressed," rarely underlying pain recognized. We learn through our culture to be angry in response to being emotionally wounded, because it is not acceptable to be hurt and in pain. The natural combustion of dishonored and hidden pain and fear of being overwhelmed by our hurt feelings often results in rage and violence. While violent outbursts temporarily discharge some of the explosive pain we hold inside, these eruptions only superficially relieve our distress. Anger is externalized inner pain. *Violence is the cry that expresses hidden pain we feel helpless to bear and powerless to heal.* In his 1970 Nobel lecture, Alexander Solzhenitsyn spoke of violence in the context of dishonesty: "Let us not forget that violence does not have its own separate existence and is in fact incapable of having it: It is invariably interwoven with falsehood."

Thomas Gordon, creator of parent effectiveness training (PET), calls anger a "secondary emotion" that is triggered by "underlying feeling – fear, hurt, frustration, embarrassment, grief, shame – which you find [even] more threatening or difficult to cope with." Thus, he concludes, "Vented anger alone does not heal your real wounds." Similarly, John Ruskan, founder of Integrative Processing Therapy and author of *Emotional Clearing* (2000), says that contrary to Western philosophy in which expression of feelings is viewed as the route to their clearing, talking about and acting our negative feelings don't ultimately provide relief. In fact, notes Ruskan, these activities can reinforce the very feelings we wish to resolve.

The cultural disposition to hide and fear our pain begins as a self-protective defense mechanism. By not naming or limiting pain we allow it to gather power and to fuel desperate destructive acts toward ourself and others. Gordon observes that "Both violence and depression stem from painful emotional wounds we are unable to heal." It is denying these hurt feelings, he says, that predisposes youth and adults to hide their real feelings.

In his 1984 book, *The Viscott Method*, psychiatrist David Viscott describes the sequence of inner reactions to wounding events, such as loss, which lead to anger. He says, each loss is a hurt. Each hurt causes pain. Each pain increases our fear of further hurt. Each fear of further hurt calls for defenses to hide the stored, unacknowledged hurt. Often, the only way those disabled by EDH can express their underlying pain is to "cry out" with anger. This anger is a form of retaliation to "get even" for suffering our original pain. Cognitive psychologist Aaron Beck (*Love is Never Enough*, 1988) explains that angry and defended persons tend to see other people not only as having "wronged" them, but as also trying to manipulate or deceive them. *Anger is a common reaction when we mistakenly believe that others control what we are feeling.* A dramatic example of this was found in the videotape made by Dylan Klebold which was found after the Columbine school killings. "I'm sorry I have so much rage, but you put it in me," the teenager accused.

When we are suffering from emotional wounds, it does little good to know that many other people every day encounter the same kinds of painful experiences and deal with them without getting angry or depressed. In *Anna Karenina* (1875-77), Leo Tolstoy wrote, "Happy families are all alike; every unhappy family is unhappy in its own way." The way we react to our pain is one of the characteristics that makes us unique individuals.

To protect ourselves from emotional pain we must be constantly on guard against further threats to our emotional safety. And sure enough, every new loss, rejection, or other wound we suffer *further justifies our need for even greater vigilance.* Heavily defended people are usually on alert and prepared to retaliate with anger for any emotional injury they suffer. Each painful wound reminds them of a vulnerability they arduously deny. The steady public demand for guns for self-protection may be not so much a sign of physical insecurity as emotional insecurity. Guns provide a sense of power to those who feel powerless and incapable of dealing with their pain and vulnerability.

Anger is linked to being in emotional **danger**. Angry/violent responses or being withdrawn/depressed are two of the most common ways of not acknowledging pain from wounding experiences. Both violence and depression stem from unacknowledged pain from ignored wounds. Both of these destructive behaviors provide a precarious sense of safety and security. Defenses hide the real fear and shame connected to our pain – that we may deserve our hurt and suffering because we are an unacceptable or unlovable person. EDH also traps us in destructive behavior patterns for we feel powerless and incapable of honestly dealing with and recovering from our pain.

Unfortunately, we live in a society that shows more interest in controlling violent behavior than learning how to deal with underlying painful feelings that often fuel harmful acts. When we are hurt, each wounding experience creates a series of powerful inner reactions we must understand in order to safely recover from the emotional injury. EDH is one of our most critical inner reactions to pain. By devaluing the importance of feelings that lie behind destructive behavior, we inadvertently reinforce EDH. Is there a common pattern for perpetrators of workplace violence, adolescents who shoot classmates, and those who assault their mates or children – the growing incidence of domestic violence? There is one correlation in these brutal acts: *Perpetrators of violence tend to substitute anger for pain.* They can't acknowledge their painful feelings, nor take responsibility for them. These are characteristics of EDH. Rage and violence are a means of seeking retribution against those whom perpetrators feel are responsible for their own feelings. Blaming and wanting to harm others for our own pain reveals an inability to accept and own our feelings. Anger is the disguised emotional response to wounded feelings we cannot own or understand.

In his 1999 book, *Nonviolent Communication*, Marshall Rosenberg describes a key principle about feelings that lies at the root of most violent conflict: "We are never angry because of what someone else did." Dr. Rosenberg cautions that by blaming others for our pain, we confuse the stimulus with our emotional response. "What other people do is never the cause of how we feel," he reminds us. "The more people use blame and judgment, the more defensive and aggressive they become."

The irony of violence is that perpetrators find it easier to express pain through rage because they cannot accept their hurt, nor recognize the painful wounds they inflict on others. Disabling feelings keep us from experiencing our hurt. We believe others are responsible for our painful feelings that arise from emotional injuries. Violence punishes others for our pain. Columbine High students Harris and Klebold could only sense the release of their rage, not the agony of those hit by their bullets. *How can we feel someone else's pain when we are obsessed with hiding our own?* These are some of the many tragedies of EDH.

Those who work with people in treatment for domestic violence report that often batterers are also unaware of their victim's emotional pain. After violent outbreaks, batterers may plead with victims to forgive them and not leave, but later continue their abusive behavior. The chain of family violence and abusive behavior is transmitted to children who, suffering from the disability of EDH, later become perpetrators of violence to also express their pain.

Teens who are confronted for verbally abusing peers remark that they had little idea how much their taunting hurt other students. An inherent part of EDH is not only distancing ourself from our *own* feelings, but being unaware of the feelings *others* experience as the result of our actions. Disconnecting from feelings allows violent persons the "emotional impunity" to act out their rage without regard to consequences. By dishonoring feelings we may become incapable of genuine compassion and empathy.

School counselors report that verbal abuse – put-downs and name-calling – are the most common distressing events that students report during counseling sessions. Dr. Gerald Amada, founder and former co-director of San Francisco City College Mental Health Program, reports that a very high percentage of the 5,000 students he saw over a 30-year period had reported suffering extensively from being victims of hostile verbal assaults from adolescent classmates during their middle and high school years. In counseling they vividly recall their distressing wounds years later as college students.

Why it's difficult to name our pain

We might say that each emotional injury comes embedded with a secret message that we may deserve our suffering because we are an unworthy person. Emotional wounds are not only painful, but each wound also reminds us about our "shameful" vulnerability. Upon being wounded, our first instinct, as with physical injury, is to hold onto and cover each painful emotional wound. EDH literally comes to our defense by allowing us to cover up or lie about what we are feeling. It therefore appears to reduce our pain through pretense. Pain is treated with a vow of silence. This lie allows us to act as though we were not wounded. We put on a front, not only to deceive ourselves, but to deceive others that we really don't feel hurt when we may be devastated. This pretense, which initially serves as self-protection, ironically carries with it the seeds of destructive behavior. Emotional pain that is ignored and stored continues to haunt us. It only appears to have been removed since we haven't named or claimed it. Just as the baseball player shrugs off the pain of being hit by a 95 mile per hour fast ball from the pitcher, while trotting to first base, we may develop a compelling need to hide our pain whenever we are emotionally hurt.

II. Root Causes of Violence

There are two, distinct conceptual approaches for identifying the root causes of violence. Each approach dictates the type of prevention efforts that are taken to reduce the growing violence in our culture. One is the bio-medical model which is primarily based on probing the physiology of the human brain for probable causes. Another approach is to view violence and destructive behavior – toward oneself and others – as being linked to an *acquired, functional, emotional disability.*

The bio-medical model leads to identifying physiological abnormalities in the structure and pathways within the brain. The functional emotional disability model examines the human inner reaction to experiences that leads to violent, destructive or otherwise antisocial behavior.

The bio-medical model focuses upon the scientific search for disease or genetic, biologically inherited physical characteristics that may be related to violent behavior. The functional emotional disability model is more disposed to examine how individuals acquire adaptive patterns for processing feelings that lead to acts that are harmful to themselves or others.

These two methodologies for preventing violence are significantly different not only in their approach, but in the types of "solutions" they seek. The bio-medical model, which searches for abnormality and pathology, seeks to eliminate the biological-physiological causes of violence through use of chemical, surgical or genetic intervention. The emotional disability model seeks to train or educate individuals through *self-awareness to self-correct* or re-program their acquired dysfunctional manner of processing feelings that leads to violent or self-destructive behavior.

The primary assumption underlying this book is that EDH is an acquired pattern of processing feelings, which, if not corrected, may lead to self-destructive or violent behavior. It is a natural, self-protective process that in excess or over time may get out of control and become disabling. EDH has similar characteristics to the biological (immune) protection system in that both can automatically "overre-act" to a threat of danger (infection, disease or emotional injury), and by doing so cause even greater pain or disability.

Being controlled by unattended pain

Each experience of emotional pain arises from specific wounding events. However, when painful injury isn't named and defined, it's not "realized," given form, and therefore is unspecific and uncontained. If we cannot "get hold of" pain, it may remain a free-roaming phantom continuing to assault us long after the original wounding event. *Hurt feelings that we neglect will continue to cry out to us for attention!* This avoided and unattended pain is often treated like an orphan, never truly embraced, seen or heard. It's not accepted as our own true experience. When we feel too ashamed to acknowledge being wounded, the pain we deny remains in a suspended and unreal, ghostlike form. These unattended individual experiences of pain over time coalesce into a single, overpowering source of pain, much like a cancer metastasizes from a localized point in our body. Unnamed and unattended pain from recurring wounds, if allowed to grow within us, can become an all-consuming, unbounded source of anger and hate.

In this manner, emotional pain becomes transformed from a single experience into an *uncontrollable, undefinable, and unbearable general distress.* It is no longer connected to a particular wounding experience. The overwhelming, generalized pain can then fuel a desire to rid ourselves of it by punishing ourselves or others.

Each self-destructive or violent act is an attempt to rid ourselves of unbearable emotional pain. These harmful acts are done without acknowledging or naming the real pain that prompts them. *Denied pain never leaves us; it only changes form!*

When we're able to name our pain, it remains localized (to the wounding event) and is prevented from spreading into a more pervasive emotional distress. By respecting and giving pain a name we limit its damaging effects upon us and other innocent persons.

For example, among the most common emotional wounding experiences is being betrayed by an unfaithful mate. In the aftermath of the disclosure of infidelity, the wounded partner typically reacts protectively by being angry with the philandering partner. The anger seems to release the victim's distress. But the real hurt of betrayal – being hurt by one we love and trust – is not acknowledged by the victim. The last thing a betrayed partner feels safe in revealing is that they're vulnerable and emotionally devastated by their mate. When we're in pain and feel unlovable or unacceptable, we're also too ashamed, threatened and devastated to admit the real reason that we hurt. Our love and trust of another – the most precious, intimate disclosure of vulnerability – has been betrayed. And so we typically lash out with verbal or physical retaliation, or retreat into depression – both of which mask the real pain we cannot name and claim as ours. While we may not be able to repair the relationship, we can heal our own pain by having the courage to be emotionally honest.

The terrifying secret of murderers

Psychiatrist James Gilligan, who has studied violent inmates for over 25 years as former State of Massachusetts Mental Health director, and director of the Center for the Study of Violence at Harvard Medical School, learned previously undisclosed motives for harming others. By carefully listening to inmates who murdered and brutalized innocent people, he discovered a pattern of what these violent men feel but can't reveal. He discovered that most violent acts are a form of ritual for quieting others whom they believe are responsible for the murderer's own unbearable sense of shame.

In his 1997 book, *Violence – Reflections on a National Epidemic* (Appendix IV), Gilligan observes that murderers feel the need to kill because they "have no other choice" (the precise words 15-year-old killer Kip Kinkel repeated during his confession after killing his parents and classmates in Springfield, Oregon in 1998). Gilligan concludes that people who commit violent acts do so to ward off tormenting feelings of being ridiculed. They feel accused of having shameful and painful character faults. His discussions with violent inmates reveals that *devastating feelings about themselves causes their murderous rage against others.* Their desperate acts come from feeling they can no longer suffer their humiliating "loss of self-respect," says Gilligan. Inmates the psychiatrist interviewed disclosed that the primary triggering experience for their violence was *being laughed at!* Gilligan's in-depth interviews with violent men revealed that they shared a common inability to express their tormented feelings in words, and so they voiced their pain by violent acts. He sees the inability of violent persons to identify their emotional wounds as a key for preventing violence. This suggests that both psychotherapy and education are effective, preventive strategies.

Gilligan disputes conventional ideas that perpetrators of violence carry biologically inherited tendencies, are mentally ill, or are "evil" persons – contentions he says keep our society from taking preventive action to bring violence under control. He notes that the U.S. murder rate is 5 to 25 times higher than any other industrialized nation! "The only way to explain the causes of violence so that we can learn to prevent it, is to approach violence as a problem in public health," says the noted authority on violent behavior.

Gilligan states that despite conventional wisdom, violence isn't a sign of mental illness. He reminds us that most violence is not committed by the mentally ill, and that only a very small percentage of mentally ill people are violent. He declares that "the emotion of shame is the primary cause of violence, whether toward others or towards the self." Shame is a necessary but not sufficient cause for murder. By disclosing their closely guarded secrets, violent inmates have given us new insights for preventing violence. Gilligan emphasizes the powerful effects of shameful feelings. He says the inmates' admission of emotional pain underlying their murderous rage is so shameful that "many of them would rather die than reveal it."

Rage from cumulative pain

On the surface, it may seem incredible that experiencing shameful rejection or humiliation could trigger the act of murder. Gilligan's research offers insights to help us understand this apparent absurdity. Violent people are not violent most of the time, he says. "It only happens when an incident occurs that intensifies their feelings of being humiliated, disrespected or dishonored." He emphasizes that often the very triviality of a wounding incident is what provokes deep shame that precipitates their violence. It is as though we feel more shame when we feel pain from a minor incident. Each minor incident may seem insignificant, for what we don't see is the accumulated pain people carry from previous wounding experiences that remains denied and unnamed. Therefore, what may seem like an insignificant slight, a passing criticism or cutting remark made in jest can open similar hidden wounds that have been stored for years.

This is why it is so difficult to reconstruct the underlying cause of violent outbreaks, such as the school killings that have shocked America in recent years. *It is futile to try and tie a specific wounding experience to a violent act.* In most cases it is the accumulated past pain that has been denied and hidden that is the most troubling. Pain from any individual injury may, in itself, appear as trivial, but EDH has a tendency to connect stored wounds to each other. Each of us give our pain its meaning, for it is we who feel unacceptable and unlovable when we are hurt. No one else can truly "feel our pain."

The cultural tendency to deny and lie about our pain conditions us to devalue our feelings and ourselves. By dismissing our emotional pain and lying about having it, we place ourselves and others in jeopardy for paying the price of our suffering. Painful feelings arising from emotional wounds are often stored as resentment. Unattended, accumulated pain from separate experiences coalesce until each is no longer associated with the original emotionally hurtful events. Dylan Klebold's prerecorded videotaped "confession" of the Columbine High School massacre states, "I hope we kill 250 of you." He said, "If you could see all the anger I've stored over the past four f____ing years . . ." He also recounted his hate for kids who had shunned him going back even to his *day-care* years. Eric Harris, who had been prescribed anti-depressants, had stopped taking them, according to his videotaped "confession," so he could fully release his rage. It was undoubtedly not his rage he had difficulty getting in touch with; it was his pain.

When accumulated, unattended emotional pain reaches an intolerable level, individuals generally respond in one of two ways: *They may ignite into blame-filled rage or cause withdrawal into shame-filled depression. Both are protective behaviors that avoid confronting the real wounding experiences, which are the true source of their pain.* Disguised responses to hurt feelings mask the real, underlying cause of their pain. This escalating pain may accumulate for months or years until it becomes unbearable and overwhelming.

Chronically upset people who suffer from EDH, typically withdraw into depression, suicide or other self-destructive behavior rather than lash out in violent rage. Both violent and self-destructive acts indicate individuals are unable to connect their harmful behavior with the fear and shame of their hurt feelings. *Whenever we express uncontrollable anger, the level of rage correlates to the depth and severity of underlying emotional pain that we are unable to acknowledge, honor and contain.*

The EDH epidemic

The spread of EDH throughout our culture may help explain the rise of civil rage: violence in America's schools, homes and workplaces, as well as the upsurge in depression that now disables one of every six Americans. The cumulative effects of denied, unattended hurt are passed down from parent to child, generation after generation, in the form of self-protective EDH. This is what makes EDH such a "contagious" disability that grows at an exponential, compounded rate.

When we are emotionally injured and engage protective defenses and pretenses, we often believe there is often some person, some group, or some institution to blame for our pain. The rise of Nazi Germany, may in part, be explained by this fatal inner confusion. *When people deny responsibility for what they feel, their suffering must be someone else's fault!* If we act on this misguided belief, the thirst for revenge against those we hold responsible for our pain can never be quenched. Vengeance never brings closure because our true, painful feelings are disguised as destructive acts toward others and ourselves.

Harboring a grudge against others in this manner hides our own hurt and disowns our feelings. Emotional defenses seem to work because they disguise hurt feelings with resentment against those whom we mistakenly believe control our persistent, escalating pain. As we so often see in chronically angry or violent people, *EDH retains the desire for vengeance because retaliation never ends the suffering.* Stronger and more violent measures seem to be the only recourse. In *The Art of Forgiving* (1996), author Lewis Smedes refers to this escalation of violence as a cycle of retribution – a desire to cause as much hurt as we feel. It is the ancient punishment of "an eye for an eye, a tooth for a tooth." In effect, we cannot forgive and accept ourselves for our pain and shameful vulnerability, so we must blame and punish others for it. *Our war inside leads to war outside.*

Violent or hostile consequences may follow whenever we routinely blame others for what we feel. Gilligan (Appendix IV) asserts that the tortuous, shameful sense of self prompts the act of murder to "symbolically" silence the ridicule killers have endured. He states that "Behavior can be just as symbolic as words." By punishing others for our sense of shame, violent actions are used to express our nameless, unattended pain.

The value of pain

In our society, there is one place where emotional pain and suffering are valued – our judicial system. Putting a price tag on this otherwise devalued experience, is the task of judges and juries who decide awards in personal injury lawsuits. Our judicial system is given the task of quantifying how much financial compensation a person is entitled for emotional pain and suffering they experience from an injury or accident. Perhaps we need to take a cue from our judicial system in this area. For if pain and suffering do, indeed, have value, we need to pay more attention to learning from feeling hurt. This is one benefit from being emotionally honest about our pain.

III. When Shameful Pain Becomes Self-Destructive

All self-defeating behavior is protective.
– Laurie Ashner and Mitch Meyerson, *When is Enough, Enough?* (1996)

Expressing pain with self-destructive acts

Self-destructiveness is self-punishment for the "crime" of feeling unlovable or unacceptable. In both chronic self-destructive behavior and chronic violence against others, we surrender the self to EDH. We have seen that violent behavior is often the result of blaming others for the emotional pain we feel. However, we also punish ourselves for being emotionally wounded. In effect we further harm ourselves for being hurt. Preventing *self-destructive behavior* – the more subtle types of destructive acts – has received far less attention than the subject of preventing violent behavior.

Self-destructive acts are based on the self-devaluation that occurs when we are emotionally wounded. Deeply painful experiences often trigger our primal fear that we may deserve the pain from wounding experiences because we are unlovable or unacceptable. Pain is interpreted as punishment for our unworthiness. Self-destructive acts are used to take control of our own punishment. In a bizarre way, self-punishment serves as a self-protective measure. *No longer are we at the whim of others who hold the power to cause us pain!*

Storing unattended pain for too long a period leads to a sense of helplessness: We are unable to escape from our shameful suffering. In this abyss of feeling pain and being helpless and hopeless to recover from it, several recourses are within our power. We may disconnect our feelings, and/or cut off the pain by punishing ourselves. Often we do both.

1. Disconnecting our feelings. When we "don't care anymore," we give up the freedom to feel. Suicide is often the final, desperate act to end one's unbearable, emotional pain. However there are many less severe self-destructive acts associated with EDH. These include depression and abuse of drugs, compulsive behavior such as workaholism, and other measures taken to quell the throbbing, unbearable pain that we are neither able to accept nor escape. These are attempts to bring about emotional numbing.

2. Self-punishment. EDH confuses the meaning of our emotional pain. Anger is the pain we deny having. Turned against ourselves, our denied pain harms us twice. The first wound is the actual experience of pain that usually comes from one or more of the four core wounding events. But we also interpret the pain as being deserved or "our own fault." Pain is judged as being our punishment for being an unlovable or unacceptable person. In effect, we punish ourselves for being ashamed and fearful of our pain. Self-punishing people become "victims," self-injure and even sabotage their love, happiness, or success.

In *The Language of Feelings* (Appendix IV), David Viscott explains the cruel logic behind self-destructiveness:

People who put themselves down and protect their inferiority are really saying, "Don't bother attacking me, I have already attacked myself and done a better, harsher job." They deal with a potential hurt by trying to neutralize it in advance, by outdoing any potential critic.

All self-destructive acts are driven by a confused logic that the more losses, rejection, betrayal or humiliation we experience, the more reasons we have to numb our pain or mistreat ourselves. When the pain that we've tried to hide continues to broaden, it's common to believe: "There must be something fundamentally wrong with me to keep on hurting like this." This belief often leads to despair. EDH thereby compounds rather than relieves our distress and suffering.

Withdrawal and Depression

> To each person some pity is due. If not from others from
> self will do.
>
> – poem written by Ronald Brill at age 15

Disconnecting our feelings, being depressed and living in "victim mode" engulf us in self-pity. On the surface this may seem to be a loving and consoling act toward ourselves. Since EDH continually fools us about our feelings: *Self-destructiveness is punishment masquerading as protection, and self-pity masquerading as love.*

Depression is a crushing sadness that disables spontaneous feelings of millions of Americans. It is particularly devastating and widespread among adolescents and seniors. Depression is the most common self-destructive response to being wounded. It is a severe protective measure for denying agonizing, emotional pain. EDH disables by trapping its victim in a state of helpless anxiety, much the same fear that dependent infants experience when they feel abandoned by their parents. Depression may also be a form of ritualistic self-sacrifice: an attempt to stave off emotional devastation. Withdrawal from feelings leaves a sense of emptiness and grief – a mourning of one's loss of emotional vitality and responsiveness. There is also more shame added to our original pain by feeling sad, alone, or emotionally empty.

David Viscott (*Emotional Resilience*, Appendix IV), describes the way we respond to pain by adopting a posture of indifference. When we say to ourselves, "I don't really care" or "That's what I expected" following a devastating emotional injury, he says, we are covering up our wound without acknowledging our hurt. Depression is a natural, protective reaction that "shuts down" feelings when emotional pain becomes unbearable. Self-pity, like anger, grows from a devastating fear of being a worthless, unlovable or unacceptable person. Self-pity only appears to be "taking care of myself." Depression is a feigned way of feeling love for oneself to compensate for a gnawing inner sense of unworthiness. Whatever spurious comfort we obtain from depression, it is self-destructive to cut off our emotional connection with ourselves, spouse, family or friends.

One of the reasons depression is so difficult to cure is that by giving it up we become vulnerable to all the pain we have been denying and hiding. In an emotionally dishonest society, rather than work on strengthening our ability to honestly deal with pain from wounding experiences through emotional education and self-awareness, millions of people become addicted to anti-depressants, alcohol and other drugs. Anti-depressants are the most frequently prescribed medicines in America today. The current U.S. depression rate is 10 times greater than in the days of our grandparents. Some of the increase may be due to the condition being more frequently diagnosed today.

Depression and withdrawal behavior patterns are particularly resistant to self-help or therapy, since emotional health requires recognizing and honoring feelings in the present. In an attempt to escape the emotional present, withdrawal into depression disables our spontaneous, full range of feelings, from pain to joy. This form of EDH appears to be self-comforting, but it comes at a high price. Periods of depression keep us in a frightened, helpless state, unwilling and unable to deal with our terrifying emotional reality. As we relive the terror of past hurts we fearfully await future ones.

Defenses drain emotional energy from the present and create anxiety about the future. We cling to our defenses with a persistent fear that something even worse is about to happen to us.

Most depression is not long lasting since EDH provides us with so many other forms of self-destructiveness which can be used to keep from dealing with painful, wounded feelings. Among the other disguised behaviors used in conjunction with withdrawal and depression are victimhood, workaholism and compulsiveness, eating disorders numbing substance abuse, self-injury and suicide.

Victimhood and martyrism

> Self-pity means holding our pain with fear and judgment.
> Self-compassion means embracing it with love.
> –John Amodeo, *Love & Betrayal* (1994)

Both depression and feeling victimized outwardly appear to be taking care of ourselves. Indeed, defenses seem to keep us from experiencing what we fear most – a primitive survival terror that we are likely to be annihilated because we are unacceptable and unlovable. Once we fall into either victim mode, depression or "righteous" anger, however, recovery is difficult. For if we acknowledge our vulnerability and discontinue the pretense of ignoring our pain, we fear being further wounded. People who play victim roles truly don't want to be rescued from their self-inflicted misery, any more than angry or violent people can be satisfied by emotionally or physically harming others one more time.

Feeling victimized, just like sorrowful depression, may appear to be a form of knowing and owning one's feelings. But, being a victim is an insidious form of EDH. Rather than deal with hurt feelings with the intent of healing emotional wounds and moving on to self-acceptance, victimhood is a seductive delusion that prevents recovery. It does this by mimicking vulnerability and self-compassion.

Victimhood seems like one is being emotionally honest because the victim truly appears vulnerable. But the victim's long suit is suffering, which is different from acknowledging their vulnerability. Victims parade their suffering just as a young child throws a tantrum, overreacting to frustration, physical or emotional pain to get a parent's soothing attention and love. The last thing victims are capable of admitting, however, is being terrified of confronting their real pain and emotional vulnerability. Were they able to be emotionally honest and exercise the right to claim their feelings, they would no longer feel like a victim.

Depression is a companion of victimhood. When victims don't receive the desired frequency or level of concern from others for their exaggerated wounds, they feel further rejected or unacceptable. Victimhood/Depression are twin self-defeating behaviors, for there is never enough sympathy to make the victim "feel better." This behavior pattern often entraps family members or loved ones who are unable to help victims recover from their pain. Sufferers of victimhood place those who truly care about them in a perplexing predicament. Too much sympathy and attention only feeds and perpetuates victim mode; too little is interpreted by victims as further evidence of their being unlovable persons. In addition to their original distress they also will tend to be "abandoned" by those closest to them who become frustrated by their inability to console the victim.

EDH convinces victims that they are martyrs. Rather than confront the terrifying pain of feeling unlovable or unacceptable, they may endure horrible physical or emotional abuse from others. In their twisted logic, the emotionally defended person wears suffering and martyrism like a badge of honor. Enduring an abusive relationship or marriage, or tolerating an abusive boss makes them into compliant victims. This may be the only way they feel entitled and "worthy" of being loved and accepted – except that they can't feel worthy of having it when it arrives!

Workaholism and compulsiveness

In his book *No Place to Hide* (Appendix IV), Michael Nichols says, "Obsessional people must always be in control. Of what?.

Their own feelings of inadequacy of which they are ashamed." He
calls compulsions "traps we walk into and are afraid to break out
of." For many, burying themselves in work is an effective way of
distancing the wounded feelings that accumulate in their more
emotionally vulnerable relationships outside of work.

In his brilliant and insightful analysis of the hidden distress
that many highly successful professionals and business executives
suffer, Wall Street psychiatrist Jay Rohrlich, in *Work and Love* (Appendix IV), describes how work addiction provides emotional safety
in contrast to the "danger" of being emotionally vulnerable and
"naked" in loving relationships.

Those who are capable and successful in more superficial relationships at their workplace often use their work to escape from
their insecurity and inability to share deeper intimacy in close
relationships. Emotional intimacy requires accepting one's vulnerability. In his penetrating analysis of this dichotomy, Rohrlich
observes that the structure, goals and success criteria in work are
particularly alluring to those who feel less capable of dealing with
the risk of unexpected pain, hurt and disappointment that occur
in spontaneous personal relationships. *Emotional honesty is certainly
not a requisite for work success. But it is essential for having trusting
and intimate personal relationships.* Chapter 13 focuses on the key
role emotional honesty plays in relationships.

Work routine can be used to anesthetize us from psychic pain,
notes Rohrlich. Intimacy and emotional spontaneity have no goals
or structure, they just happen. Emotional defenses, which may be
an asset in work, make intimacy a far more risky situation. Careers
often flourish in relation to one's ability to "put aside feelings" and
do what is necessary. In addition, at work we play roles (called
jobs) which often require pretenses about what we really feel. Office politics and emotional deception are constant companions in
our worklife.

Compared to other self-destructive, disguised behaviors, compulsive and obsessive disorders are more openly acknowledged in

our society today as disguised distractions that keep us from dealing with disturbing feelings. The obsessive-compulsive curmudgeon played by Jack Nicholson in the 1998 movie "As Good as it Gets," is able to acknowledge his vulnerability by feeling love and loss after returning his neighbor's dog that he had grown attached to while caring for it. Whether it is being compulsively neat and orderly, structuring our day so stray, troubling feelings don't intrude upon our routine, or adhering to an inflexible regimen that keeps our mind off of painful feelings, regimented behavior primarily keeps us in a state of feigned emotional indifference so we don't acknowledge our real feelings.

Alcohol and other drug abuse

The use of alcohol and other drugs, workaholism and compulsive behavior to escape from or numb our emotional pain are prevalent in any society or segment of the population where EDH is rampant. Adolescents often use alcohol and drug abuse to mask their disturbing, painful emotional pain and insecurity. Jan Ardell, director of substance-abuse recovery services for the Family Service Agency of Marin County, believes that "The devastating effects of alcohol and drug abuse can tragically mask other primary problems, making recovery more difficult." She states that teens are more likely to relapse to drug use if their underlying emotional pain is not effectively addressed.

Driven by their need for acceptance, teenagers are likely to seek chemical relief when their fear and anxiety of not being acceptable and lovable surfaces. This is similar to the way adults often rely on prescription medication, alcohol and other drugs to temporarily numb their unbearable, hidden pain. Adolescents are much more likely to risk substance abuse and chemical addiction because of their intense emotional insecurity and shameful fear of acknowledging their vulnerability.

Adolescents are drawn to emotionally numbing substances for

they are often unprepared for, and unable to understand and accept, the normal pain from wounding experiences. Also, as teens pull away from dependence upon parents, they encounter loss of familiar love and acceptance. All of this occurs as they seek to develop a sense of self and respect from peers. Combine these distressing events with their frequent encounter with rejection, criticism, put-downs, and commonplace humiliated by peers, and we can understand why adolescents are not only at risk of alcohol and other drug abuse, they are prime candidates for all types of emotional numbing, self-destructive behavior. For this reason, they can particularly benefit from emotional honesty training as part of drug and substance abuse programs in middle and high schools.

Eating disorders

There are significant sex differences in self-destructive behavior. Girls tend to internalize ostracism, rejection and shame rather than turning it into anger and violence. New York psychotherapist Steven Levenkron states that the incidence of cutting (self-injury) and anorexia for girls is about the same, one in 125. In his 1998 book, *Cutting*, Levenkron calls both types of self-destructive behavior "acts of emotional desperation." Eating disorders, overeating as well as bulimia or anorexia, are unquestionably self-destructive. Abusive use of food is self-punishment and self-sacrifice to alleviate otherwise unbearable emotional pain. Overeating and anorexia involve different dynamics related to one's acceptability. Though both raise physical health concerns, anorexia is mistakenly seen as a way to achieve social acceptability by being thin, while overeating is often self-sabotage since it reduces both one's longevity and social acceptability. In both cases, eating significantly less or more than is required for physical health is a serious, self-inflicted injury. Girls or women who suffer accumulated wounds of rejection, failure, betrayal, or criticism tend to feel shamefully unacceptable or unlovable.

Some new approaches that focus on developing self-acceptance as the key factor in recovery from eating disorders (e.g., Peggy Claude-Pierre's *The Secret Language of Eating Disorders*, 1997) show promise for helping individuals to manage their compulsive behavior around food.

Self-Punishment and Suicidal Wishes

> Suicide victims do not wish to end their lives but, rather,
> they wish to end their overwhelming pain.
> —Karen Theobald, Sonoma County, California suicide prevention worker

All of us know people who seem to cause themselves pain through some form of self-punishment. Constantly berating ourselves for shortcomings with self-criticism and even self-injuring behavior indicates an inability to deal with the real, underlying emotional wounds. Direct self-punishment clearly reflects the torturous belief that we deserve our pain and suffering because we are an unworthy, unlovable or unacceptable person. EDH further self-punishes by causing us to torture ourselves with unreasonable self-demands or expectations. Each failure to fulfill impossible expectations results in a further sense of unworthiness. The cycle is difficult to end for the greater our sense of unworthiness, the more punishment we believe we deserve.

Self-injury such as cutting, burning, or other self-inflicted wounds expresses a sense of helplessness and inability to relieve painful emotional wounds from loss, rejection, betrayal or humiliation. *The ritualistic, self-destructive pattern of self-inflicted pain is penance for feeling guilty, shameful and flawed whenever we are hurt.* As long as EDH continues to prevent us from dealing with injuries from each wounding experience, we may substitute self-inflicted pain for the anguish we cannot name, accept, or escape.

EDH places all feelings under suspicion. Chapter 13 discusses how this disability may sabotage relationships. When we don't feel deserving of success or love that may come our way, we often discount it when it arrives. This is another common form of self-defeat and self-punishment. EDH leads to distrusting and ruining positive feelings about ourselves that might affirm our happiness and sense of accomplishment.

Females are much more susceptible to self-inflicted injury, particularly ritualistic cutting. However, while four times as many men kill themselves as compared to women, three to four times as many women attempt suicide. Wishing to no longer live – to permanently escape from our feelings – is the ultimate self destructive urge. "Wishing we could die" is how we express our reaction to extreme humiliation. But wanting to actually end our life is connected with a more desperate need to annihilate our emotional pain. When heavily emotionally defended people are devastated by an accumulation of painful experiences that overwhelm their defenses, they may "unconditionally surrender" and release their unbearable emotional agony. This condition is commonly referred to as an emotional breakdown. It might more accurately be called *a breakdown of emotional defenses.* For it is this breakdown that releases the hidden, raw fear and shameful pain we have been struggling to deny. An accumulation of unbearable levels of emotional pain may lead to taking "the only way out" to permanently escape from it. Those unable to accept and recover from devastating pain may prefer to die. At this time of deepest despair, when we most need emotional honesty and courage to accept our feelings and ourselves, EDH again betrays us.

IV. Violence and Self-Destructiveness During Adolescence

Adolescents need to hide their real feelings more than younger children or adults do. They often feel trapped by EDH, since they lack the experience and confidence that would allow them to overcome tendencies to be depressed, or seek revenge when wounded. Youth suffering from EDH are attracted to violent portrayals of revenge since they often feel others are responsible for their hurt feelings. Chapter 14 focuses on helping adolescents to understand and confront their EDH tendencies.

Even more shocking than the death toll from teens killing their peers is the more common tendency for emotionally wounded teens to express their silent suffering through self-destructiveness. Self-destructive behavior by teens is thousands of times more prevalent than their violent acts toward peers or adults. The U.S. Department of Health and Human Services, Centers for Disease Control and Prevention reports that the rate of American youth suicides has tripled over the past three decades. Adolescents typically lack the ability to acknowledge, honor and accept hurt feelings that lie at the roots of both youth violence *and* self-destructiveness. By the time they reach adolescence, most youngsters have learned practical ways to cover up their emotional pain. Alcohol, drugs, depression, eating disorders and self-injury help them to conceal their unhealed pain. Because of their increased exposure to emotionally wounding experiences that they are unprepared to deal with, adolescents are more likely than other age groups to try and kill themselves. This is true despite a wide variety of other methods available to them for avoiding their often unbearable, painful feelings. A 1999 national poll of U.S. students aged 12 to 17 reported that over 25% of respondents knew a teen who had contemplated suicide.

The roots of teens' destructive behavior towards themselves and others lie in their inability to safely discharge accumulated pain from "shameful" emotional wounds. In particular, teens tend to deny their troubling pain from rejection by school peers. They quickly learn to not show vulnerability to common rituals of name-calling, rejection, and taunting by classmates. While we cannot eliminate ridicule, rejection, or bullying on the school campus, we can teach our children principles for openly and honestly dealing with their pain from these wounds before it erupts into destructive behavior. Those who learn and practice emotional honesty principles are more likely to accept their feelings, even their hurt, and in so doing accept themselves. Furthermore, they become more accepting and tolerant of others. *Emotional education gives teens the tools to mend themselves and help mend our society.*

Rage and Violence at School

> Bullies may feel powerful, but they do not feel accepted or loved.
> – Lillian Katz, Ph.D.

The recent rash of adolescents killing their classmates raises the question of what is the root cause, and how can we prevent such tragic violence? Adolescents carry a lethal combination of emotional insecurity; a gut-wrenching need for acceptance by peers; and a fear that their shameful vulnerability and hurt feelings will be revealed. Students with this potentially dangerous mixture are often caught in the trap of EDH. Moreover, these volatile youth are all concentrated in the nation's middle and high schools. Here emotionally fragile kids are routinely subjected to rejection and ridicule, rituals of exclusion, name-calling, and humiliation by their typically insecure peers. Whenever an individual's pain from loss, rejection, betrayal, or shameful humiliation reaches intolerable levels, destructive behavior is likely to follow. Couple this explosive emotional chemistry with the tendency of schools and parents to avoid the critical importance of emotional health education for teens – helping them to safely recover from painful wounding experiences – and you have a recipe for disaster.

In the aftermath of the Littleton, Colorado massacre, a Denver Police Department gang expert cautioned the public to not jump to a conclusion and blame guns and violence in media for causing the school tragedy. He stated that, in his experience working daily with teens, underlying most teen violence are emotional problems rooted in the adolescent's intense "need for acceptance, a feeling of self-worth, and a sense of identity." *Guns and portrayals of violence may induce emotionally troubled teens to act on their desire for revenge, but they are neither the cause of this desire nor the source of their emotional distress.*

All adolescents are "at risk" from EDH

Simplistic solutions for curbing teen violence do not address one core issue: *All adolescents are at risk today!* Adolescence is the most emotionally insecure period of life. Not only are adolescents bombarded with the glorification of violent revenge in the media, they and adults also have access to a variety of "weapons of lethal destruction" to carry out their rage from unhealed pain. Emotionally distressed teens are driven to seek violent revenge when they can no longer endure their emotional pain. Indiscriminate revenge killings take place at school because this is precisely where most will experience emotional wounds, particularly rejection and humiliation from peers. Many teens are not capable of understanding or handling the emotional pain they suffer from taunting peers, for example. Rituals of exclusion, name-calling, put-downs, and embarrassing criticism are emotional assaults tens of thousands of middle and high school students experience everyday. The focus on violence among boys ignores the fact that girls now represent 25 percent of the adolescents arrested for violent crime, according to Deborah Prothrow-Smith of the Harvard School of Public Health.

Psychiatrist Gilligan (Appendix IV) says that an adults can often see their way to restoring a sense of self-worth through success in work or love. Children, however, usually lack the emotional maturity and skill to do that. The very schools where teens suffer daily emotional pain, is where students should be learning the vital emotional skills necessary for identifying, expressing and healing their hurt feelings in healthy ways. While emotional health education is needed today more than ever, rarely is it provided for adolescents by parents or schools.

On that fateful day in April 1999, when two teenagers shot to death themselves, 12 students and a teacher at Columbine High School, 685 teens across America attempted suicide. According to the National Institute for Mental Health, 250,000 teens attempt suicide each year, and 2,000 die from these attempts. The leading cause of teen death after accidents is suicide. Unlike the very small percentage of emotionally troubled teens who kill their peers, *most adolescents silently suffer in lonely depression from the painful wounds resulting from rejection, name-calling, embarrassment and despair.*

Anger and violence among teenagers, once considered an inner city problem, has now spread to affluent, well-educated households in suburbs that are generally considered safe havens from violence and crime. All of the school murders in recent years, which have occurred in average, middle-to upper-class suburban schools, were perpetrated by teens who had been repeatedly ridiculed. Unable to deal with their own pain, they desperately sought to avenge their suffering by killing innocent classmates – a symbolic punishment of all those taunting classmates whose remarks and acts over the years caused them such humiliating, unbearable pain.

Most of these teenage killers' painful, emotionally wounding experiences of rejection and humiliation took place in school. Once they gave up trying to belong, these alienated and tormented youth took action to avenge their own pain by returning "to the scene of the crime" against them. Innocent classmates were killed at point blank range. The victims, however, were actually symbols of the emotionally disabled youths' inability to deal with their frustration, rage and sense of helplessness. The victims represented all those peers from whom the teen killers craved and failed to receive acceptance and respect. As the pain of feeling unworthy and lack of social acceptance destroyed their remaining sense of self-acceptance, they retaliated. They had nothing to live for but one final act to avenge their unbearable pain.

Given these circumstances and the small chance that social conditions will change considerably, adolescents will continue to face devastating, periodic emotional assaults for which they are not prepared. Tragically, many teenagers have not learned honest and healthy ways at home or school for attending to their pain from emotionally wounding experiences. These youth are a high risk for expressing their pain through behavior harmful towards themselves and others. Violence in our culture appeals particularly to youth. It is their inability to take responsibility for dealing with their pain that leads to their burning need to avenge it by punishing their peers. *Their entertainment, filled with thrilling displays of violence and acts of vengeance, appeals to emotionally wounded youth who suffer from not having learned safe and honest ways of healing normal but painful wounds.* The mounting horror of good kids with"bad"feelings killing their peers in schools across America suggests that all children need to learn *emotional survival skills for adolescence.* For an emotionally insecure teen desperately striving for acceptance, there is nothing worse than feeling unacceptable or rejected. For them, it can be a life or death issue.

The student massacre in Littleton, Colorado and other school shootings by adolescents are not so much about violence in our society, as it is about our children and their parents being unable to cope with their hurt feelings. What is it that makes some kids unable to tolerate painful experiences? The same type of tormenting emotional pain which likely fueled the Littleton killers' rage is similar to that experienced daily by the tens of thousands of teens who endure these wounds in shameful silence.

V. The Tragic Killings in Springfield, Oregon

The January 18, 2000 PBS Frontline television program featured a 90-minute documentary examining factors leading up to 15-year-old Kip Kinkel murdering his parents and indiscriminately killing two and wounding over 20 of his classmates at Thurston High School in May, 1998. The shy but otherwise normal, insecure and emotionally confused Springfield, Oregon boy encountered a series of emotionally wounding events not atypical for most adolescents. The documentary prompts viewers to ask questions which all parents of teens might asks themselves:

- Am I a good enough parent?
- Is there something I need to know to help make my child more resilient to rebound from emotional distress?
- What can I do to help prevent my child from engaging in destructive (e.g., violent or depressed) behavior?

The emotionally wounding events preceding young Kip's tragic acts in Springfield, Oregon fall into the four core wounding experiences addressed earlier – loss, rejection, betrayal and humiliation. These experiences most often trigger a protective response that disables the healthy emotional processing and recovery from painful experiences.

The PBS program carefully documents and attempts to recreate Kip's inner reactions, as well as his behavioral responses to wounding events using interviews with his friends, neighbors, police records and excerpts from his private diary. The documentary skillfully portrays the youngster's torturous pain without theorizing or offering psychological interpretations how it might have triggered his violent acts. The documentary, for example, failed to probe whether a functional disability such as EDH might have prevented him from dealing more safely and effectively with his painful feelings.

Being an accomplished athlete, Kip's father was disappointed at his son's lack of athletic prowess. Slightly built Kip behaved in a timid manner which was reflective of his father's lack of acceptance of him. Both father and son were shown as being uncomfortable with openly or honestly discussing their feelings. For example his father reportedly spoke disparagingly of psychologists. As Kip encountered more and more taunting by his peers, he became increasingly obsessed with guns and violence. In an effort to satisfy the withdrawn boy's fascination with firearms, his parents, described as ardent opponents of guns and violence, reluctantly capitulated and his father gave him several of his old guns. This attempt to reach his son and lift him out of his sadness and withdrawal was short-lived.

Eventually, Kip's parents agreed to have their boy enter therapy despite his father's low regard for these practitioners. The psychologist prescribed Prozac for Kip who was diagnosed as having a "depressive disorder." Kip remained on the anti-depressant for three months before being released from treatment when he had apparently recovered from the diagnosed disorder. Kip then discontinued the medication and soon thereafter relapsed into his previous reclusive pattern. No effort was made to assist him with the functional emotional disability which prevented Kip from effectively dealing with his troubling and painful feelings. The boy had secretly acquired an arsenal of weapons and explosives. Long before shooting his parents and classmates, Kip exploded some of these devices in an isolated quarry. He noted in his diary "feeling better" after these incidents.

The documentary reconstructs events at Kip's home and school which may explain his later rage. The murders of his parents and classmates were preceded by a series of wounding events that, in retrospect, may have added devastating "evidence" to the emotionally insecure teenager's sense of being unlovable and unacceptable. In his diary Kip referred to "my cold black heart that cannot love." It is clear that Kip was unable to recover from the mounting assaults of painful experiences that occurred in months (and perhaps years) preceding his tragic actions. The following is an account, from the documentary, of the four types of core wounding experiences – loss, rejection, betrayal and humiliation – which could have finally overwhelmed his protective defenses and might have led to the mild-mannered boy's desperate acts of violence:

• **Loss.** Several friends of Kip and his family noted that his demeanor began to change shortly after his older sister left home for college. This was a significant and painful loss for she was one of his most important emotional attachments other than his mother. Otherwise, the adolescent seemed completely emotionally isolated and withdrawn.

• **Humiliation.** Kip is known to have experienced at least two major humiliating experiences within months preceding the killings. One of these was a classmate calling him names on the school bus. We can assume that the reclusive teenager had suffered many such humiliating verbal attacks by peers who frequently ostracize and belittle weaker classmates. These wounding acts typically take place in front of the very peers from whom adolescents most ardently seek acceptance. This time, however, Kip's reaction was different. He kicked the taunting classmate in the head.

• **Rejection.** Kip was temporarily suspended from school following this violent act against the student on the bus .

• **Humiliation.** Based on his father's concern that Kip needed to develop his confidence and physical ability, he was encouraged by the high school football coach (a friend of Kip's father) to have the boy join the team. The result was yet another public humiliation. The slightly built 120 pound boy was overmatched and belittled by much larger and stronger players.

• **Rejection.** Kip not only suffered humiliation by the public exposure of his lack of physical prowess, the football team failure gave his father one more reason for being disappointed in his underachieving child. Kip had failed once again to live up to the expectations of his successful and athletically talented father.

• **Rejection and betrayal.** Kip then had his first adolescent romance. He finally met a girl with whom he could feel close. The girl, who initially befriended him and accompanied him to a school dance, was later described by Kip's friends as having "led him on" and then teasing him and refusing to talk to him. Kip was broken hearted. While he claimed feeling love for her, he wrote in his diary "she could never love me." This wounding experience was doubly painful to Kip for it must have deepened his fear that he was truly an unacceptable and unlovable person.

• **Rejection and humiliation.** In addition to the preceding event, there was one added emotional assault that seems to have finally overwhelmed the troubled teenager's tenuous control of his emotional pain. As a result of the school's discovery of a gun in Kip's locker, he was permanently expelled. The expulsion was not only the school administration's rejection of him, but probably symbolized his rejection by the all-important peers upon whom he was dependent for social acceptability and sense of his own identity.

- **Rejection.** Kip's humiliating expulsion from high school was compounded by his father's reaction. Following the gun incident, the documentary suggests that Kip most likely endured the rage and scorn of his father during their long ride home from the police station to their secluded residence. The documentary surmises that Kip's father was undoubtedly unable to contain his anger and disappointment in his son. His father was reported by friends to have been humiliated by Kip's expulsion from school. Not only had his son ruined his own opportunity for success in school, his father felt he had irreparably damaged his and the family's reputation in the community.

Detonation of accumulated pain

Following Kip's suspension, his enraged father confiscated the guns he had given his son. However, later one fateful day in May, Kip retrieved a gun from his hidden arsenal, went downstairs and shot his father in cold silence as he sat reading at the kitchen table. After his arrest, the sobbing 15-year-old described his following actions to police:

- He was terrified of confronting his mother after having killed his father. He reportedly was so fearful of his mother's reaction (the thought of being rejection by the only remaining person with whom he had any emotional connection) that he waited until she arrived home. He then shot and killed her after telling her he loved her.
- The following day the 15-year-old assembled his cache of weapons and ammunition and drove the family car to school where he opened fire on students in the final act to avenge all the pain and suffering he was no longer able to contain. After his arrest, he kept repeating to police the haunting reason for his acts: "I had no other choice!"

Achieving a violence-proof society

How can this tragedy help us to learn how to prevent future teen violence?

• Could all children, including emotionally confused students like Kip, be taught healthy and honest ways of dealing with and recovering from their inexpressible pain? Could they learn how to become more resilient and recover from wounding experiences, so they become more resistant to destructive acts, and more self-accepting?

• Could emotional health education programs for parents and students at the high school have demonstrated emotionally honest ways for dealing with painful feelings arising from predictable wounding experiences during adolescence (including family losses and rejection as well as student rejection and humiliating acts by peers)?

• Could simple, preventive training measures based on general knowledge of adolescent emotional dishonesty tendencies have spared Kip, his classmates and parents from the awful, violent expression of his fear, rage and overwhelming shame for having painful feelings he couldn't understand, name or accept?

Rather that try and bullet-proof our schools, wouldn't it be more wise to violence-proof our students? If we could help teens recover from their hurt feelings without hiding their pain, or expressing it in anger, they would have no need to harm themselves or others. Removing guns may be a worthy cause, but it will not end a child's needless distress from EDH, nor will it remove their misplaced desire for revenge.

I believe that all adolescents and their parents can benefit from emotional education that helps them to develop basic skills for recovering from common wounding experiences. Emotional health education of this type is essential for enabling adolescents to understand the dangers of EDH which can fuel explosive violence or self-destructive behavior.

Can we afford to withhold essential emotional education from teens and adults when we know many are in danger of being disabled by EDH and are likely to express their pain through destructive acts? Because few schools and parents teach healthy and honest ways of dealing with everyday hurt feelings, most teens are easy prey for hate-mongering media influences which glorify the powerful force of vengeance through violence. Adolescents who learn and practice skills of emotional honesty will help to make schools a more safe place. They will also become future parent-models capable of helping their children deal more honestly and effectively with their hurt feelings.

It's possible to learn how to prevent hurt feelings and emotional pain from turning into destructive behavior. The lessons of emotional honesty are not contained in some obscure, technical treatise on psychology. We're capable of violence-proofing our children and future generations, rather than focusing primarily on removing *the instruments of violence* that in our culture will always be available in some form. It comes down to being aware of the real cause for humans *needing to punish others or themselves with destructive behavior.*

We know, for example, that fear of vulnerability and pain is disguised by destructive acts. We also know that it is our natural tendency to hide our vulnerability. In her November 1995 *Cosmopolitan* magazine article, "I'm Sick to Death of Being Vulnerable," Susan Jacoby writes:

> Some degree of vulnerability – the capacity to suffer along with others as well as to feel one's own pain and disappointment – is a crucial component of emotional health. "Vulnerability does make us feel weak and exposed," says New York City psychiatrist Willard Gaylin [Appendix IV], "but it's also one of the qualities that makes us fully human. We've all read about invulnerable people – the serial killers, Ted Bundys, Charles Mansons – who can't be hurt or feel the pain of others."

Emotional honesty requires seeing through our defenses and pretenses by recognizing how they control our lives and can lead to mounting anger and rage. Unfortunately, untold millions of people daily try to discharge their outrage because they are unable to honestly deal with their emotional pain. The spread of road rage, work rage, school rage, and the rage that results in the growth of domestic violence is strong evidence of increasing EDH in our society. Airlines also report increasing incidents of passengers exhibiting rage against flight personnel or fellow passengers. Harboring unhealed hurt feelings has become the source of an epidemic of social incivility, rage and violence. It is also a major factor in self-destructive behavior.

Psychoanalyst Arno Gruen, in *The Betrayal of Self* (1988), refers to "the often unconscious feeling of impotence which stems from the crippling of our genuine human potential [to feel] that fills us with rage. Unaware of the source of this rage, we inevitably turn it against ourselves or against another person."

Sometime they'll give a war and nobody will come.
– Carl Sandburg, *The People, Yes* (1936)

Pulitzer Prize winning poet and biographer Carl Sanburg suggests in the above powerful line about the vision of a little girl,* that violence itself would have fewer patrons were we to have less need to use it as a means of expressing our pain. The question of why violence is so prevalent in our society is debated following every mass shooting of innocent people by some "crazed" gunman in our communities. Is violence against innocents "craziness" that can be prevented only by taking away guns? Or, do we need to look at helping people to be more responsible in dealing with their hurt feelings?

Violence in society has become prevalent, in part, due to the mistaken belief that guns make us seem invulnerable. We cannot both be human and invulnerable. And so we must learn to live with our natural vulnerability, and use our emotional freedom to honor what we feel. Otherwise, when we become injured and don't know what to do with our pain, the self-protective instinct of EDH is likely to disconnect and disable our feelings to protect us from emotional devastation. Destructive behavior may then become the only way to express the denied, disowned pain that builds up within us.

If we practiced emotional honesty when our feelings are injured we could become a far less violent society. If we learned to acknowledge inner pain directly and honestly, we would have less need to avenge our emotional wounds. This, I suggest, might do more to prevent gun violence than all the social and political action seeking to remove guns and violent entertainment from our culture.

The most powerful violence prevention tool schools have at their disposal is emotional health education. Schools are the natural place for teens to learn how to honestly deal with troubling feelings *before* they lead to destructive behavior. Schools and parents need more resources and new strategies for teaching teens how to understand, accept and express their hurt feelings in safe and healthy ways. We can no longer ignore our social responsibility to offer preventive emotional education programs so teens and adults can learn essential emotional skills. These skills enable more of our people to honor and accept hurt feelings without shame or judgment. Littleton sounded a national alarm that we must begin this education process.

Our teens, their parents and teachers have the ability *and choice* to develop their capacity to accept and own their emotional pain without blame or judgment even though they won't always be successful in accomplishing this goal. But by making a start *we can soon become a nation where people do not need to punish themselves or others for their pain.*

*The full context of this line is:

"The little girl saw her first troop parade and asked, "What
    are those?"

"Soldiers."

"What are soldiers?"

"They are for war. They fight and each tries to kill as many
    of the other side as he can."

The girl held still and studied.

"Do you know . . .I know something?"

"Yes, what is it you know?"

"Sometime they'll give a war and nobody will come."

PART THREE

*Strengthening Emotional
Honesty and Self-Acceptance*

CHAPTER 10

Ten Capabilities of Emotional Honesty

Emotional honesty is a capability that can be developed through emotional education and practice. By developing these 10 primary capabilities we become more skillful in using emotional honesty with ourselves and with others.

1. Ability to distinguish feelings from thoughts, behavior, beliefs and values
2. Ability to acknowledge having hurt feelings when we are wounded
3. Ability to accept feelings without judgment (right or wrong; bad or good)
4. Ability to own our feelings as an integral part of who we are
5. Ability to honor vulnerability in ourselves and others as a valuable part of being human.
6. Ability to name and express hurt feelings without blame or shame
7. Ability to detect our emotional dishonesty (EDH) and defenses that deny what we really feel (even if we are presently unable to stop the pretense)
8. Ability to recognize our disguised behavioral responses to painful feelings
9. Ability to validate feelings of others to help them own what they feel
10. Ability to not take responsibility for other's feelings

The Emotional Honesty Journal process discussed in the next chapter can be a helpful tool for becoming more aware of practical applications of these lessons. Emotional Honesty Discussions Groups (Appendix III) are also useful for applying these lessons in a group of compassionate learners.

I. Distinguish Feelings from Thoughts, Behavior and Beliefs

Feelings come from a different place than thoughts. Yet we often mistake thoughts, acts and beliefs for feelings. What we think about our hurt feelings is sometimes different from what we feel. In his 1998 book *Love & Survival*, Dr. Dean Ornish says "To feel that you're wrong" is not a feeling. It is a thought masquerading as a feeling. He cautions that when we say "I feel like . . .," "I feel that . . ." or I feel as though . . ." we are expressing judgment, not feelings. Ornish says, "Feelings are true. Thoughts can be argued about. Feelings are an experience. Feelings keep us in the present moment." He also emphasizes that "Emotions influence us more than thoughts." In *The Resilient Child* (1994), Joanne Joseph notes that children starting at age 10 or 11 are capable of grasping relationships between thoughts, feelings and actions.

When we rationalize away what we feel by thinking we don't feel it, our actions are often at odds with how we feel. And, most important, our beliefs about "good and bad," "right and wrong" feelings can lead to censoring our emotions, particularly those which we have learned are embarrassing or socially unacceptable. Since we live in a society more interested in what we do or think rather than what we feel, it is easy to become confused whether we are having a thought (I think I'm mad), a feeling (I feel hurt), a belief (I must be a terrible person), or a value (that hurtful experience doesn't matter). To heal our hurt feelings, we must first recognize that what is bothering us is an emotional wound, or perhaps a series of painful experiences. We need to concentrate on examining the raw feeling unembellished by what we believe, think, or how we have been taught we should feel.

II. Acknowledge Hurt Feelings

Why do we find it so difficult to acknowledge when our feelings are hurt? We often feel it is something "we must get over." Psychotherapist Michael Nichols (*No Place to Hide*, Appendix IV) notes that often the primary way parents react when their child is sad or wounded is to say or do something to talk them out of their hurt: "Well, it's not that bad." "You'll feel better soon." "Who cares about what that persons says, anyway?" To children these are signals that they should not feel their real distress. If we shouldn't feel it, then it must be bad. Nichols notes that when adults tell a friend that they feel bad about themselves, most likely he or she will try to cheer them up. He warns, "The trouble about reassurance is that it doesn't last." The missing element that well-meaning parents, partners and friends don't consider is that "feeling bad, hurt or emotionally wounded" is a danger sign to our inner sense of self. The more we try to dismiss our pain, the more it secretly intensifies. Accumulated and hidden hurt feelings may become so frightful and anxiety-producing that we fear we must be an unacceptable or unlovable person just for having them. It takes courage and emotional honesty to admit that our feelings hurt. Emotional wounds that are never acknowledged remain haunting evidence that we are an unworthy person. We feel we must then make up for our inherent sense of unworthiness. We may bear this terrible burden throughout life because we live in fear of the consequences of being emotionally honest.

III. Accept Feelings Without Judgment

The first rule about having feelings is that they exist despite how we might judge them as being right or wrong. We need to catch ourselves when judging a painful feeling as shameful, for example, for then we are likely to judge and dismiss it. This leads to distancing ourselves from our real feelings. Once judged as "bad," painful feelings are banished to an inner hell where they remain unaccepted and unhealed. By accepting hurt feelings as a normal and natural part of being human, we won't separate our feelings from who we are. Our feelings make us unique individuals. They tell us what is important to us. We are neither a good or a bad person just for what we feel. Feelings evolve and change. What we originally felt as painful and potentially devastating may later be recognized as a wounding but not fatal experience. When we no longer experience being hurt as shameful or bad, we'll be less likely to screen or censor what we feel. By honoring rather than judging painful feelings, we allow them to be part of us so that we can know them and understand their message.

IV. Take Responsibility for Owning Feelings

Taking responsibility for what we feel, particularly the pain from being emotionally wounded, is different than blaming ourselves. If we recognize that our hurt comes from within us, we can distinguish between being wounded by words or actions that are beyond our ability to control, and our pain, which is within our control. Emotional pain is our inner reaction to a wounding event. While we may try to protect ourselves from the pain we experience from emotional wounds by blaming others for what we feel, the process mistakenly gives others responsibility for our feelings. Our emotional states are deeply personal, valid, and valuable responses to our experiences. By owning our feelings we accept whatever we feel just as we accept what we see, hear or taste. If we believe others control what we feel, then we lose the power to heal our pain. By recognizing and taking responsibility for our feelings, we also realize that we have little control over what others may do or say that may wound us and trigger our emotional pain. But it will be our pain to heal. We may rightfully blame others who emotionally wound us, but we need not blame ourselves or others for the pain we feel from the wound. Of course, we can be hurt and feel pain. We are vulnerable and we hurt when wounded. This does not make us a weak or flawed person. It means we are human.

Disowning our hurt feelings often replaces pain with an angry desire for revenge. There is no need to blame others or avenge our pain when we take responsibility for what we feel. We can learn to recover from emotional distress by focusing on what *we* can do, rather than trying to change other people's behavior. Denying that we're hurt only intensifies and lengthens emotional distress. We become more guarded, fearful and ashamed of feeling hurt, which causes us to transform innocent remarks that are not intended to cause us harm into devastating assaults. When we take responsibility for our ability to be hurt, we seize the power to recover from it.

V. Honor Vulnerability in Ourself and Others

Unfortunately, we live in a culture where exposure of vulnerability and feeling hurt is primarily seen as a weakness and a character flaw. Emotional honesty uses a process of honoring our vulnerability and hurt feelings rather than hiding them. By honoring our vulnerability, we no longer need be ashamed when we are hurt. Suffering the emotional wounds from rejection or loss is bad enough. But our emotional distress is compounded and intensified when we feel embarrassed by our human vulnerability. We will then feel humiliated when we expose our hurt. This results in even stronger defenses and pretenses to deny the pain that we consider disgraceful.

The more we practice honoring not only our hurt feelings, but those of others, the more open and honest we can be in acknowledging our vulnerability without shame. Families and couples can help each other to practice emotional honesty by openly talking about how they feel when their feelings are hurt. This helps to honor our universal ability to be vulnerable, which is our emotional birthright. The honoring process is powerful. It allows for the flowering of emotional intimacy and encourages family members and loved ones to take further risks in being more emotionally honest and trusting of their feelings.

Even in the safe and trusting climate of the therapist's office, hiding hurt feelings and vulnerability is a common occurrence. The late psychiatrist David Viscott wrote in his last book, (Appendix IV), that clients who were asked to review their taped therapy sessions were surprised by how much they routinely lied about their feelings.

VI. Name and Express Hurt Without Blame or Shame

Being able to identify how we really feel when we're emotionally wounded, is the first step in healing our hurt. If there is nothing wrong with being in emotional pain, then there is no need to blame others or shame ourselves. In *Being Intimate* (Appendix IV) John Amodeo says that disclosing our vulnerability to ourselves and others allows us to "appreciate our strengths and recognize our limitations."

It is not that we hide our hurt feelings which perplexes us and perpetuates our emotional distress; it is that we aren't aware we've hidden our real hurt and mistakenly believe it has been banished. The next chapter describes keeping an Emotional Honesty Journal of Hurt Feelings which begins with practicing naming your hurt. Does your pain come from experiencing a loss, rejection, betrayal or humiliation? We are more likely to attend to painful feelings if we first name them, and then claim them as ours to heal.

In order to express and recover from hurt, we need to name what we fear when we are emotionally wounded. By acknowledging our fears and shame of being vulnerable and hurt, we lessen the tendency to replace our pain with anger and then try to punish others our ourselves for what we feel. Once we can name our pain, by removing most of its mystery we limit its power over us. The unknown is frightening and anxiety producing. Naming feelings is much like the relief we feel once we know what is causing our physical pain. Even though knowing that doesn't cure the pain, we at least understand what it is we are dealing with. Naming each hurt we feel helps to release the fear and shame we may have for feeling it.

VII. Detect Emotional Dishonesty (EDH)

Emotional dishonesty (EDH) always involves self-deception. Defenses and pretenses are hard to detect because their purpose is to fool ourselves about what we feel. There are four types of emotional defenses:

1. **Feelings withheld, silenced, unstated or unacknowledged.** This self-deceit is pretending that our feelings are not hurt when

they really are. In his book *No Place to Hide – Facing Shame So We Can Find Self-Respect* (Appendix IV), psychotherapist Michael Nichols calls this type of EDH "disavowal." He describes it this way:

> Shame, the prototype of painful feeling, is not about what we're doing, or even thinking about, it's about who we are . . .In disavowal, shameful memories [of experiences] are conscious, but the painful emotion is split off: "Oh, yes, I was a klutz in junior high, but it didn't really bother me . . ." We take in the facts, but not the feelings that go with them.

2. Feelings distorted or obscured by generalizing. The most common type of deception that hides our hurt feelings is to confuse feelings with our self-worth. The mere fact that we feel wounded by a rejection or loss may be distorted into "There must be something terribly wrong with me to have so much pain." We never get to dealing with and healing our real and specific pain, because we are too frightened to acknowledge that it means we are an unworthy, unlovable or unacceptable person.

3. Disowning feelings. One of the most convenient ways of disowning hurt feelings is to blame others for the way we feel. This accomplishes two objectives: First, we fool ourselves into believing our feelings are not really our own, not real or genuine; and second, someone else is always at fault whenever we feel hurt. In the latter case, we bury our pain, substitute anger and perpetually carry grudges, seek revenge and expend effort plotting ways to retaliate for the way we feel.

4. Pretending about what we feel. Humans are endowed with a creative and imaginative sense that makes it easy to pretend about their feelings. Why? Because pretending is the easiest way of hiding what we don't feel capable of handling. And hurt feelings, as we have seen, are the most threatening aspect of our emotional life. They make us seem flawed and vulnerable. And so we "put on a good face," and are told to "Cheer up, it's nothing," and "toughen up" rather than recognize and deal with a burning pain inside that may feel devastating.

VIII. Recognize Disguised Behavioral Responses to Painful Feelings

The previous chapter explains the range of destructive behavior that may result when EDH distorts the pain from wounded feelings that we're unable to acknowledge or heal. Self-destructive acts include depression, being a victim, emotional numbing through alcohol or other drug abuse, compulsive behavior that distracts us from feeling our pain, self injury, and suicidal wishes. Destructive acts include anger and violence toward others, and being filled with an unquenchable desire for revenge and retaliation against those we feel are responsible for our own hurt. In both cases we need to clearly see the connection between the "disguised" behavior and unbearable pain that we are afraid or ashamed to acknowledge. The more honestly and capably we can manage our hurt feelings, the less we will resort to destructive behavior.

IX. Validate Others' Feelings

In parenting and in adult relationships we have a great opportunity to reflect to those we care about the feelings they may have that are the most troublesome to accept and express. When a loved one seems hurt, defensive, angry, or withdrawn, validating their underlying pain allows them to own and recover from it. Validating is not fixing someone, it is merely being a sensitive mirror to reflect what you imagine they must be feeling. We can validate loving feelings as well as hurt feelings: "I see in the way you touch me, or what you said, how much you love me." "I see that the business you lost really hurts you inside as much as it is a loss of money." Both statements validate what might otherwise be difficult feelings for another to articulate. By validating the feelings of others, the better we can recognize our own. This also helps us learn to more precisely articulate our deeply troubling feelings.

Conversely, when we invalidate our own or another's feelings, the real emotional response is nullified. Not only is the specific hurt feeling discredited, but other positive feelings such as love and happiness may come under the same suspicion and distrust.

X. Not Taking Responsibility for Others' Feelings

When we feel responsible for another's feelings, particularly for being the cause of their happiness or unhappiness, we become subject to being trapped by co-dependent and manipulative relationships. If we have not learned to take responsibility for our own feelings, we may also be induced to feel guilty for what others feel. If *our* pain is always somebody else's fault, then we may wonder what we may have done or not done that causes a parent or loved to be sad or angry. Knowing how to sort out our genuine feelings from emotionally dishonest denials of hurt feelings, helps keep us from being deceived into assuming responsibility for what others feel.

In relationships, when we learn to take responsibility for our feelings, by our example we influence those we love to also take responsibility for theirs. Emotional honesty flourishes in families and adult relationships when each person is encouraged to recognize that they're accountable to heal their own hurt, and refuses to blame others for what they feel. Two healthy and emotionally honest people can learn to share and honor each other's pain without feeling responsible either for their joy or sadness. It is one of the enduring myths of our culture that we marry someone because "they make me happy." In our early courtship, I said to my wife during a blissful walk in the woods, "You say that you feel so happy being here with me. I am overjoyed by your delight, not that I have caused it, but that I have helped you to bring out your own happiness and am here to celebrate it with you."

CHAPTER 11

The Emotional Honesty Journal of Hurt Feelings

The tendency to hide pain is deeply embedded in our culture. We may not properly attend to and learn from our painful feelings when we are emotionally wounded, because doing so requires that we acknowledge our vulnerability. Keeping an Emotional Honesty Journal of Hurt Feelings will enhance self-awareness of your inner reactions, defenses and disguised behavioral responses to each wounding experience soon after it happens. It will allow you to stay with your hurt long enough to learn its message, to honor and accept it as yours. It will facilitate your becoming more emotionally honest with yourself.

Specifically, the journal process will help you apply the lessons of emotional honesty listed in the previous chapter. It also serves as a chronicle of your progress as you move toward becoming more emotionally honest. Generally journals are used to help focus on our thoughts, values and behavior. The Emotional Honesty Journal, however, helps us to also monitor our feelings. It's a useful tool for becoming more self-aware of, and eventually changing unhealthy and often destructive inner reactions to emotionally wounding experiences. Documenting wounding experiences and your inner reactions to resulting hurt feelings helps to uncover your unique, hidden process of emotional self-deception and dishonesty.

The Journal is a way of discovering your unique blue print of emotional dishonesty. This helps you to dismantle your defenses, which in the end, are often more destructive to yourself, your children and loved ones than the original pain you may be shielding. The Journal may also help you identify the areas in which you most need support and encouragement to take more emotional risks. Community agencies and mental health professionals may be able to assist you in these areas. When you catch yourself thinking or declaring that a rejection or significant loss doesn't matter to you, it's a tip-off that emotional defenses are at work to protect yourself from your pain.

Keeping the Journal with utmost emotional honesty requires a certain amount of courage. Looking into the deep well of your true emotional pain can be frightening. You may fear falling into the place where our denied hurt is stored. You may feel anxious about being devastated as you first acknowledge your fear of being unlovable or unacceptable. You may wish to have companions on this journey. Consider forming a group or inviting close friends to also use the Journal so that you will have people with whom you can discuss the process (see Appendix III). Initially as you start each Journal entry, you will may find it difficult to name and document your inner reaction to each painful experience you encounter. Remember, the naming of pain is the first step toward healing it. The more practice and experience you have doing this, the more it becomes a natural process.

The Journal process involves five self-observation steps:

1. Name your hurt
2. Disempower the self-messages from hurt feelings
3. Identify judgments of feelings
4. Identify defenses
5. Recognize disguised behavioral responses

I. Name your Hurt.

Begin your Journal by listing the of the most painful emotional experiences of your life. As you progress in the journal process, you may recall more events to add to your list. List these painful events under the four types of core wounding experiences: loss, rejection, betrayal and humiliation. Arranging wounding experiences under the four categories will serve as a reference point for identifying those new wounding experiences you encounter and enter into your Journal.

When your feelings are hurt, try to stay with the pain at least long enough to identify which of the following four core wounds are involved. Some emotional injuries involve more than one of these core wounding experiences. After awhile you'll become aware of how often the same categories of wounding experiences reoccur and create distress. In *Emotional Resilience* (Appendix IV) David Viscott suggests that when we practice acknowledging hurt feelings, we start to take responsibility for them even if the feeling may be unacceptable to express to the people they involve.

These are the four core wounding experiences you will be documenting. Again, remember you may often have more than one of these involved when you are hurt:

Loss: Loss of a parent, family member, loved one; health or functional loss (through injury, disease); as well as loss of job, income or money, valued possession, or loss of innocence (child abuse, rape, etc.)

Rejection: Hurt from prejudice, spurned romantic efforts, having feelings ignored, social rejection, failing to be approved for a job, raise, new position, etc.

Betrayal: Hurt from actions of those whom you trust or have significant influence or power in your life, including being lied to or deceived by parents or family members, or romantic partners; having agreements broken or confidences breached by bosses or business colleagues, lovers, or close friends

Humiliation: Exposure of your "shameful" secrets, vulnerability, incapability; being ridiculed, belittled, laughed at or called names in front of others

II. Disempower Self-messages From Hurt Feelings

If you're injured emotionally, you need to know the source of your pain, as well as the fear and shame that your hurt brings up. Declare which of the following disempowering self-messages occur within you when you are hurt. Does my hurt make me feel:

Sad
Sorry for myself
Ashamed
Empty
Fearful or anxious
Flawed, wrong or unworthy
Taken advantage of
Weak or devastated
Helpless, hopeless or powerless
Unlovable
Unacceptable

For each wounding event practice naming the fears and shame you experience. This will then help you identify the types of defenses you use to protect yourself from these fears. Remember that fear paralyzes and keeps us from knowing our emotional truth. While this process may seem frightening, *your unknown fear has much greater power in your life than any fear you reveal in the emotional honesty process.*

One way of doing this part of the exercise is to use "If I'm . . .then" statements. For example, following a rejection by your boss who does not accept your proposed plan for solving a problem at work, you may first write that this rejecting experience caused me pain or made me feel weak. Following you might write: "If I'm weak, then I'm afraid others will not think I'm strong enough to protect myself and will try to take advantage of me." Of course, you may have more than one "If I'm . . .then" statement for each wounding event.

The "If I'm . . .then" statements not only describe the underlying fears and shame that arise when you are wounded, they tell you why you are afraid to acknowledge your painful or shameful feelings. Play out the "If I'm . . .then" scenario. For example, "If I'm unlovable and don't defend against feeling the pain, then what might happen is . . ." Another example is: "If I'm being taken advantage of, and acknowledge my vulnerability, then he/she won't respect me any more."

III. Identify Judgments of Feelings

Remember that our feelings are neither good nor bad, they simply are emotional experiences. Notice that the first sign of EDH is judging the hurt feelings we have as being wrong or not acceptable. Distinguish between self-judging evaluations (shame) and judging of others (blame).

• **Self-judging (shame): Do your hurt feelings make you feel you are unacceptable or unlovable because you are:**

   A bad (or evil) person
   A bad parent
   A bad child
   Faulty, defective or flawed
   Not good enough (person, child, parent)
   Undeserving, worthless
   Incompetent
   Deserve to be punished

• **Judging others (blame): Do your hurt feelings make you feel that others:**

   Have power over my feelings
   Cause my hurt
   Are overly critical
   Are bad, evil or rotten persons

Are faulty or flawed
Are insensitive to my feelings
Are unable to understand how I feel
Have something wrong with themselves

IV. Identify Defenses that Protect us from our Hurt

The purpose of our emotional defenses and pretenses is to fool us into believing we don't hurt when we really do, we don't care when we really do, or that we don't feel what we really feel. Pretenses will be hard to identify initially, but with practice you will begin to see a typical response pattern each time your feelings are hurt. Review the list of defenses and emotional dishonesty (EDH) syndrome in Chapter Six. These are some of the most common pretenses that invalidate your feelings:

It (wounding experience) really doesn't hurt
I can take it
I don't really care (about the misfortune or wounding incident)
I don't really love . . .(a specific person)
They aren't really concerned for or care about me
No one really cares about my feelings

• Devaluing or disowning our feelings

When we're defending against feeling or owning our hurt, we often devalue our feelings in general. Note when your defense pattern includes these types of devaluing beliefs:

No one thinks my feelings are important
He or she is responsible for how I feel!
No one cares what I really feel
My feelings don't count

• **Recognize Disguised Behavioral Responses**

In response to being hurt, you may recognize *patterns of disguised behavior* that convert the pain – which you cannot accept – into a harmful action toward others or yourself. By noting these reactions to your hurt feelings, you'll soon discover how predictable your disguised, behavioral responses are. One of the key ways of determining if our feelings (or feelings of others) are hurt is to identify these overt behavioral responses that are often cover-ups to avoid experiencing our pain. The behavior is disguised because the original hurt we have hidden is replaced by an action. By observing and noting our typical reactions to hidden pain (anger, depression, drinking, victimhood, etc.) you may observe yourself blaming others for your hurt and harboring resentment, or numbing your feelings to shut down a sense of shame for being vulnerable. The Journal process may help you detect repetitive, disguised behavior patterns – toward yourself and others – that may be destructive.

• **Some destructive, disguised behavioral responses to hurt feelings:**
  a. Destructive behavior toward others
  Anger, violence, abusive behavior toward others
  Blaming others along with a desire for revenge
  Being hypercritical/disapproving or disrespectful of others (di
      rectly or secretly behind their back)
  b. Self-Destructive behavior
  Depression or withdrawal
  Suicidal wishes, self-injury practices and eating disorders
  Numbing addictions: alcohol or other drugs
  Compulsive, repetitive behavior: workaholism, sexual compul
      siveness

IV. Journal Uses for Groups, Couples, Parents and Adolescents
By reviewing your Journal every week or so, you should begin to see a pattern of your responses to hurt feelings. By periodically reviewing past entries in the Journal, you will be able to see progress toward emotional awareness and honesty. As Robert Burney says in Codependence: *The Dance of Wounded Souls* (Appendix IV),

"There are times when it is not safe to be vulnerable and emotionally honest." Remember, overcoming EDH is incremental. Be self-forgiving when progress is slow.

You will still feel hurt by wounding experiences. But reviewing your Journal of hurt feelings will help you to deal with your *real* pain, identify your defenses, and document your self-deceiving reactions and responses. Over time you'll see how your responses to wounding experiences begin to change. The lingering, stinging pain and emotional distress that might have previously hung on for days or weeks may begin to feel less threatening. You will begin to recognize the danger signal your inner sense of self sends to warn when your emotional pain indicts you as unlovable or unacceptable (see Chapter Five). In particular, you may become more capable of shortening or reducing the episodes of shame, blame, anger and resentment that may have been automatic responses when you were previously emotionally wounded.

Remember that the Journal process will not prevent you from being emotionally wounded. It can, however, protect you from self-destructive or harmful tendencies by increasing your awareness of self-deception about your hurt feelings – pain that arises when you're hurt by loss, rejection, betrayal or humiliation.

Using the Journal in Emotional Honesty Groups

Emotional Honesty Discussion Group participants (see Appendix III) are encouraged to keep journals. As we are able to note and share our difficulties and successes in becoming more emotionally honest with ourselves, we may be encouraged by others who are committed to the same objective. Making it a joint effort also helps empower us to change. There is always risk in being vulnerable, but being part of a working group that acknowledges the challenge *and rewards* of emotional honesty helps to further our effort toward self-acceptance. The self-awareness journal process reminds us that *all growth requires taking risks*. This process becomes easier when we know others who are taking the same risk.

The journal process for couples and parents

Couples may prefer to keep separate personal journals and periodically share their insights, progress, or difficulties in dealing with painful feelings arising from wounding experiences. Some of each partner's hurt feelings undoubtedly result from their interaction as a couple. Journal sharing may serve as a platform for more open discussion about each partner's vulnerability, fear and anxiety about revealing their inner processes. The greatest reward for couples doing Journal sharing, however, is that they have the benefit of knowing each other well enough to recognize and honor their changes in behavior and emotional processes as they increase their emotional honesty. Discovering and sharing inner processes for dealing with hurt feelings naturally deepens trust, love and caring for each other. Practicing emotional honesty is an experience that deepens intimacy.

Parents will find that Journal sharing helps keep them more aware not only of their inner reactions to each other, but emotional defenses and pretenses that arise from interactions between themselves and their children. The more openly we can acknowledge, respond to, honor and support our children's hurt feelings, the better parent and teacher we become. We are also better able to model emotional honesty for children to emulate. Children also benefit by knowing that their parents' Journal-keeping helps to keep adults more open and responsive to their own and other family members' feelings. As the Journal process generates more open discussion of emotional dishonesty and hurt feelings, these subjects become normalized and destigmatized within the family.

The journal process for adolescents

Parents may want to discuss the Journal process with older children, and particularly adolescents. Emotional education programs and school classes can integrate the Journal of Emotional Honesty into their program. The Journal helps students apply emotional honesty general principles to everyday life experiences. Initially, groups of adolescents may be reluctant to reveal their vulnerable feelings and EDH tendencies for protecting themselves. After all, these are secrets that allow them to cope with adversity. But their resistance may be overcome by curiosity as they learn more about the way emotional honesty can lead to greater self-acceptance and developing healthy relationships. These are very big issues for all adolescents!

Emotional honesty health education programs in middle and high schools can help break down the natural barriers that prevent teenagers from having more open discussions of this type. Emotional honesty naturally makes the subject of hurt feelings more safe to talk about. Adolescents who keep an Emotional Honesty Journal can accelerate their self-awareness and more quickly learn how to control EDH tendencies that exacerbate their emotional distress.

At some point during emotional education programs, while adolescents are being encouraged to keep a Journal of Emotional Honesty, they may want to participate in small, peer Emotional Honesty Discussion Groups (see Appendix III). These discussion groups provide an opportunity to share their problems, questions and accomplishments as they work toward understanding their own or others' hurt feelings. Adolescents are normally responsive to the group process with their peers. They may find it refreshing to have their feelings valued, respected and honored. Teens may often be too frightened to broach the sensitive issues of painful feelings and vulnerability with peers who may be the sources of painful rejection and humiliation. Once they join Discussion Groups, however, they have a safe place where everyone plays by the same rules of honoring feelings. This is an effective way for teens to appreciate the complexity and depth of their emotional processes. In their groups they may also discover their untapped wisdom and strength for dealing with troubling feelings in more healthy and productive ways.

The journal process for practicing self-acceptance and forgiveness
The journal process takes us from being hurt by wounding experiences to accepting ourselves and others. An integral part of this process is learning to forgive ourselves for our self-deception and disavowal of our feelings when we have been hurt. EDH is not a flaw in our character. It is a disability we've acquired from both our culture, parents, and our instinctive survival fear. Forgiveness is a part of letting go of resentment, blame and shame when we are hurt. It is often necessary for achieving greater self-acceptance. The Journal keeps us on alert so we do not summarily reject our feelings and ourselves when we become hurt. We learn through practice to honor not only what *we* feel, but the feelings of *others*. Gradually, we will come to recognize that painful feelings are neither good nor bad. Only our judgements make them so.

Emotional honesty is self-affirming for it allows us to trust and accept what we feel, both our hurt and our love. All of us can become more emotionally honest, spontaneous and present. As we learn to stop blaming others for what we feel, it's easier to attend to our hurt feelings and release our pain. If we no longer feel ashamed of being hurt, we can remove self-damaging and destructive behavior as our response to it. If there's no one at fault for our hurt feelings, then all of our feelings are acceptable. When this occurs, we become more free to accept and love ourselves and others.

Self-acceptance is a natural outcome of emotional honesty. Learning to become more emotionally honest leads to discovering and honoring who we really are by knowing what we really feel. In a more self-accepting society, there will be less need for anger, violence, the tragedy of suicide and self-destructive behavior. In the end, emotional honesty is a healing process for our community, nation and world.

CHAPTER 12

Parenting With Emotional Honesty

When parents hide their true feelings, a child is deprived
of hearing honest emotions and feels there is no safe place
to express them.
– David Viscott, *Emotional Resilience* (1996)

I. Parents, Our First Emotional Honesty Teachers

It is important for parents to learn, practice and model skills for acceptance of hurt feelings. Parents are the child's first and most important model of emotional honesty.

A primary rule is that to be emotionally honest we must learn to counteract natural, instinctive urges that cause us to protect ourselves by distorting or disguising the meaning of our emotional pain. It is normal for children to construct defenses against experiencing their truly painful feelings. Parents cannot take for granted that their children will learn emotional honesty principles through daily experiences. In fact, the more contact children have with others, the more likely they are to adopt ploys of pretense about what they really feel. Parents must take responsibility for teaching and modeling emotional honesty from earliest childhood through adolescence.

Chapter Five explains the instinctive emotional survival need of infants that triggers defenses. These protective instincts remain with us throughout life, and cause us to react with self-deceptive emotional dishonesty (EDH) when we feel endangered and frightened by pain from wounded experiences.

While their defense mechanisms may temporarily relieve some emotional distress, young children primarily rely upon their family for emotional security. In 1999, the Washington-based Institute of Youth Development reported results from a survey of 90,000 adolescents to determine which home conditions and circumstances increased the chances of risky behavior – drug or alcohol abuse, sexual promiscuity, violence against others or themselves. A key finding was that emotional bonding with parents was a major factor in the family life of those children who avoided risky behavior. The bonding allowed them to feel more safe and secure, as well as emotionally connected to others and themselves. Parents who are skillful in honestly dealing with their own feelings and those of their children can significantly influence their children's emotional health and development.

By observing how parents interact between themselves and deal with their own hurt feelings, children learn more by example than from instruction. Parents who demonstrate healthy ways of accepting feelings without judgment, honoring their own and their child's feelings, are a powerful role model for their children's emotional resilience. Parents who honor and accept their own and other's feelings allow children to value and accept even their most troubling feelings. Parents cannot always be there to help their children when they encounter painful wounding experiences. But parents can set examples that enable developing children to become more aware, accepting and confident of recovering from their painful feelings.

Therapist and author John Bradshaw conducts recovery workshops to help adults overcome self-acceptance problems that arose during childhood. In his program announcement, he recognizes the vital role parents play by their validation of the child's painful feelings. He states: "As children we often felt ashamed for feeling the way we felt. We were told that our feelings were illegitimate." Many of us never realize how well we learned to disown our feelings by following our parents' example. Bradshaw says that validation from others helps us legitimize our feelings and allows us to begin our "grieving process" for the loss of our true feelings during childhood.

John Gottman, in *The Heart of Parenting* (1997), recounts some common false and potentially dangerous beliefs parents have about children's anger and sadness:

- Children acting sad are usually just trying to get adults to feel sorry for them, get attention or get their way.
- If you ignore a child's sadness or anger it will go away in time.
- I help my child get over sadness quickly so he can move on to better things.
- When my child gets angry my job is to get him to stop.
- Focusing on a child's uncomfortable feelings is like watering weeds.

Distinguishing between behavior and feelings

Our society focuses on rewarding and punishing *behavior*. In their role of teaching right and wrong, parents may fail to distinguish between disciplining a child to stop "wrong" or "bad" behavior, and invalidating or disowning feelings that prompted the behavior. John Bradshaw observes that in many households, there is an implied "no-talk-rule" about feelings. In early childhood, we may not be capable of distinguishing between doing "bad things" and having "bad feelings." Parents need to be aware and sensitive to a young child's confused interpretation of rewards or punishment for behavior as also being a judgment that their *feelings* are unacceptable. Bradshaw notes a major difference between misbehaving, which is "making a mistake," and feelings we have about ourselves when we do it – the self-belief that "I *am* a mistake."

Children who learn to judge and question their feelings will tend to become emotionally dishonest. Children who are fortunate to have parents and teachers who understand and practice the honoring and acceptance of feelings, will more likely value emotional honesty. As these children grow into adulthood, they are also more likely to be more emotionally honest parents and role models for their children.

II. Emotional Honesty in the Family

> The emotionally honest family discusses and honors feelings without judgment. It does not permit hiding from one's own or other's feelings. It recognizes feelings as being part of who we are. Such a family creates a safe environment for feelings by not blaming or criticizing; by reserving judgment to behavior.

The above statement from David Viscott's powerful book, *Emotional Resilience* (Appendix IV), reflects the important role parents play in shaping their children's emotional honesty. Viscott emphasizes, "Each person's defensive style is an adaptation which mirrors their family experience . . .The emotionally insecure child becomes emotionally deprived. His secret anger drains his capacity for self love and loving others."

Parents cannot prevent themselves or their children from being emotionally wounded by experiencing loss, rejection, betrayal and humiliation. *Emotional health is not the absence of having hurt feelings. It is our ability to respect and acknowledge these wounds as part of us, so that we can recover from them.* Johns Hopkins University studies have found that emotionally healthy people experience the same stress as others, but have less severe reactions, because they are able to let go of them earlier. Emotional honesty is not a magic solution. It is risky and difficult work. Were it not so, we could all easily disarm our defenses and simply refuse to be captives of EDH pretenses.

Emotional distress is our natural reaction to danger – any threat to our survival need for feeling acceptable and lovable. Antoinette Sanders (*The Stress-Proof Child* in Appendix IV), a child psychologist and pioneer in the field of stress education, speaks of the fundamental value of children learning emotional resilience: "When

[emotionally] capable kids get hurt they don't get damaged."
Emotionally capable kids bend, while others break from the weight
of life's wounding experiences. Sanders explains the EDH trap that
catches youngsters who do not develop emotional resilience: "It
becomes easier and less threatening for them to keep feelings inside and deny that they even have them than to acknowledge them."
The former University of Illinois psychology professor notes that if
emotionally healthy people stop practicing emotional honesty, they
eventually lose the ability "to distinguish how and what they are
feeling."

Emotional fitness at home and school

Certainly, we cannot be emotionally honest all the time. Emotional honesty is not being perfectly truthful about every pain we
feel when we are emotionally wounded. *Practicing emotional honesty is more like physical fitness.* The more we do it the easier it
becomes. Also, if we don't use it, we lose it. Modern parents certainly understand the benefits of their children being physically
fit. Children can also develop emotional fitness with encouragement and participation of parents and schools. Emotional fitness
is self-conditioning through repetition and practice that develops
our capability to ward off unhealthy defenses and pretenses. If we
do not use this capability, we lose the strength needed to recover
from inevitable hurt feelings and emotional distress.

Nearly all schools today are committed to offering a wide
variety of physical education programs. Shouldn't parents demand that they also offer emotional education – or emotional
fitness – in the same spirit of helping children to develop resistance and stamina to recover from emotional distress? When I
address parents and educators about the need for emotional
education, I emphasize that emotional honesty is not beyond
the average person's ability to learn and practice. This aspect of
human nature can be developed and strengthened. The com-
petence required for emotional honesty involves recognizing and
strengthening the capacities we all possess to some degree.

Americans have become avid devotees of physical fitness, flocking to gyms and using personal trainers for conditioning and strengthening. Perhaps, someday soon, we will use emotional fitness training in a similar manner, and become more resilient and resistant to EDH and emotional distress.

Parents and teachers are necessary models and coaches of emotional honesty and fitness for children. In his 1997 book, *The Heart of Parenting*, John Gottman says the most effective type of parenting is "emotional-coaching" which values the child's feelings, and even uses the child's "negative emotions as opportunities for intimacy." By contrast, Gottman recounts the reaction of the mother of seven-year-old pilot Jessica Dubroff who died while trying to become the youngest pilot to fly across the U.S. In a *Time* magazine interview following the tragedy, the mother says, "I know what people want. Tears. But I will not do that. Emotion is unnatural. There is something untruthful about it."

Unfortunately, due to the cost and social stigma that is still associated with "psychological therapy," families may be reluctant to use these professional services on a *preventive* basis. Yet, this type of preventive education and personal development can help families to become learning centers for acquiring and practicing the principles of emotional honesty. Families are logical and natural places for children to develop emotional honesty and resilience.

Parents can also become advocates to insist that schools sponsor or provide students, particularly adolescents, with preventive educational programs for emotional health. Emotional health education can be offered in a natural, non-stigmatizing way by trained coaches just as schools now provide physical education experiences. For this to happen, however, a new education emphasis is needed to develop "emotional fitness trainers" who are skilled in helping children learn how to develop safe and emotionally healthy practices for dealing with their troubling feelings.

III. Honoring and Affirming a Child's Emotional Rights

All children have what I call *emotional rights*. All children have a right to not have their feelings neglected, ignored, dismissed, or discounted. They deserve to have their feelings honored, acknowledged and accepted by their parents without judgment. They have a right to not be held up to ridicule or made to be foolish for having a feeling. They have a right to be emotionally upset, and have those feelings honored, even though their resulting behavior may not be acceptable. The also have a right to not be "talked out of their feelings" by parents. In her 1990 book, *Shame & Guilt: Masters of Disguise* (Appendix IV), which deals with childhood emotional issues, Jane Middleton-Moz discusses many of the life-long traumas that arise from having one's feelings shamed during childhood.

In *Emotional Resilience* (Appendix IV) David Viscott states that: "Our personality as an adult reflects how well we've adapted to childhood stress; how much we were supported and encouraged to risk being open with feelings." Children develop judgments about how to react to wounded feelings, and how they "should" feel, which is primarily based on their parent's example. These judgments can lead to a life of censoring feelings and the damaging self-belief: *If my feelings are not acceptable, then I am not acceptable as a person.* When wounded, this torturing self-belief exacerbates normal emotional distress, causing children (and later as adults) to replace their denied, emotional pain with destructive behavior. Children eventually lose their ability to spontaneously experience feelings in the here and now. In the phrase of our age, they "become emotionally unavailable" and are incapable of honest emotional responses even to those with whom they have close relationships.

There are simple questions parents can ask children to help them honor and accept their feelings, remain emotionally present, and deal with emotions honestly:

Honoring and affirming questions, statements and responses:
1. How do you *feel* about what happened . . .?
2. Did I do or say something that makes you hurt inside?
3. When I say . . .how does that make you *feel?*
4. It's okay to cry if it makes you feel better.
5. Do you feel that way a lot of the time?
6. What would make you feel better?
7. That must really make you feel . . .?
8. I can see how that *would* make you feel . . .
9. It's okay to feel the pain when you are hurt inside.
10. Your feelings are important. I'd like to know how that [event] makes you feel. .
11. I don't feel that way, but its okay if you do.
12. You're such a good person. I'm sorry I hurt you (or that it hurts you so much).
13. Something must be hurting inside you; can you tell me what it is?
14. I know that you feel (hurt, rejected, sad, etc.), but you don't have to act this way.

Some ways we dishonor and invalidate feelings of children (and adults):

1. I don't like it when you're that way (hurt, needy, crying, moody).
2. Why are you so unhappy when everyone else is not?
3. I don't have time to hear that (emotional expression) now.
4. I like it (I love you) when you're not . . .(crying or express ing upset feelings).
5. Look, Johnny isn't upset by that. (Why can't you be more like him?)
6. Why not look on the bright side (ignore your pain or loss)?
7. Just forget it; or, you'll get over it.
8. You're just too sensitive. Don't let it get you down. It shouldn't hurt that much.

9. Grow up. Stop being a baby!
10. When you're that way (sad, withdrawn, etc.) it makes me mad at you.
11. You're too wrapped up in your own feelings.

It may seem more compassionate to try to talk children *out* of their hurt feelings, rather than talk them *into* feeling their hurt. In fact, on the surface, many of the above dishonoring statements may, indeed, be intended to be helpful. But these responses are not likely to help children (or adults) to "get in touch with" and accept their real feelings. Parents can help children to realize their hurt by honoring their those feelings. Respecting painful feelings might seem as though this would make children feel worse. Parents may worry that helping children honor their feelings will turn them into self-pitying "victims." Incredible as it may seem, honoring has the opposite effect. *Children should never have to feel guilty or ashamed of their feelings!* It is the responsibility of parents to respect children's emotional upsets and by doing so encourage them to take responsibility for recovering from their painful experiences.

Author Rolland Parker, in *Emotional Common Sense* (1973), warns of the dangerous consequences of well-meaning parents: "Sometimes parents tell the child to cover up conflict . . .so that they, the parents, do not experience shame. The child is thus taught that the only way to have self-respect is to conceal pain and weakness." Robert Burney, in *Codependence: The Dance of Wounded Souls* (Appendix IV), says we believe that to be good parents we need to teach a child to be a well-behaved "good boy or girl." Because, if the child acts out and misbehaves, there is something wrong with the parents. Children conditioned in this manner, he says, lose touch with their emotional honesty. Parents may also use their "love" to control the child ("I love you when you feel . . .") or conversely, "It makes me unhappy when you feel . . ."

Psychology professor and author John Gottman (1997) recounts the way parents invalidate a child's feelings. Parents often dismiss children's fear and upsets as though they don't matter. "There's nothing to be afraid of," they say to a five-year-old. This makes the child question his own fear and lose trust of feelings that are constantly invalidated.

In his 1991 book, *No Place to Hide* (Appendix IV), Michael Nichols discusses the importance of honoring a child's feelings and inner reactions to wounding experiences, particularly when they are different from the parent's emotional responses to the same wounds. He says "An effective parent communicates understanding first . . .and allows children to differentiate feelings distinct from parents." He points out that a parent's "understanding and tolerance of what children feel has such profound consequences because children cannot control who they are. They cannot control their feelings."

IV. Opportunities for Children to Develop Emotional Honesty

Learning about emotional defenses

The goal of learning about emotional honesty is to better understand what goes on inside us when our feelings are hurt. This involves learning about how we develop emotional defenses to protect ourselves from feeling endangered when we are emotionally wounded. Understanding the general principles of emotional honesty, and then comparing them to our own emotional reactions to being wounded takes a certain level of sophistication. This is why I advocate teaching the principles of emotional honesty as part of emotional health education for students in middle and high schools. Prior to adolescence, children are best taught by parents who understand the principles and are able to model as well as explain them to children during their younger years. Following this book, I am planning a "read together" emotional honesty storybook for children 8 to 11 years old and their parents.

By learning the general process by which we protect ourselves from painful feelings, and the dangerous consequences of defenses (covered in Part Two of this book), parents become more confident in discussing their own feelings with their children. Children, in turn, are more likely to follow their parents' example, and with encouragement begin to more openly share their feelings with parents as well as with their peers.

Parents do not have to be perfectly emotionally honest to be good models and teachers for their children's emotional health. But it is important that they honor painful feelings and become aware of the dangers of ignoring them.

Parents play an important role by encouraging their children's emotional self awareness and helping them to more clearly recognize and distinguish between healthy self-protection of feelings and EDH distortions, which weaken or destroy self-acceptance and intensify normal emotional distress.

Dealing with the rejecting adolescent

The transition from child to adult can be terrifying not only for adolescents, but quite unsettling to parents. During this emotionally turbulent period, the fear of being unacceptable and unlovable intensifies. No matter how careful parents have been to offer love, understanding and acceptance, adolescence is a whole new game in terms of emotional distressing experiences. Adolescents are apt to unleash a barrage of critical judgment aimed at adults and other authority figures. Parents, whose own sense of self-acceptance may have been wounded by a painful divorce, separation or death of a spouse, must now additionally endure their teenagers' assaults. The adolescent's rebellion, though not aimed solely at parents, can be particularly painful for child and parent. When children become adolescents, no matter how much parents may have encouraged their independence, parents and children will experience a sense of loss. The times of trust and closeness with their children during earlier ages can become a distant memory. These tender memories are replaced by petulance, rudeness, distance and worst of all, silence punctuated only by loud and raucous music.

Because the trauma of adolescence creates losses and pain for both teenager and parent, it is an opportune time for them to "get real" about having hurt feelings. Parents during this period can offer to share their pain from "loss of their child" to adolescence, and soon to be adulthood. Children naturally feel confused, vulnerable and emotionally insecure as they separate and individuate from their parents. During this period, San Rafael, California adolescent psychologist Trout Black says "Teens will point out the part of the parent that is not well developed." He urges parents, *"Do not lie to your kids about your feelings! They need your honesty."* When parents can be open with their real feelings, they give permission to their teens to do the same, even if they are often too embarrassed to do so. The youth therapist also cautions parents of adolescents to never betray their child's confidences. Teens are terrified of betrayal when they risk disclosing their real fears and revealing their "shameful" vulnerability. *It is also important that parents honor and respect their teenager's fear of being emotionally honest.* Teens need parents who are trustworthy confidants for youngsters who desperately need a safe and secure place to reveal their painful, secret feelings.

To the extent parents can be open and reveal the painful wounds they experience, they help their growing child to break away from home and family in a more emotionally safe way. Adolescents need permission to acknowledge their vulnerability during this painful period. One of the greatest gifts parents can give their adolescent children is permission to honor and accept their own hurt feelings. The more parents can openly discuss the ways in which they feel hurt – doing so without shame, blame or anger – the easier it will be for their children to value and develop emotional honesty.

Chapter 14 offers examples of how parents and teenagers can use principles of emotional honesty to deal with the unique challenges of adolescence. I also plan a follow-up book on parenting with emotional honesty.

V. Surviving "The Not Good Enough Parent" Trap

Before leaving the topic of parenting with emotional honesty, adults are reminded that they do not always deserve their burden of guilt. In their 1996 book *When is Enough, Enough?* (Appendix IV), Laurie Ashner and Mitch Meyerson remind us that "Parents can rarely attend to the child's [emotional] demands all the time." Parent guilt, "the not-good-enough-parent" trap, is the insecurity of never feeling we've done "a good enough job" raising our children. This insecurity may be related to the parents' core fear of being generally unacceptable or unlovable. Parents who feel undeserving, may carry a shameful sense of themselves that can turn real or imagined criticism into a devastating indictment of their worthiness as a parent.

With the intense time and economic pressures on today's parents, they deserve to be self-forgiving for not being perfect. Most parents do the best they can with their awesome responsibility of helping to shape a new human being into a happy, healthy and well-functioning person.

The late humorist Erma Bombeck, who helped many a parent survive the worrisome guilt of possibly disciplining their children incorrectly, had a wonderful retort to the parenting gurus of the 1960's and '70's. She recalled the popular child rearing advice of the time which admonished parents to never spank children while angry over the child's misbehavior. Her response was: "What better time!"

In his 1997 book about understanding guilt and forgiveness, *How Good Do We Have to Be?* (Appendix IV), Harold Kushner tells the story about a mother's anger brought about by her small boy wandering away and disappearing in a department store. The boy's mother is undoubtedly distraught over losing her child, filled with fear that maybe he is injured or kidnapped. A feeling of guilt arises and painful feelings of "not being a good enough parent" may flash through the mother as she desperately searches for her child. She is filled with anxiety about not only her possible loss should some harm come to her son, but that *this frightening event also proves that she is an incompetent mother by failing to properly watch her child.*

Finally, the boy is found wandering in another part of the store. The relieved mother's reaction – immediately after initially hugging her offspring – turns to anger as she chastises the child for wandering away. No one can dispute that the mother loves her child, and that she was filled with fear when her child disappeared. Yet her distress of losing her child and confronting her own painful fear that she may not be a good enough parent unleashed a "cover up" of anger against the frightened, innocent child.

Of course no one, including well-meaning and conscientious parents, are free from reacting with anger when an unruly child misbehaves. What parents need to ask themselves, however: Is their angry behavior toward their child the parent's way of disguising and expressing their hidden, painful sense of "not being a good enough person?" While there may be a factor of EDH in being angry at a child, parents may be forgiven for occasionally being upset and responding with anger so long as they do not harm their child. *However, anger can easily cross a line and escalate into punishment of a child for the adult's own fearful sense of being an inadequate or incompetent parent.*

Young children need to have their feelings acknowledged and accepted even when parents are angry at them for misbehaving. And older children need to know that parents may have concerns about sometimes feeling ashamed or "not good enough" when youngsters exhibit what they have been told is unacceptable behavior.

In the case of the department store mother, what she failed to do is help the child understand *both of their fears.* This was likely an emotionally wounding event for the child who feared losing (being abandoned by) his mother. Not being able to find mother and being frightened by the anxiety of being abandoned, the child may suffer from the frightening fear that "There may be something wrong with me for Mother to abandon me." This emotional reaction to traumatic loss is characteristic of the way our inner sense of self (see Chapter Five) senses danger to our personal survival. Childhood trauma of loss under these circumstances is sometimes humorously placated by store security personnel who announce on the public address system, "We have a four-year-old boy named Adam whose mother is lost."

When you excessively worry about being a good enough parent, it may be useful to remember that being an emotionally honest person with yourself and your child goes a long way toward compensating for any shortcomings you have in parenting skills. After the trauma of the department store incident passed, the mother might have used the frightening episode to model and teach emotional honesty by talking about her own fears and hurt feelings. "I was so frightened that I might have lost you, it made me feel deeply worried and hurt inside. That's why I was angry. I'm sorry that I behaved so angrily when I was frightened and feeling hurt." The lesson from this upsetting experience is: Though emotional pain is often frightening or shameful, we do not need to be angry about having hurt feelings. Each day, parents can use emotionally wounding experiences as opportunities to show their children healthy and honest ways of acknowledging while not judging their emotional distress.

Parenting with Emotional Honesty discussion groups

When we become new parents, it is important to examine the legacy of EDH we may be carrying from our parents. This is a critical time to reassess how we deal with painful feelings from emotionally wounding experiences. This EDH self-assessment will help us to recognize how much energy we spend maintaining defenses to guard against emotional pain. We may then decide that we want to prevent this legacy from being passed onto our children. *We can ask for Emotional education programs for parents, which can take many forms:*

1.   Adult education offered by colleges and community agencies
2.   Parenting classes provided by schools, PTA's and children's organizations
3.   Parent support groups

I particularly advocate Parenting with Emotional Honesty discussion groups which can be helpful ways for parents to learn together how to uncover their patterns of emotional self-deception and dishonesty so they are not transmitted to children. These types of groups (described in Appendix III) provide opportunities to practice skills for becoming more emotionally honest adults. These discussions enable parents to share techniques and problems they encounter in trying to help their children development emotional honesty skills for dealing with ordinary but painful or fearful childhood experiences.

These discussions are not traditional group therapy. Rather, they are useful for learning to openly share personal experiences, problems and successes in overcoming emotional defenses and pretenses. This open process enables parents to be more aware of how they may be inadvertently influencing their children's emotional dishonesty. *Group discussions can also have an emotionally liberating effect upon the relationship between parents.* This educational "no fault" process is non-judgmental, for its underlying message is that neither children or adults should be blamed or shamed for having hurt feelings. One of the greatest strengths parents can help develop in children is their ability to honestly and safely recover from emotional pain. By understanding effective, healthy ways of dealing with wounded feelings, parents are able to help their children develop both emotional honesty and self-acceptance.

A child's emotional growth and development is enhanced by parents who respect and understand the importance of their own feelings and the feelings of others, including their children. Parents invariably model or transmit to children their own emotional honesty or dishonesty. As they learn about their critical role in this aspect of child development, parents will be able to help new generations avoid devaluing and dishonoring their feelings. *Parents who understand the preventive value of emotional health education provide children with the gift of emotional health insurance.*

CHAPTER 13

Developing Emotional Honesty in Adult Relationships

> Our relationships are reflections of our inner lives . . .If we
> feel weak and emotionally fragile, we'll think that others
> are dangerous; and if we're convinced we're unlovable,
> then we won't believe that anyone could possibly love us.
> – Scott Wetzer, *Is It You or Is It Me?* (1998)

I. You Always Hurt the One You Love

It is human nature to fear taking risks. One of life's biggest risks is emotional intimacy, the foundation for deep friendship and romantic relationships. If the people we choose for close relationships value and practice emotional honesty, they allow us to do the same. If our friends, family and partners support and encourage being open with our feelings, we will feel safe revealing our vulnerability and fear of being hurt. Marriage and committed adult relationships become complicated by the interaction of two opposing dynamics. On the one hand, we desire to be joyously close, trusting, sharing and accepting. On the other, we fear risking disclosing feelings that give the person closest to us the power to betray our trust by manipulating our feelings and vulnerability. We fear being rejected and thereby losing – being left or abandoned by – someone we love. In his 1991 book, *No Place to Hide* (Appendix IV), Michael Nichols states: "The intimate other we allow inside our boundaries has the capacity to . . .inflict more pain . . .One of the secrets of a successful relationship is learning to rise above [fear of] hurt, vulnerability, and rejection."

Close relationships reveal how safe we feel being emotionally honest. In his 1977 book *Risking*, David Viscott says that admitting hurt to a friend or partner is a test of trust in a relationship. Being close to someone, whether a spouse, a loved one, a best friend, our parents or children creates a bond of trust and emotional intimacy that makes us vulnerable to betrayal. When we are open with our feelings, we permit others inside our defenses that protect us from hurt. We call it "falling in love" because as we open ourself to emotional intimacy we sense danger whenever we lower our defenses. Loving someone is filled with excitement because when our vulnerable inner self is unguarded, "out of control," and exposed to emotional danger, we experience both the joy of liberated feelings along with fear of our vulnerability to devastating hurt.

In the 1940's popular song made popular by the Mills Brothers, "You Always Hurt the One You Love," writers Doris Asher and Allan Roberts remind us that it is impossible to avoid hurt feelings with those to whom we are most close and vulnerable:

> You always hurt the one you love,
> The one you shouldn't hurt at all.
> You always take the sweetest rose
> and crush it till the petals fall.
>
> You always break the kindest heart
> With a hasty word you can't recall.
> So if I broke your heart last night
> It's because I love you most of all.

Fear of intimacy

In their 1986 book, *Being Intimate*, marriage counselors John Amodeo and Kris Wentworth describe a misconception of close relationships: "One of the most destructive romantic myths is that if we truly love someone, we should never experience 'negative' feelings in relation to that person." Because intimacy cannot exist without the potential hazard of being emotionally wounded, EDH and protective defenses arise in most relationships. The authors expose a prevalent myth that "Experiencing or expressing anger, hurt or fear is seen as indicating that something is terribly wrong with the relationship, or that our love is no longer true." In all close relationships there is both excitement and risk, for by opening our vulnerable self to another we also give them the sword to wound us.

What makes adults decide upon the person they chose to be close to in a primary relationship? Everyone has a need to experience feeling accepted and loved. *When we find someone with whom we can be emotionally open and honest, the floodgates that protect our vulnerability open.* We are overjoyed by filling our deep emotional survival need to feel lovable and acceptable. Openly discussing and sharing this deep need creates an even deeper bond between intimates. While we can experience the sense of self-acceptance from a religious/spiritual experience, we may also experience it through emotional honesty that fosters the joy and warmth of feeling accepted and loved by someone we value. When we genuinely feel loved by our mate, we feel secure that we are a lovable and acceptable person.

This is why the pain of rejection or betrayal in relationships can be so devastating: We may vow to never again let down our defenses, trust our feelings, or reveal our emotional vulnerability. We retreat into EDH, hiding behind protective defenses that disable both painful and joyful feelings. Losing the love and acceptance of an important person in our life can diminish our self-acceptance, at least temporarily. We desperately need to feel lovable and acceptable for our emotional survival. If we do not, a persistent nightmare tells us we are *unworthy* of being loved and accepted. Amodeo and Wentworth explain the dilemma:

> We all want to feel cherished for who we [really] are, without resorting to pretensions and manipulations. However

the bind we are in is that we can also be rejected for who we
are . . . Of course, in reality, we have absolutely no control
over other people's reactions to our unguarded inner selves,
or whether they will give us the acceptance, respect and love
we want.

Psychiatrist Jay Rohrlich (Appendix IV) distinguishes between our
sense of lovability as an adult and the love relationship with our
mother. A mother's love is controlled by the child's wishes, he
says. Adult love is not. It is based on mutual empathy between
"autonomous equals" who can be critical of each other without
feeling devastated. Codependence counselor Robert Burney (Appendix IV) describes how terror of unlovability spoils love: "At the
core of my being, at the foundation of my relationship with myself, I feel unworthy and unlovable." Therefore, he adds, "It felt
that anyone who loved me would eventually be disappointed, would
learn the truth of my shameful being."

When we are wounded and emotionally dishonest, we must
deny our pain for it is accompanied by the fear of being an unworthy person who deserves punishment. Needing love, but feeling
unlovable, leads to a self-destructive trap of devaluing the persons
who value you: *There must be something wrong with them to like a
person such as me.* This corrosive self-belief, which robs us of the
ability to experience intimacy, becomes disguised in relationships
as "emotional distancing." Rabbi Harold Kushner (Appendix IV)
says, "There are few emotions more capable of leaving us feeling
bad about ourselves than the conviction that we don't deserve to
be loved." When having hurt feelings make us seem unacceptable,
we sabotage any feeling of love and then complain that "nobody
loves or understands me."

It is difficult to risk expressing or owning the feeling of love
for another when powerful inner warnings tell us to not expose
our vulnerability. Denied and unhealed pain can haunt every
new relationship. Protective defenses prevent us from facing

our real fear of intimacy. It is the familiar fear that when we allow ourself to feel love we become apprehensive that it's not genuine or will be taken away. This paralyzing fear prevents us from fully experiencing love or happiness without the accompanying terror of possible loss or betrayal.

Amodeo and Wentworth emphasize that "Trusting others may not be possible without . . .the full range of feelings that will inevitably arise." Once we can trust our feelings, "We then have the strength and ability to be vulnerable with others because we know we can be with hurt and sadness if they happen to arise." Amodeo and Wentworth state, *"In order for others to care about us they need to know what we are feeling."* To have an open and honest relationship in which intimacy deepens and flourishes, we also must be capable of confronting the fear of emotional devastation that may arise when we are emotionally wounded by someone we love and trust.

II. Emotional Rights and Responsibilities in Relationships

> I want to know if you have touched the center of your
> own sorrow, if you have been opened by life's betrayals or
> have been shriveled and closed from fear of further pain! I
> want to know if you can sit with pain, mine or your own,
> without moving to hide it or or fade it or fix it.
> – Oriah Mountain Dreamer, *The Invitation* (1999)

The emotional defenses that appear to protect us against experiencing the pain of our hurt feelings also keep us from acknowledging and sharing the very emotional vulnerability necessary to maintain close and trusting relationships. Vulnerability to being hurt is the risk we all must bear to achieve true emotional intimacy.

> If we can own hurt feelings without blame,
> We will encourage our mate to do the same.

When we become emotionally wounded, typical reactions include feeling ashamed or being consumed with rage and blaming others. *To dull our anguish when feeling sad or in pain we may renounce our emotional rights.* Emotional honesty, which helps us reclaim these rights, is the ability to honor and accept feelings particularly when we hurt! We have a right and a responsibility to accept our hurt feelings. It is awareness of these emotional rights and responsibilities that enables us to develop and maintain healthy and emotionally honest relationships.

Dr. Dean Ornish (in *Love & Survival*, 1997) discloses his battle with EDH and fear of intimacy which led him to choose women who had similar problems. We became "unhealthy mirrors for each other," he says: "I had to [learn to] coexist with emotional pain without trying to numb it or distract myself from it. I was incapable of being in an intimate relationship with anyone, no matter who they were. It was not about finding the right person; it was about being the right person." He describes the emotional dishonesty and deception that prompted his fear: "If you really knew me, you wouldn't want to be with me, so I have to create a façade of who I want you to think I am that is more lovable and acceptable than who I really am."

Before we can be free with our feelings, we must know what we feel. We must also be willing to ask others how they feel. EDH dampens our curiosity and hampers our freedom to probe emotional truth in ourself or others. The more adept we become at rejecting and renouncing our feelings, the less we want to know what others are truly feeling. Since self-deception leads to distrusting our own feelings, we also become suspicious of other people's feelings toward us. In relationships, this leads to questioning another's love and misinterpreting comments as rejecting and disapproving even when there is no such intention.

In emotionally honest relationships we can hold onto our love for another even if we may disapprove of specific things they do. Relationships also provide opportunities to exercise our right to own and reveal our pain with emotional honesty.

When one partner withdraws or hides their pain, the other is deprived of a chance to validate it and have the process reciprocated. We can validate another's pain without encouraging self-pity or a victim complex by saying: "You have every right to be hurt. You are responsible for healing your hurt, but how can I support you in recovering from it?" This is what every partner in a relationship needs to hear, but rarely does.

Emotional rights and responsibilities in adult relationships

We all have a right to feel hurt when we are emotionally wounded. In adult relationships, conflicts and wounding interactions between partners are normal. In healthy relationships, partners honor and respect the hurt feelings of each other, just as they honor each other's love. Honoring a partner's emotional pain, however, does not include taking responsibility for "fixing" their hurt feelings. When painful conflict occurs, partners may need time to work through the pain, their emotional withdrawal or even anger and rage. *When we have difficulty dealing with our underlying pain, angry behavior seems therapeutic.* When we are deeply hurt, anger makes us "feel good" because it is often the only way to express our hidden pain. The less we are able to accept and take responsibility for our hurt, the more anger we use to disguise our pain.

When conflict occurring in close relationships opens up unhealed wounds, good partners help the other to stay with their hurt. By recognizing the right to own our painful feelings, we have less need to blame others, lash out in anger, or shamefully withdraw into depression. Partners who are aware of their own and each other's EDH patterns – denials and pretenses about feelings – are able to keep from driving wedges between themselves. Even if they never learned as a child to honor their hurt feelings at home, adult partners who practice emotional honesty can learn to honor each other's rights and responsibilities for healing their pain.

Dealing with inevitable relationship conflicts

The primary gift of loving relationships is not unconditional love and acceptance, as desirable as that might be. It is using our love and compassion to honor and respect each other's feelings, particularly hurt feelings. Truly loving relationships are healing relationships. They are safe places to practice risking emotional honesty with oneself and trusting that our vulnerability and honesty will be honored.

We bring our flaws, our unhealed pain and fears of unlovability and unacceptability into every close relationship. It is a fantasy to expect that loving someone will wash away this pain and fear. But we can be a good and honest mirror, reflecting back to our partners their right to their feelings. In emotionally healthy relationships, partners help each other to develop courage to accept their pain without judgment, blame or shame.

When conflicts arise, misunderstandings abound and one or the other is likely to feel resentful that their feelings are not being honored. In all adult relationships it is likely that one or both partners' hurt feelings will be ignored, unacknowledged and thus dishonored. Without being accusing or placing blame, we can practice revealing to our partner that we are upset or hurt by what they said, did, or did not say or do. Use of the Emotional Honesty Journal of Hurt Feelings (see Chapter 12) helps partners practice this process.

Reactions to hurt feelings in relationships

When we are emotionally wounded in a relationship, we can react and deal with our pain in one of three ways:

1. Hide our real pain.

Rather than admit or disclose our pain, we avoid acknowledging it by harboring resentment toward others for their behavior or words that wound us. Since we do not honor the pain as our own, we cannot express it to those who fail to recognize or respect our wounded feelings. We may react with either *silent rage* (depression or self-destructive behavior) or *angry behavior* toward others we believe are the "source" of our pain. These reactions are disguised or disconnected from the original wound because we are too ashamed and fearful to acknowledge our pain. Since EDH disables our ability to respect our own feelings, violence toward others is often rationalized as retribution. Hostility hides the real wound we avenge. Rather than acknowledge our pain, we disguise the real hurt and substitute avenging actions to punish others for our suffering.

2. Honor and acknowledge real pain without blame.

When a person close to us says or does something that wounds us, we must acknowledge the pain to ourself. But to prevent future injury, we also need to tell our partner, friend or family member when we feel hurt. By saying "My feelings were hurt when you . . .," we claim our feelings and reveal them without judgment or blame. We can eliminate the need for angry revenge or self-loathing whenever our feelings are hurt. David Viscott (Appendix IV) suggests using this type of social discourse to determine whether another's wounding action was done intentionally to harm us. Letting another person know that their behavior has wounded us, discloses our pain and vulnerability. After this disclosure, if they continue the same behavior that has wounded us, we know by their actions that they are intentionally trying to hurt us. This exercise of emotional honesty can make a partner aware of and cease their abusive behavior, or provide us with a convincing reason for leaving the relationship.

3. Mutually honor and respect painful feelings.

Healthy relationships are ones in which partners agree to honor and respect their own and each other's painful feelings. When loving partners disclose that they are wounded by something the other says or does, they can clarify: "Though I am hurt, I do not hold you responsible for my pain. What you did was a wounding experience that made my feelings hurt." This allows a partner to recognize the other's pain and the specific incident that injured them.

With practice, we can learn to identify and share our pain arising from loss, rejection, betrayal or humiliation that has triggered our hurt feelings, without placing blame or having shame for being wounded. We may even be able to share our terrifying sense of self-endangerment that tells us that we deserve this punishment. When we no longer need to be shaming and blaming to cover up and protect our feelings and anxieties, we will create more freedom for intimacy.

When our pain and our happiness is validated and honored by those important to us, we become more free with feelings and vulnerability. Arguments and conflicts take us into our feelings, not away from them. Our love and caring is deeper when we honor each other's hurt with emotional honesty. The following poem illustrates what a healing process this is.

Though It May Not Always
Seem That Way . . . I Really Do Love You

Sometimes it may not seem
that I love you
Sometimes it may not seem
that I even like you
It is at these times
that you really need to
understand me more than ever
because it is at these times
that I love you more than ever
but my feelings have been hurt
Even though I try not to
I know that I am acting cold and indifferent
It is at these times that I find it so hard
to express my feelings
Often what you have done to
hurt my feelings is so small
but when you love someone
like I love you

small things become big things
and the first thing I think about
is that you do not love me
Please be patient with me
I am trying to be more honest
with my feelings
and I am trying not to be so sensitive
but in the meantime
I think you should be very confident that
at all times in every way possible
I love you
— *Susan Polis Schutz*

In her beautiful poem, Susan Polis Schutz eloquently expresses both the complexity and simplicity of pledging emotional honesty to a loved one. In a loving relationship, emotional honesty is a joint effort. Though we may bring EDH patterns into the relationship, we can overcome them by using the bond of love to jointly honor genuine feelings including pain. Bringing hurt feelings out into the open allows our feelings to breathe more freely. *Emotional honesty makes more of yourself emotionally present and available to love.* By acknowledging painful feelings, we share our sense of endangerment when we are emotionally wounded. We remove the blame and shame by honoring both our own wounds as well as the emotional injuries of our partner.

III. Drowning Intimacy with "Carefulness and Caution"
The risk of being emotionally honest creates so much anxiety during the inevitable times of distress in relationships that we seek refuge by becoming emotionally distant from ourself and our partner. Once emotional separation occurs, physical separation is likely to follow. When we are offended or wounded by a critical remark,

a lack of consideration, an insensitive act, or an angry outburst, defenses tend to go up. Both the relationship and our ability to be emotionally honest are tested. The test is, "Can we be with our pain, take responsibility for it, and heal it?" Or do we have resentment toward our mate for doing or saying something that triggers our fear of being an unlovable or unacceptable person.

Close relationships create new wounds and open old ones. When loving relationships start to come apart, the unhealed pain from the past is again present. We begin to withhold expressing our painful feelings because we fear they will overwhelm us and drown our love. Instead, we drown intimacy by being careful and cautious with each other. We choose having a "safe" relationship over having a "satisfying" one. We sacrifice emotional truth for safety and security. Relationships become empty shells, devoid of intimate sharing of feelings since we fear both being hurt and hurting a loved one. In his 1988 book, *The Betrayal of Self*, Arno Gruen warns: "The price we all must pay in this game is the loss of self and, consequently, the loss of closeness to the other person." He describes how fear keeps people in unhealthy, emotionally dishonest relationships:

> We are afraid to start over, afraid to change, because we do
> not believe anyone could love us for being ourselves. And so
> we go on playing our self-destructive games, believing that
> the best teachers are those . . .who show us how to play the
> game better.

Since intimacy requires being spontaneous and vulnerable, EDH often becomes the destroyer of relationships. Being emotionally honest in intimate relationships is forever difficult because vulnerability always entails risk. The choice is between jeopardizing intimacy and closeness by being careful and cautious, or trusting our partner to honor our vulnerability. Beneath the silent pact to be careful and cautious with each other lies a fear of losing a loving partner. Loss, as we have seen, is one of the core wounding experiences that triggers EDH and defenses. Past experiences and painful emotional wounds from failed relationships keep us in "careful and cautious" mode. *The fear of losing yet another loving partner keeps us from taking risks by revealing our real feelings to ourselves and our partner.*

There is always a certain "carefulness" in codependent relationships, whether they involve physical or emotional abuse, alcohol or drug abuse. In their 1994 *Los Angeles Times* article on abusive relationships, Judith Sherven and James Sniechowski describe what others have called "the death embrace" of codependence: "Both the male and the female are bound in their dance of mutual destructiveness, their incapacity for intimacy . . . They need each other to perpetuate personal and collective dramas of victimization and lovelessness, and so, regrettably, neither can leave."

We learned to be careful and cautious early in life when we dared not reveal our upset because our parents could not honor our hurt. Adults innocently encourage children to be careful and cautious with expressing hurt feelings because as parents it is difficult to cope with the distress or guilt whenever their child is sad or hurting.

Making relationships safe for taking risks

If emotional honesty involves risking, what can we do in relationships to make them a more safe place to take risks? Accepting our emotional wounds enables us to be more self-accepting. But we do not suddenly reverse ingrained tendencies to reject our feelings. The job of EDH and defenses is to hide our fear of being an unworthy person until it becomes secretly a part of our nature. The path to emotional honesty and self-acceptance is filled with stops and starts. Being truthful about our vulnerability and pain also involves revealing our emotional dishonesty, a treacherous and shameful part of ourselves. Being loved and accepted does not ensure that we really feel these affirming sentiments. Healing wounds in relationships requires that we learn to speak the same emotional language to name our pain and share our nightmares of being unworthy.

When defenses protect us from pain that confirms we are unlovable and unacceptable, we don't feel safe to love, or feel free to be loved. Dr. Aaron Beck, in *Love is Never Enough* (1998), describes this destructive, fear-based belief system: "If someone important to me doesn't accept me, then I am unacceptable; when they don't love me, then I'm not lovable." *Healing the Shame That Binds You* (1988) author John Bradshaw says that we are not so much ashamed of admitting a mistake, as fearful that *we are a mistake.*

By validating our partner's hurt feelings, we can help remove the fear that making mistakes renders us unlovable. Failure is part of the learning process. In his 1963 book, *Self-Renewal*, John Gardner writes about our need to cultivate the "courage to fail" that is needed to break through self-limiting habits. Too often relationships are doomed to fail because we fear that a failed relationship proves we are "not good enough" to be loved. This fear sends us searching for "safe" solutions. In relationships we settle for "safe", instead of risking being vulnerable and emotionally honest, which is essential for true intimacy. Laurie Ashner and Mitch Meyerson say, in their 1996 book, *When is Enough, Enough?*, "Being rejected or unappreciated in a relationship," appears to be "the ultimate proof that we're really not good enough." They say, "When we feel 'lonely in love' we may be avoiding the risk of dependency, hiding our vulnerability. We refuse to feel or try to hide how much we love another for fear of being hurt, betrayed, abandoned and therefore disappointed or manipulated by our own true feelings."

For relationships to be safe places to practice emotional spontaneity partners must learn to honor and validate each other's feelings. Asking our partner, "How does it make you feel when . . ." gives them permission to access their inner feeling process. Emotional honesty is living with feelings in the present. Though we may still carry the heavy baggage of past unhealed hurt, we can begin dealing with each wounded feeling when it occurs. David Viscott reminds us that we were not born knowing how to handle our feelings, we just have them. Relationships are one of life's greatest learning opportunities. Along with showing kindness, consideration and love, partners who are emotionally honest respect each other's emotional rights. This frees them to be emotionally honest with themselves and with their companions in healing.

Gradually, with a partner's encouragement and honoring mutual capabilities to recover from our emotional wounds, we may begin to take steps toward self-acceptance. Use of the Journal of Hurt Feelings described in Chapter 12 is a safe way to start naming and taming the tortuous inner demons that convince us we are unlovable or unacceptable because we experience emotional pain.

There will always be a risk of partners falling into old patterns of seeking safety and security behind defenses to protect themselves from more emotional injuries. During these times loving partners can encourage each other to forgive themselves for not always being strong enough to be emotionally honest.

IV. Seven Rules for Dealing With a Partner's EDH

1. **Don't criticize or denounce a partner's EDH. It just raises their defenses because that's how they survive!**

We cannot make someone more emotionally honest by criticizing them. EDH is not a fault! In fact, the point of emotional honesty is that it avoids the need to find someone at fault when we hurt. Parents, former lovers, or tyrannical bosses may have done or said things that wounded us and made our feelings hurt. But when we have not learned to deal openly and directly with our hurt, EDH becomes the way we protect ourselves so we can cope in the world. The problem with EDH is that it can be a life-long, addictive trap that keeps us imprisoned in defenses and pretenses. This self-deceptive trap prevents us from knowing what we really feel and recovering from emotional distress. We thereby renounce our emotional rights and freedom to honor what we really feel. Unless we recognize that our defenses provide a *false sense of security*, we will continue to use them to hide our hurt.

2.   **Expect anyone trapped by EDH to feel that "nobody understands me."**

Perhaps the most universal sign that we are emotionally dishonest is a pervasive sadness and frustration that we are not understood. "Not being understood" is the code for fearing that if anyone really knew me they would know that I am an unlovable and unacceptable person. When we are emotionally dishonest, of course, we never feel understood. For how can anyone else know who we are when we're masters at hiding and disguising our real feelings from ourselves? Our feelings are an important part of who we are. To deny them makes us an impenetrable enigma to others. When we are protected by emotional defenses, a part of us doesn't want anyone to know what we really feel.

3.   **It is easy to misread or be misled by someone who disguises their hurt in anger or depression.**

Living or working with someone who uses emotional dishonesty for self-protection tends to also make us reluctant to reveal our real feelings. We feel hesitant to acknowledge hurt feelings to someone who doesn't seem capable of recognizing theirs. People who are heavily defended tend to react to painful experiences through the mask of anger or depression, sulking or swearing. When we see a self-destructive or outraged person's behavior, it is useful to ask, "What underlying hurt feelings might they be hiding?" Both their expression of anger through hostile behavior, as well as using depression to withdraw from their feelings, are acts that disguise emotional pain. We may never be allowed to get inside to see what feelings are behind the angry or depressed person's behavior, but we can be sure that lurking deep within is hidden hurt from wounding experiences too painful and frightening for them to acknowledge. Anger is the disguised response to self-messages that warn us we are in **danger.**

4. **A person trapped in EDH may love you more than they can show. They fear that expressing their love exposes their vulnerability.**

    It may not be much comfort to recognize that an emotionally distant parent or partner may love you more than you realize by their words or behavior. Yet this is often the case. When terrorized by fear of our vulnerability to being hurt, the only way we feel safe is by not exposing our love or pain. Part of the EDH bargain of not feeling our pain is that neither can we trust our feelings of love and happiness. Partners who cannot freely show their love, live in a tenuous world of carefulness and caution.

5. **The best way to help someone caught in EDH, is to keep affirming their feelings without judgment, blame or criticism.**

    The simple process of helping a loved one to affirm their right to have and name their pain without blame or shame is effective for helping them to recover from their emotional distress. Emotional honesty works by affirming all hurt feelings as valid and normal. We honor feelings of a loving partner by saying, "Of course, you feel bad;" or "That must make you feel terribly hurt;" or "I can imagine how painful that must be for you." The next step is to help them name each wounding experience, such as "Not being selected for the job must feel like a painful rejection." Helping them name the loss, rejection, betrayal or humiliation helps a partner reduce the wounding event's mysterious and frightening power. This process of affirming emotional honesty helps to contain the devastating impact from painful injuries. Couples are encouraged to separately maintain their own Emotional Honesty Journal of Hurt Feelings (see Chapter 11) to help practice the "naming and taming" of hurt feelings when they are wounded.

6. **When someone you love is hurt, reassure them they don't deserve their pain.**

    Unfortunately, EDH converts normal painful experiences into an indictment of our unworthiness. Caring people reassure those in pain that they are lovable and acceptable despite the wounded person's fears to the contrary. We all need help to counter secret fears that we deserve the pain we feel. It is living hell to be tortured by EDH and the shameful sense that our emotional wounds are deserved punishment for being an unacceptable or unlovable person. Healing is impossible so long as we believe that something must be wrong with us to hurt as much as we do. People suffering from EDH need someone to console them by affirming that even though they hurt now, they do not deserve to suffer. This is why people in pain find such relief from receiving loving and caring attention. When we reassure a loved one that we care for them and want them to feel better, we should not hide the fact that their pain is real. When we cannot accept our hurt feelings without judgment, shame or blame, we need to be encouraged to honor and accept our pain, so we won't fear the next hurt as much.

7.   **Honoring our own hurt feelings helps other's get in touch with theirs.**
       One of the best ways of helping someone close to you to recover from EDH is by demonstrating that you honor and accept your own hurt feelings. In his 1988 book *Resilience*, psychiatrist Frederick Flach emphasizes that when it comes to feelings, "disclosure begets disclosure." In relationships, we model the healing process by revealing to our partner the pain and shame we secretly feel when we are hurt. Close relationships provide the best opportunities for emotional honesty. Partners who use emotional honesty to share frightening and disquieting feelings help each other by recognizing and honoring vulnerability. Knowing what we feel when we hurt, and honestly dealing with the pain, keeps our relationship partner from feeling isolated, helplessly sad or angry when they are injured.

CHAPTER 14

Helping Teens Handle Hurt Feelings

I've ever met anyone who wanted to go through adolescence again!
  – David Viscott, *Emotional Resilience* (1996)

I. An Emotional Road Map for Adolescents

It is often the task of therapy to re-examine our adolescence and how we survived the assaults to our identity and self-acceptance during the perilous passage from child to adult. In his revelatory book, *Emotional Resilience* (Appendix IV), psychiatrist David Viscott notes that during adolescence emotional defenses become entrenched and emotional dishonesty (EDH) patterns become more evident. Adolescents are easily upset by even the most common emotionally wounding experiences. At this time of heightened emotional vulnerability they are assailed by the compounding effects of raging hormonal changes, challenges to their emerging but frail sense of identity, and their driving need to separate from their parents.

Psychiatrist Frederic Flach (*Resilience*, 1988), lists the four main stressful events that adolescents must come to deal with:

1. Loss of childhood
2. Physical and psychological aspects of sexual maturation
3. Individuation and attainment of autonomy
4. Expanded social relationships

In relation to the last point, Dr. Flach states: "Acceptance by peers seems a matter of life and death . . . The teenager experiences wide swings in self-appraisals as he becomes much more reliant on a wider circle of other people whose opinions he values to help him define his own worth."

In *Emotional Resilience*, David Viscott portrays the emotional agony of adolescence: "Your ideals may have been crushed as you begin to see your parents and heroes as having feet of clay. The whole world seems phony, and what's worse, you don't know who you are." Adolescence is filled with emotional dishonesty. Self-deception about what teenagers feel is part of their role-playing, always trying on new identities to see which one will make them feel acceptable and lovable. Adolescence is a precarious rebellion, struggling to know what you feel while compelled to separate from your family whose love and acceptance you need. Viscott cites this wisdom about adolescent rebellion: *"It's been said that an adolescent is grown up when he can do what he wants even if his parents are in favor of it."*

By the time children reach middle school they have been charged with hormonal imperatives that create more intense experience of feelings. Following their struggle to cope with emotional wounds during earlier childhood, the young person arrives at adolescence greeted by a crippling sense of vulnerability coupled with a desperate need for social acceptance – all this just when they thought they'd finally grown up! The teen years are characterized by intense sensitivity and frequent use of defenses and pretenses to mask the fears that arise when feeling hurt and vulnerable.

As toddlers, children begin testing their capabilities and powers, struggling between feelings of autonomy ("the terrible two's", the "no" period) and dependency (desire to be protected and comforted). By the time they reach their third year, children have become veterans of encountering feelings of shame and doubt that color the meaning of their hurt feelings. In their classic book, *Childhood and Adolescence: A Psychology of the Growing Person* (1968), developmental psychologists L. Joseph Stone and Joseph Church say that despite these troubling early childhood experiences, "they have not yet learned the duplicity and guile, the masks and disguises and evasions of later years." They are naturally emotionally spontaneous since they have not yet become fully invested in defenses that will later serve to protect them from their hurt feelings.

The pre-adolescent school years, kindergarten through fifth grade, are on the surface "periods of innocence." Yet during this period children become moralistic and attach value judgments to their feelings as being right or wrong. They also begin judging and comparing themselves with others. They start honing skills of denial and indifference to hurt that become lifelong habits. Rationalization and self-deception hide and disguise inner pain, allowing it to be expressing primarily through anger. These defensive mechanisms may relieve some emotional distress. But even at this young age children will have begun accumulating and hiding hurt feelings – stored in a flammable reservoir of resentment that is likely to be ignited during adolescence.

During the formative years before the child's distressing encounters with school peers begin, parents teach which feelings are acceptable and which are not. Children naturally learn to imitate how parents cope with their losses and hurt feelings. Sadly, most emotionally dishonest parents are also unaware of their powerful influence upon their children's emotionally dishonest (EDH) patterns – denials and pretenses that may convert painful emotional wounds into anger and self-destructive behavior.

Psychiatry professor Michael Nichols, author of *No Place to Hide* (Appendix IV), describes the painful social adjustment during pre-adolescence:

> At age 10, teasing [by classmates] reaches its peak and becomes pointed and hurtful . . .Between 5-10 percent of children in elementary school have no friends; many are disliked or rejected. By fifth grade children have learned the rules of peer acceptance, how to fit in, what to wear and how to behave to avoid mockery and ostracism. Children's

defenses are well developed. Teasing becomes a playful way
of acknowledging insecurity. Standing out and making a
mistake is now considered funny, like all other things that
are in reality frightening and profoundly shameful.

Adolescence is filled with anxiety and insecurity – a voyage into
unchartered waters. As they leave the safe harbor of family in quest
of their separate identity from parents, adolescents are consumed
with apprehension. *Adolescence is a crucible for testing one's sense of
being acceptable and lovable in the hostile world beyond family.* After
age 12 or 13, children spend more time away from than with
parents. It is a period of uncertainty, brutal emotional assaults by
peers, fear of not measuring up that test self-acceptance, and anxiety about social acceptance by peers, teachers and authority figures. By adolescence, says *The Lonely Crowd* (1963) author David
Reisman, "A child has ingested significant messages about the
importance and necessity of being accepted and belonging, but
struggles with deficient skill for achieving self-acceptance."

During this period of self-discovery, teenagers are generally capable of recognizing that defenses hide their feelings. In fact, adolescents are super sleuths at uncovering and criticizing any kind of hypocrisy or pretenses, particularly those of adults and peers. *But many
youngsters enter adolescence lacking the capacity to change their self-deceptive responses to emotional wounds.* They have little awareness of the
reasons for their sensitivity, which makes wounding experiences all
the more devastating. Their lack of emotional self-awareness places
great responsibility upon adults to provide teens with an emotional
road map that identifies the emotional pitfalls and barriers that can
exacerbate their distress from wounding experiences.

While children tend to adopt their parents' emotional defenses
and coping styles, adolescence is an opportune time to introduce
emotional education so they develop their own way of dealing with
painful wounding experiences. When teens are wounded they often
feel helpless about dealing with their emotional pain. This makes
adolescence the perfect time to learn the value of practicing emotional

honesty, as well as the dangerous consequences of substituting anger and other pretenses for their hidden pain. The very fact that teens are engaged in developing a separate and distinct identity from their parents provides schools with the opportunity to teach, coach and model emotional honesty. Before their adolescence, children could learn emotional honesty by parental example. After the onset of adolescence, however, teens turn outside the family for models, and become caught up in rebellion that devalues parental influences.

During adolescence, when children have the greatest need for emotional self-understanding, peers, teachers, emotional coaches and educators will have greater success than parents in reaching teens with emotional health education. Adolescents want to be grown up and be treated like adults. Emotional health programs, presented in a non-stigmatizing, educational manner for all teenagers, will help them become more aware of ways they hide and judge their feelings.

The challenge for developing emotional honesty during adolescence

During adolescence children begin to attach new meanings to their hurt feelings. In the abyss between childhood and becoming an adult, two powerful forces intensify adolescents' emotional insecurity. One is their desperate search for belonging and acceptance in the hostile world outside their family. The other is their drive for independence and forming their identity as an individual. *Adolescence is the most vulnerable period for experiencing hurt feelings.* The four types of wounding events that trigger emotional defenses – loss, rejection, betrayal and humiliation – become teens' four horsemen of the apocalypse. To deal with intense pain from rejection, particularly by peers, teens typically mask their suffering with pretenses of not caring and "being cool."

The primary social game played in adolescence is "If I'm an insider, than somebody has to be an outsider." School becomes a venue for dividing peers into insiders and outsiders, and castigating those who do not fit the insider profile. Belonging is power. Not belonging is traumatizing and humiliating. Kids who become outcasts not only feel like outsiders, but they begin acting like renegades. While they put up a front that not belonging doesn't bother them. They conceal a devastating and shattering sense of being unlovable and unacceptable when experiencing emotional pain. It takes a lot of defenses and pretenses, at age 12 or 13, to cover the devastating shame that one does not fit in coupled with a fear of being unworthy.

One teenager who participated in a 1998 national girls summit convened by the American Association of University Women Educational Foundation (AAUWEF), stated, "Media messages tell us to be a certain shape and size, our friends and peers tell us to be like them, our parents wish we'd act a specific way. With all the different messages from all different angles, it is sometimes hard for a girl just to find the person she really is."

In their 1991 book, *Self-Defeating Behaviors* (Appendix IV), Cudney and Hardy say that adolescents "fear that if you abandon the pose you present to the world, you will have no identity whatsoever." Adolescents strive to become "their own person" separate from their parents, but this drive can create confusing ambivalence. They need to become independent but are still emotionally dependent upon parents and others for a sense of being lovable and acceptable. The resulting conflict is a hallmark of teen emotional distress: confused feelings; ambivalence, and uncertainty about their identity; EDH; and heavy use of defenses to cover-up fears and insecurity.

Adolescents are quick to point out hypocrisy in themselves and others, and are highly critical of those whose actions don't match their words. They are both critical of others, blaming peers and adults for their own painful feelings; and ruthlessly self-critical, feeling ashamed of being sad and lonely, hurt and vulnerable. They become experts at hiding painful feelings and fooling themselves. Adolescents become easily trapped in EDH, denying their hurt feelings then hating themselves for lacking the courage to be honest about their true pain. Their keen sense of criticism flares up as harsh judgments of themselves, their peers, parents, teachers and other adults. They often distrust and reject the world that seems to be rejecting them.

Emotional honesty education programs for junior and senior high school students are essential for adolescents to understand why they adopt defenses to protect their vulnerable feelings. In middle (junior high) schools, students need a basic understanding of their inner process of dealing with feelings, which includes the principles of emotional honesty. They need to recognize the dangers of emotional defenses and pretenses including the link between them and destructive behavior. It is crucial that they learn the relationship between accepting hurt feelings and achieving self-acceptance. Building upon this basic introduction, the high school level emotional education program can go on to explore the more complex challenges of becoming an emotionally honest adult, which involves the role of emotional honesty in establishing healthy and emotionally fulfilling relationships.

Commenting on the responses of 2,100 teenage girls participating in their national summit, AAUWEF president Sharon Schuster summarized one major area of concern about schools. She says sex education in schools needs to move beyond "just say no" and abstinence training for adolescents. They should "help them better understand the *complex social and emotional nature of relationships, not just the basic anatomy and biology of sex.*" [My emphasis.]

The rejected adolescent

No matter how carefully and lovingly parents try to understand and support their children, adolescents daily face threats of peer rejection, betrayal and humiliation that challenge the insecure individual's fragile sense of worthiness and belonging. Parents during this time also endure rejecting behavior by their teenager. Adolescent rebellion, while not directed solely at parents, may particularly wound parents who most need their child's closeness and acceptance. Parents, like their children, cannot avoid the strife of adolescence

Strain and distress surround the teenager – at home and at school. During the teen rebellion stage, parents and adolescents often become more verbally abusive and unsympathetic toward each other. Just at the time when children need reassurance, the parent's cold judgment, "it's your own fault," adds to the adolescent's nagging fear and suspicion that the reason they suffer such torturous feelings is due to something being wrong with them. To compound the family turbulence during adolescence, parents often develop emotional distance and defenses to protect themselves from their teenager's assaults and criticism. The emotionally wounded teenager's parents may feel betrayed and abandoned as their child emotionally and physically separates. Most adolescents spend as much time as possible away from home as a symbolic statement of their drive to become independent.

The more secure parents feel about acknowledging and honoring their own vulnerability and pain at the "loss" of their child to adolescence and share these feelings, the more permission they give teenagers to accept and value their fears and insecurity about growing apart. Emotionally honest parents can openly acknowledge and grieve their loss of the separating child. This allows their children to deal with their own loss of childhood. Parents who take responsibility for their own feelings, without blaming children or shaming themselves for what they, themselves feel, demonstrate to teenagers an important capability of emotional honesty. (See Chapter 10.)

When teenagers observe their parents openly and non-defensively experiencing painful feelings and not being devastated by them, they are encouraged to deal honestly with their own emotional wounds. They learn how to acknowledge and accept what they feel. When given an opportunity to speak with adolescents about emotional honesty, I begin by asking, "How many of you have ever heard your parents talk about their hurt feelings in an accepting and honoring way, without getting angry, blaming others or themselves; or trying to escape from their pain with alcohol or other drugs, etc.?" Very few hands go up.

Talk about emotional insecurity!

"Say, Mom and Dad, I just want to tell you I was rejected at school today and, you know, I'm beginning to feel seriously distressed, sad and worried about my sense of being worthless and unacceptable."

This is an unlikely scenario for to be this disclosing and revealing of teenage vulnerability, the adolescent would have to understand what really happens inside when their feelings are hurt. This is why emotional honesty such as this is not likely to take place. When adolescents are emotionally hurt, they usually suffer in silence. This is due, in part, because they literally have no words to describe their shameful and fearful pain. For adolescents, this time of struggling to define themselves and identify what they are feeling is made more distressing by not having learned a language that gives meaning to emotional pain. When you ask teens, "What's wrong?" as they listlessly mope around the house, either angry or withdrawn, it's likely you'll get no answer. This typical lack of response, which can frustrate and infuriate parents, is often misinterpreted as yet another teenage refusal to comply with adult requests.

Teenagers are often bound by a protective pact with EDH which typically requires a code of silence to protect hurt feelings and vulnerability. The rules are: You must not appear to be fazed by a peers' taunting, rejecting or humiliating acts. Nor shall you by hurt by a friend's betrayal, or losses such as childhood companion's moving away. Emotional defenses prevent teens from knowing what they are really feeling. Not only do they not know what's wrong (with themselves), they fear telling anyone who might "betray" their vulnerability and secret shame of being hurt.

Feelings are an enigma for most adolescents. And so they are drawn to pretenses and EDH to remove their devastating fear and shame when they are emotionally wounded. Sometimes, the only way their pain and sense of helplessness can be expressed is through rage and revenge against others, or by withdrawing into depression or other self-destructive behavior that provides a way of "controlling" their pain.

The following are some of the most common anxieties that contribute to the adolescent's emotional insecurity.

1. Being rejected or ignored by someone I'm attracted to.
2. Being criticized or rejected by an authority figure or a group I want to belong to.
3. Not fitting in; not being like others.
4. People may find out about my most private feelings.
5. Believing nobody likes me because something is wrong with me.
6. Being made a fool of; being embarrassed in front of others.
7. If I fail it proves that I'm not a smart or competent person.
8. I want to be accepted and liked, but I don't want anyone to know that I want it.
9. Admitting that I need my parents' love and approval, even though I want to be independent of them.
10. Being sad, alone or lonely.

Adolescents tend to treat these anxieties as though they are life-threatening. They are at once tortured by emotional frailty, and desperate for acceptance by peers and the adult world whom they hold up to ridicule. This is a no-win situation, a painful Catch 22. Every rejection, loss, betrayal and humiliating experience seems like a fatal wound. And to make things worse, each new wounding experience and resulting pain makes the uncertain teenager seem more flawed, unacceptable and unlovable.

The confusing insecurity of adolescence was aptly captured in the musical, Chorus Line, which features a song sung by adolescents who described themselves: "Too young to take over, too old to ignore; I'm almost ready, but what for?"

II. Preventing Teen Self-Destructive and Violent Behavior

The puzzling horror of incidents where junior high and high school adolescents kill or assault innocent classmates should cause us all to question if certain functional emotional disabilities may be linked to destructive adolescent behavior. Psychiatrist David Viscott emphasizes that emotional vulnerability and its disclosure can be particularly troubling for adolescents. Michael Nichols describes teenagers' "Thin veneer of insouciance behind what appears to be a knowing, imperturbable and self confident person – everything they are not." Adolescence is a time of pretense, a time of EDH.

Adolescents need to deal with painful wounds from rejection, their fear of humiliation and emotional devastation from losses and betrayal, because their lives and the lives of their classmates may depend upon it. By unlocking the prison and confronting their hidden and denied pain they can learn to remove the crippling effects of EDH. They are able to defuse the explosive mixture of hurt feelings and emotional insecurity before it explodes. Those teenagers who lack the capabilities of emotional honesty are the ones most likely to act out their emotional pain in destructive behavior toward themselves or violence toward peers and others. Chapter Nine deals with this dynamic in more detail.

Learning to practice emotional honesty is critical for teens whose defenses may otherwise become a costly, lifelong habit. Society, teenagers and their families pay a high price by allowing EDH to distort even one person's private, emotional pain into public tragedy. *Teens will continue to be drawn to violence because anger speaks for their silent pain.* Each added hurt that is not dealt with honestly during adolescence, will require more emotional defenses to keep the vulnerable teenager from feeling devastated and desperate for relief. EDH in adolescence as well as adulthood actually deepens our insecurity since denials of feelings keeps us from trusting our ability to deal openly and honestly with every wounding experience.

Teenagers can understand these dynamics and begin to unlock the mystery of their misery. Teens want relief from their daily dose of distress from crushing disappointment, shameful pain and a burning need to seek "revenge" against others whom they blame for their pain. Hate crimes and murders of peer are not random adolescent acts. Rage comes from the painful, but normal feelings we have not learned to name and accept. In *Emotional Resilience*, David Viscott describes teen violence as coming from adolescents who do not know who they are; who are afraid of expressing their feelings; and so act them out instead. He calls adolescence a time of "emotional disorientation." When they cannot accept and honor their hurt, teens turn to drug and alcohol abuse, depression and other self-destructive behaviors to try to numb or control their pain.

San Rafael, California family therapist Stephen Christofferson, who specializes in counseling adolescent boys, has written about the societal and peer pressure that keeps teenagers prisoners of their hurt feelings (*Marin Independent Journal*, December 12, 1999):

> Hurt people hurt people. Someone who is feeling pain inside is likely to inflict that pain on someone else. But the trick is to be able to see that the teen-age boy is feeling any pain at all. Adolescent boys are masters of hiding their emotions. The more painful the feeling, the deeper it can submerge...For the teen-age boy to admit pain, confusion, fear, sadness or sorrow is to admit weakness. To be weak is to be a wimp, a punk, an outcast and an object of ridicule by everyone.

Christofferson adds that adolescents "must learn that they are not alone in feeling scared, hurt, betrayed, lonely or any of the myriad emotions that are taboo to the adolescent American male."

Dealing with feelings that precede violent acts

Rather than blaming adolescent violent behavior on all sorts of external factors – from guns to violent video games – we need to consider the teenager's fragile inner sense of self, their over-reactive emotional control center. What drives teenagers to kill or assault their peers is unbearable pain. If we can help adolescents learn healthy ways of dealing with their painful feelings, they will have no need for retaliation. *True prevention requires finding inner causes of the student's violent behavior.* Yes, there are too many guns available, too much violence in media, movies and video games. But, what drives young, emotionally insecure persons to seek revenge against peers is not explained by external factors. Their unheeded and ignored painful feelings are often what prompt young persons to commit violent behavior, or become self-destructive.

School violence is a threat because teens carry accumulated wounded feelings into their schools where these wounds are further inflamed by peer rejection and humiliation. The pain from social rejection is to be expected, for the rituals of put-downs and exclusion are commonplace and largely unpreventable. Family therapist Michael Nichols (Appendix IV) reminds us that social failure is the number one fear of adolescence. Parents and school officials can help teens become more aware of their inner reactions to wounding experiences at home, at school and in social situations. Learning emotionally honesty is a safe way of dealing with painful feelings that helps teens become more prepared and less fearful of their inevitable upsetting experiences. By learning to name and acknowledge feelings preceding and connected to behavior, we and our children can more capably deal with and heal hurt feelings before they erupt into destructive acts.

Teens, parents, schools and law enforcement agencies need to recognize the relationship between the inner effects of emotional pain and the outer behavior that results from EDH.

We have legal procedures, both juvenile justice and adult law enforcement systems, to punish *behavior*. However, we lack an effective *preventive, education strategy* to strengthen emotional skills that can keep the adolescent from accumulating painful feelings that later explode into violent behavior. Most schools lack these types of programs, and many teenagers lack family role models for learning emotional honesty. The combination of these two inadequacies has devastating effects upon our society today, and will only increase when today's youth parent the next generation.

Preventing adolescent self-destructiveness

While researching this book I contacted dozens of centers, foundations, commissions and organizations purporting to be working on youth violence prevention. There is scant mention of functional emotional disabilities in connection with prevention of youth violence. Few even identify emotional disabilities as worthy of mention, funding or research. There is little attention given to learning about preventing acquired functional disabilities like EDH in training parents, teachers and teenagers. Because this disability is preventable, every year we fail to address this need, the more teens are in danger of converting their pain into destructive behavior.

It is understandable that the topic of teen violence captures public attention. The growing number of school shooting incidents over the past several years is frightening to parents, teachers and students. But a much greater tragedy than school violence is the far more common problem of youth *self-destructiveness.* The same day that 15 people died at Columbine High from student shootings, nearly 700 teens across America attempted suicide! Teen suicide rates have tripled during the last 30 years. Daily, self-destructive acts including adolescents suffering from withdrawal, depression and despair are kept a private and shameful family secret. They do not become newspapers banner headlines and evoke a call for community action.

Prevention of violence in schools should be part of a broader prevention effort to reduce *emotionally-based, self-destructive acts – substance abuse, depression and teen suicide.* Violence and self-destructive destructive behavior have common roots going back to the way we raise children to ignore, deny, judge, devalue, dishonor and disrespect their feelings – particularly their emotional pain. Self-destructive adolescents are walking time bombs waiting to explode. Thousands of times more teenagers in our nation's schools are engaged in self-harming behavior than those who might physically hurt their peers. Education programs can help students develop emotional health skills for safely dealing with their hurt feelings.

Feelings underlying self-destructive acts are often vague and misunderstood, and thereby escape detection. Emotional health education programs that address EDH are effective for preventing destructive behavior towards oneself and others. Because both types of "disguised behavior" may be used as masks to express underlying pain which cannot be acknowledged, emotional awareness can play a critical preventive role. Neither teens, their parents nor teachers may realize the depth of pain a child may be carrying because "We just don't discuss these types of issues" in our homes or schools. Since all adolescents are at risk – particularly at risk of committing self-destructive acts – emotional education programs in junior high and high schools are desperately needed. What better time and place than at their schools can adolescents learn how their normal responses to everyday emotional wounds can become twisted into self-punishing acts.

Beneath an adolescent's self-destructive acts lie an accumulation of unhealed hurt feelings. Their emotional arteries are blocked by fear of acknowledging what hurts. Well before the crisis stage, teens can learn to identify and deal with each failure, frustration and wounding experience as it occurs so their pain does not accumulate and reach unsafe levels. The less teens are able to acknowledge, accept and discuss their normal but painful feelings, the more likely they are to replace their real but hidden pain with symbolic, destructive behavior such as anger or self-punishment.

III. Teaching Teens to Accept Feelings, Themselves and Others
The principles of emotional honesty are too vital a subject to be left to chance. Emotional health education provides a basis for accepting oneself, forming deep emotional connections with others, and becoming free of the need to act out pain through rage at those whom we blame for our pain.

The author's website, emotionalhonest.com, provides an opportunity to learn more about the types of emotional health education programs that are available or being proposed. The website includes a form for registering to be part of the "Campaign for Emotional Health Education," which will gather names of a cross section of parents, educators, law enforcement and others concerned about having schools take a more central responsibility for preventive, adolescent emotional health.

Educators, parents and others who advocate helping teens to develop their emotional competency must join together to gain public support for emotional health education school programs. A growing number of groups and networks are being formed to address this educational need. The largest U.S. organization is the Collaborative to Advance Social and Emotional Learning (CASEL), founded in 1994. It is headquartered in the Psychology Department of the University of Illinois at Chicago. CASEL has an impressive roster of educators, community leaders, researchers and university professors. Their web site is listed in Appendix IV.

Adolescence is a crucial time for discovering one's acceptability in the world. Not only are personal safety and emotional health at stake, so is their ability to develop and maintain emotionally honest and healthy relationships. Adults, who have more experience in recovering from wounding experiences, must lead the way to help succeeding generations. The choice is either continuing to hide or risk exposing our real feelings. The latter is what enables us to develop more deep and rewarding emotional connections with others. Emotional self-deception and dishonesty practiced by adolescents can also affect their ability throughout life to have fulfilling and trusting relationships. Adults who are aware of the language and principles of emotional honesty in relationships can share their wisdom and awareness with adolescents who lack the trial and error experience adults have gained from dealing with their fear of vulnerability in relationships.

Emotional health is having the ability to deal with emotionally pain, not the skillful avoidance of it. It is developing the strength to become more resilient and confident that we can recover from hurt without covering it up with EDH pretenses and defenses. When teenagers learn to acknowledge, accept and honor their own feelings, they develop courage and confidence to deal with the inevitable wounds life is sure to bring. *By learning to honor feelings of others they also become more tolerant, accepting, compassionate and affirming individuals.*

Emotional honesty learning activities for teens

The Emotional Honesty Journal of Hurt Feelings, described in Chapter 11, is a simple and effective way for teens to practice observing their feelings and defenses as they occur. This is an essential first step in being able to openly discuss inner fears of unacceptability that are triggered by painful wounding experiences. Since it's private, the Journal is a safe place to practice being emotionally honest with oneself during adolescence. The Journal involves naming and owning painful or shameful feelings by identifying which of the four core wounding events (loss, rejection, betrayal, humiliation) we are experiencing. The journal process than takes us through the process of identifying our inner reactions in response to painful events.

The Journal may create a curiosity to share and compare inner feeling processes with peers, teachers and parents. Emotional Honesty Discussion Groups, described in Appendix III, are particularly appropriate for teens learning to share inner reactions to common emotionally wounding experiences. Schools, community agencies, PTA's or community youth organizations can organize small group meetings where teens can share their achievements and difficulties in practicing emotional honesty with themselves and others. As teens gather to learn about principles of emotional honesty, their discussions will bring into the open the secrecy that cloaks their feelings. These groups may be given another name, such as "Emotional Fitness", or "Surviving High (or Middle) School Stress" to make them seem less threatening to emotionally insecure and apprehensive teens.

Emotional honesty activities should not be confused with juvenile "anger or conflict management" programs. Emotional honesty involves learning basic skills to name, honor and accept our feelings, particularly those which are painful. The goal is to become more accepting of our feelings. This allows us to accept ourselves, which enables us to accept others.

"No-fault" education program

Since learning the principles of emotional honesty has nothing to do with anything being "wrong" with us, I call it a "no-fault education program . The Journal or Group processes previously mentioned are not about finding fault for what we feel. *In fact, these activities help us realize that there is no fault when our feelings hurt!* It is important to clarify that these activities are not "therapy" or remedial programs designed for changing the behavior of "troubled teens" or disturbed adults. These are proactive learning activities so that everyone can learn more clear and better ways of understanding, talking about and dealing openly and honestly with our genuine feelings which result from emotional injury.

Journal and Discussion Group activities can be effectively used together. Keeping the Journal of Hurt Feelings may develop greater curiosity about how others like yourself deal with EDH issues. Because each Discussion Group is comprised of peers, teens in groups will feel more comfortable talking about wounded feelings and defenses with those who have experienced the same painful rejections, humiliations, losses and betrayals.

The liberating power of education is that it takes mysterious secrets like hurt feelings out of the dark and moves it into the light. Through learning emotional honesty principles and practicing them in these "safe" activities, teens and adults can improve their skills and confidence to recover from emotional distress.

IV. Overcoming Resistance to Emotional Education in Schools

Marshall Rosenberg is the education training director and founder of the international nonviolent communication education movement. The organization was formed to prevent violence and resolve disputes by learning how to value our own and other's feelings. In his 1999 book, *Nonviolent Communication*, Dr. Rosenberg states:

> I went through 21 years of American schools and can't recall anyone in all that time ever asking how I felt. Feelings were simply not considered important.

Unfortunately, this is just another example in the long tradition of our culture denying or ignoring that feelings are a primary factor in destructive human behavior. The emotional health education movement, which champion's prevention strategies, is far from a mainstream force in America. A major barrier is the prevalent but misguided cultural belief that feelings are a "private matter." Considering that our adolescent youth are perpetrating ghastly violence against other students, and killing themselves in even greater numbers than ever before, we have an even greater incentive to explore the role of feelings in destructive behavior. We know that teens who fear being vulnerable and hide their hurt feelings often become angry at themselves, their peers and the world. Ignoring these teenagers' feelings will not lessen their anger nor help them heal their hurt.

More punishment and less emotional education

In the wake of a wave of school shootings by adolescents the past several years, more schools are adopting more repressive policies to "prevent" school violence. *These punitive policies against our youth amount to punishment before the crime, not prevention.* Adding armed guards, metal detectors surveillance cameras, armor plated doors, and unannounced searches of lockers sends a message to teens that they are basically too dangerous to trust.

In a recent newspaper column, Debra Saunders (*San Francisco Chronicle*, November 17, 1999) berates schools for coddling misbehaving students by having them attend programs that teach them how to deal with their feelings. The columnist condemns administrators of schools that use these programs for not holding students accountable to rules of conduct and being too tolerant of angry and belligerent behavior. She further criticizes parents for "ceding their authority to strangers" in the schools who believe "they can do something parents can't do."

Unfortunately, this mind-set reflects the beliefs of many educators and adults. Many contend that teaching about feelings has no place in the school. What kids learn about feelings should be taught at home. Schools need to maintain discipline and punish wayward students. This perspective, however, focuses on correcting problems *after* the child exhibits inappropriate or destructive behavior. It does not address underlying feelings that may precede and trigger the students' disruptive and potentially dangerous actions. Schools spend a great deal of effort attending to *behavior* problems of emotional distressed students, rather than using education programs to help youngsters understand and effectively deal with distressing feelings.

The columnist lauds Kay Hymowitz, author of *Ready or Not: Why Treating Children as Small Adults Endangers Their Future – and Ours* (1999), who writes that it is invasive, for example, for schools to ask children why they are angry. Getting involved with a student's feelings is portrayed as an authoritarian attempt by adults to control children's "thoughts," when their behavior should be the real issue. Interestingly, she confuses "thoughts" with feelings, which is precisely the type of emotional confusion exhibited in EDH. The newspaper column ends with a condemnation of adults in our society who are misdirected by putting too high a premium on feelings. Were it only so!

We live in a society where what we do, say, and think are considered far more important than what we feel. We continue to deny the importance of feelings at our own risk. Teenagers are a troubled and violent segment of our population, in part, because they struggle to conform to our bizarre "feelings don't count" mentality. We cannot have generations of youngsters rejecting their feelings as unimportant and irrelevant to their self-acceptance, tolerance and acceptance of others. We should know better. The following factors summarize why more enlightened school leadership is needed to overcome the tendency to ignore the enormous potential benefits of emotional health education.

Ten Reasons Emotional Education is Not Considered or Used to Prevent Teen Behavior That is Destructive To Themselves and Others

1. We don't understand the relationship between an adolescent's feelings and the violence and destructiveness their emotional pain and anger are capable of igniting.

2. Even if we recognize the important influence their feel ings have upon violent behavior, we don't know what to do to help teens handle those feelings in a more healthy and safe manner.

3. Schools feel overburdened with too much responsibility already. They feel it is parents, churches or other institutions that should be dealing with emotional education of their students.

4. Parents, particularly single-parent households, feel over burdened, unprepared or incapable of helping teens with their troubling feelings.

5. Teens typically do not speak openly about their feelings, particularly those who are encountering self-acceptance problems, painful losses and ridicule by peers.

6. Parents and school officials are fearful of having such programs in schools since they may appear to be providing "therapy" to students.

7. Teachers have been neither adequately trained nor equipped to discuss principles and issues of emotional health education with teens.

8. Schools feel they already provide emotional education. *Note: There is no general agreement on what should be included in "emotional health education" programs.*

9. There has been a lack of public outrage or demand for emotional education in middle and high schools. Consequently, few economic resources or incentives are being offered to encourage use of these programs and information for teens.

10. Because of the spate of middle and high school killings across America, we focus on teen violence against their peers, not adolescent self-destructive behavior which is far more prevalent.*

*   Of 500,000 Americans who attempt suicide each year, about one-half are teens. About 2,000 U.S. teens kill themselves yearly, and 685 make attempts each day. Suicide is second only to accidents as the leading cause of teen death. The rate of teen depression has tripled in the last 30 years. Alcohol and other drug abuse, eating disorders, compulsivity, self-injury and other teen self-destructive behavior all stem from the same inability to resolve emotional pain.

CHAPTER 15

Healing and Self-Acceptance With Emotional Honesty

I. Self-Acceptance and Acceptance of Others

It may be called the Master Passion, the hunger for self-approval.
– Mark Twain, *What Is Man?* (1906)

Emotional honesty is our way of healing ourselves when we are emotionally wounded. Emotional wounds, unlike wounds to our body, are mainly invisible. They are easy to ignore, deny and overlook. As we have seen throughout this book, unattended emotional wounds are dangerous to us because they weaken our sense of self-acceptance. The pain from our unhealed, unattended wounds remains with us even when we fool ourselves that it doesn't hurt. We have a critical choice in life: To either suffer emotional distress by pretending we aren't hurt, or try to recover from our wounding experiences by accepting each injury and the true pain that accompanies it. Acceptance of our painful feelings leads to genuine self-acceptance. Our self-acceptance then strengthens our ability to recover from, not fear, future emotional injuries. *Having hurt feelings is inevitable. Recovering from them is not. The difference is emotional honesty.*

While none of us is emotionally honest all the time, each of us can learn to recognize when we are being self-deceptive about recognizing when our feelings are painful and distressing to us. There is no simple shortcut for achieving self-acceptance. It comes from honoring our feelings even when they are threatening and upsetting. In the process of emotional honesty we are always seeking the real meaning of our emotional distress when we are wounded. We are continually learning about our self-deception, our fears, and our vulnerability. We are not given self-acceptance by our parents, mates or others. We must work at it. We must take responsibility for healing ourselves by honoring our hurt. *How we react to painful experiences, to a large extent, determines how self-accepting we can be.*

Many of us seek help from therapists to guide us on this journey for self-acceptance. David Viscott, author of *The Making of a Psychiatrist* (1972) and several of the recommended books listed in Appendix IV, states that "the principal directive of psychotherapy is to help the patient become more truthful about his feelings." From practicing psychiatry for over 30 years he concludes, "In nearly all the therapeutic breakthroughs I have seen, it was the acceptance of some previously concealed truth [about feelings] that allowed healing to begin." He emphasizes that emotional honesty comes from recognizing and lowering defenses, not from eliminating them. Being aware of defenses and pretenses that mask vulnerability allows us to accept being wounded without being damaged or feeling devastated. Resilient persons recover from their wounds and emotional distress more readily. They have learned that, in the long run, emotional honesty is the best policy for having healthy, accepting relationships with themselves and others.

Emotional honesty is difficult to practice, for it requires both the undoing of self-deception as well as the development of our ability to accurately sense, identify, and claim our real feelings – from pain to joy. Knowing what we feel requires naming what we are feeling when we feel it. It is difficult and takes courage to carefully listen to our pain in order to name it and honor it, but this process improves with practice. In his 1996 book, *The Art of Forgiving*, Lewis Smedes emphasizes that this is a learned, rather than an innate process:

>Philosophers have said that the purpose of all education is to
>learn how to give things their right name.

By learning to name our pain, we limit its potentially destructive influence on our self-acceptance and our acceptance of others. Naming feelings that otherwise remain vague and threatening gives us power to claim them. By listening to and respecting their message, we are able to see why emotional injuries trigger a fear of being unlovable or unacceptable. Embracing painful feelings with respect enables us to honor and accept them as part of us. By owning feelings, we more completely accept ourselves, including our vulnerability, our human capability for feeling hurt. Rabbi Harold Kushner, in his 1997 book, *How Good Do We Have to Be?* (Appendix IV), notes that "Only when we know that we are acceptable and lovable will we be able to change the things we don't like about ourselves." Treating pain as an indictment of our character leads to spending a lifetime looking for acceptance from others to make up for the corrosive fear and shame of our perceived unworthiness.

Self-acceptance is more than having high self-esteem, self-confidence, or receiving "approval" from others. As Michael Nichols says in *No Place to Hide* (Appendix IV), "Self confidence is particular to a situation; self-acceptance is who we are no matter what the situation. How we feel about ourselves affects what we feel free to do – and our tolerance for making mistakes and enduring failure."

Self-acceptance involves knowing and trusting that when we are injured, we can recover by being with our pain until it is defined. *Defining our pain limits it to the specific wound, rather than allowing it to threaten our very being.* We need not carry lifelong grudges for past assaults, for we were only wounded, not permanently damaged. If we can name and tame the fear and shame of being hurt, we can recover and move on. David Viscott, whose insights have been an inspiration for this book, says that emotional honesty "allows you to believe in yourself, accept criticism without blaming others, and take failure without being crushed" (Appendix IV, 1996). Michael Nichols points out that for healing to take place, we need to recognize: "We *are* vulnerable. Simply dropping defenses exposes us once again to the pain that was the reason for erecting the defenses in the first place. We can begin to relax the grip of shame by reaching out . . .taking risks, opening ourselves up to other people – but it's important to realize that we will get hurt along the way."

Paying attention to one's pain isn't wallowing in self-pity or over-emphasizing it to get attention. Respectfully attending to our hurt allows us to more precisely define and limit the emotional wound as an experience, not an indictment of our character. Respecting, rather than ignoring, emotional wounds keeps us from putting up a stoic front, and saying to ourselves, "If I don't pay any attention to it, maybe the pain will go away." The more we respect our hurt, the more we respect ourselves. We can then treat our injury with respect and self-compassion in order to recover from its painful effects.

The four core wounding experiences – loss, rejection, betrayal and humiliation – tells us what is important to us, what we have lost, how much we need others, how important it is to have trusting relationships, and how fearful we are of losing our humanity by being humiliated.

II. The OATH of Emotional Honesty

Despite growing up in a family where emotional *dishonesty* was the rule, you can set new rules for yourself, your own family, and future generations. These new rules can become a new family tradition. These four simple rules, which summarize main points from this book, may be used as an OATH to commit yourself to dealing honestly and non-judgmentally with feelings – yours and others'. This involves recognizing the often imperceptible danger signals of feeling unlovable and unacceptable whenever you suffer emotional wounds. Upholding the OATH means *striving* to be more emotionally aware and honest, even if you cannot always achieve these goals. This takes a commitment to yourself to accept your feelings as an important part of yourself. The OATH is easy to learn since the first letters of each element spell the word OATH:

Owning feelings
Acknowledging feelings
Trusting feelings
Honoring feelings

- **Owning Feelings**

When we own our feelings, particularly hurt feelings arising from wounding experiences, we respect and take responsibility for them for they tell us who we are. By taking responsibility for what we feel, we don't need to blame others for our emotional pain. By owning our feelings, we refuse to distance ourselves from them. We will not turn away from painful feelings by treating them as orphans, nor hide our hurt as a shameful sign of weakness. By owning feelings we affirm that we have the ability to experience painful as well as joyful responses to life's experiences.

- **Acknowledging Feelings**

When we can name our feelings, we acknowledge them and give them reality and importance in our life. We recognize what we feel when we feel it, and become more emotionally present. By refusing to judge painful feelings as "bad," we acknowledge that to be vulnerable and hurt is part of being human. This acknowledgement also distinguishes between what we *feel* and what we think, believe, do, or value. *Feelings are real and exist incontrovertibly as part of us even if we sometimes choose to ignore or discount them.* David Viscott (in his 1992 book, *Emotionally Free*) says, "Healing begins when you tell the truth about your hurt." He says it is not our anger over the hurt we need to get in touch with and express; it is the meaning of the hurt itself.

- **Trusting Feelings**

Knowing our emotional truth enables us to trust ourselves. Feelings are emotional responses we have to life. They are important messages we need to trust for they tell us what we care about. While we may not always choose to act upon our emotional truth, we won't summarily deny it, either. We may not always have the courage to risk being honest about what we feel, but we will not degrade the significance of these vital inner experiences as if they are not an important part of us.

- **Honoring Feelings**

We honor feelings by allowing them to stay with us long enough to know their meaning and significance. We neither need be ashamed of them nor apologize for what we feel, for this is our reality. Honoring the pain from losses and other troubling experiences enables us to also honor feelings that tell us how much we love, care about, and have compassion for ourselves and others. By honoring feelings, we are neither too fearful to grieve and heal our pain, nor too wary to freely celebrate and honor our joy.

III. Healing Ourselves and Our Relationships

Social dimensions of the emotional honesty OATH

Accepting our feelings not only makes us more accepting of ourselves, but we also become more free to accept others. Each of the four components of the emotional honesty OATH has applications for enhancing and enriching our social interactions:
- **Owning Feelings.** When we take ownership of our feelings, particularly our emotional wounds, we do not blame others for what we feel. By taking ownership of what we feel, we recognize that others are responsible for their own feelings, too. While we do not have the power to determine what others feel or have the responsibility to "fix" their hurt, we can help those we care about to own their emotional pain without treating it as a sign of weakness

or stigma. By encouraging others to own what they feel, we also empower them to take responsibility for their healing.

- **Acknowledging Feelings.** We can help others by asking about their real feelings, and listening as they express them. We can "mirror" their joy and pain by reflecting to them what we hear them say. We can acknowledge and affirm their feelings by recognizing "I know you must feel very sad (hurt or disappointed) about . . ." We can also show compassion and support for others and their desire to be emotionally honest by helping them identify the source of their emotional distress (e.g., "I can imagine how how much pain you feel. It must be difficult to feel so terribly betrayed," humiliated, etc.)

- **Trusting Feelings.** We can share with others that it is neither shameful nor weak for them to feel vulnerable and hurt. They are not a bad, flawed, or inadequate person because they feel pain, sadness, or otherwise suffer from an emotionally distressing experience. By talking a friend or child *into* their feelings, rather than trying to talk them *out of* their pain or grief, we help them to trust what they feel and encourage them to experience their full range of feelings.

- **Honoring Feelings.** By honoring our feelings, we can be more accepting and tolerant of others' feelings. We do not have to necessarily agree with their particular feeling of hurt or the depth of their grief. But we can help them to accept their pain and recover from it by first honoring the fact that they do hurt. When we say, "I can see how you're hurting from . . .," and "It is obvious that you feel devastated by the loss of . . .," we allow someone we care about to honor their pain as well as their human capacity to feel and heal.

One of the central tenets of this book is that *self-acceptance is necessary in order for us to accept others.* Being emotionally honest affirms not only your own feelings, but makes you capable of connecting emotionally with others – being able to empathize, feel compassion, and experience deeper emotional intimacy.

Emotional honesty affirmation (self-dialogue)

In summarizing the significance of emotional honesty for self-acceptance and acceptance of others, I have compiled a list of statements you may find useful and reaffirming. These are words to remind and encourage you to live as emotionally honest as you can, not only for yourself, but to be a more emotionally honest and supportive partner in relationships:

- My feelings are my reality and my responsibility. My feelings tell me who I am.
- My feelings are an important part of me and what makes me a unique individual.
- I will honor my feelings of vulnerability without judgment or shame.
- There are no good or bad feelings.
- Behavior is not a feeling; beliefs are not feelings; thoughts are not feelings.
- While I am *not* responsible for what others feel, I *am* responsible for my own feelings.
- Even though my parents did not accept and honor my feelings, I will not continue the chain of emotional deceit with myself, my partner, or my children.
- My life is too precious and brief to be ruled by emotional self-deception, pretenses and defenses.
- I realize it is only natural to avoid emotional pain through defenses and to fear acknowledging my vulnerability and hurtful feelings. But I can choose to accept them as part of my human experience without either blame or shame.
- I will not separate my self from my emotions by denying or disowning feelings.
- I will strive to have the courage to accept and trust my feelings. Through this honesty I can free myself to feel sorrow and pain, as well as celebrate my happiness and love.

- I will encourage emotional honesty from those close to me by honoring their hurt feelings as part of who they are – acknowledging their pain and supporting them to take responsibility for recovering from their wounds.
- The most important relationships to me are with those people who help me honor my feelings and who value my emotional honesty.
- Even though I realize the importance of emotional honesty, I'm not always able to practice it when long-held defenses keep me from knowing and owning my painful feelings.
- I can release the pain of each new wounding experience by forgiving myself for my shame of being hurt, and by forgiving others whom I blame for my own pain.
- Feelings are an important part of my humanity. By honoring my feelings without judgment, I affirm them and increase my emotional capacity to honor the feelings of others.

IV. Love, Happiness and Emotional Presence

The Faustian bargain

The right to pursue happiness is so fundamental to our lives that it is specifically proclaimed a birthright in the United States Declaration of Independence. Yet lurking within each of us is a thief of happiness – emotional dishonesty. It robs us of our basic human right – to have and accept our feelings. When we distrust our feelings or consider them shameful, the experience of happiness can evaporate in a cloud of suspicion and uncertainty. Philosophers have long struggled over the meaning of happiness and what we must do to enjoy its sweet presence. We may believe that happiness comes from within us, not from outside. Yet we may be unable to see how emotional defenses and pretenses discredit both our hurt and happiness. Our emotional sentries allow happiness and love to enter only if they pass rigid tests of authenticity.

Defenses are part of a Faustian bargain we strike: that by devaluing our feelings, we won't feel hurt when we really do. But part and parcel of that bargain is being unable to genuinely feel happiness, love, or appreciation when they occur.

Emotional pretenses are self-deceptive because they only seem to protect us. This self-deceit is fear-driven, for emotional dishonesty often paralyzes our courage, luring us to become its prisoner. Being vulnerable always entails risk. But it is a necessary risk if we are to stop squandering our emotional energy by protecting against acknowledging and healing our past hurts and fearing future ones. Our emotionally dishonest patterns may have been modeled for us by imperfect parents who were most likely unaware of their defenses. Yet each day we have the choice of confronting our self-lies and dealing more honestly and respectfully with our own painful feelings.

Feeling worthy of happiness

Emotional dishonesty undermines positive feelings about ourself, since joy can't arise from within us. Happiness is something we temporarily borrow, but can never own. *Emotional dishonesty is a declaration of dependence, causing us to believe our happiness and self-worth depend upon the whims of others.* Emotional dishonesty robs us of true happiness, for we feel we must steal moments of joy since they are not truly deserved. As Laurie Ashner and Mitch Meyerson say in *When is Enough, Enough?* (Appendix IV), "Defenses protect yourself even at the cost of your happiness." When we distance ourselves from our feelings, the source of happiness and hurt appear to come from outside us. While we still long for these rewards, gifts of joy and fulfillment may seem to slip away because we feel unworthy of them.

The only way we may feel deserving of these pleasures is to pay for them through a ritualistic self-sacrifice. Even though we know that we can't buy love or happiness, we may believe that to enjoy them we have to "pay the price." One way we pay to feel deserving is to sacrifice ourselves through self-destructive acts, being self-effacing and even self-injuring. Self-sacrifice is meant to placate the angry "gods" that we feel punish us with hurt feelings. Yet self-punishment is never enough to allow us to feel completely deserving of happiness, since deep inside we still feel unlovable and unacceptable. Prostitution is the world's oldest profession, perhaps enduring through the centuries because so many people feel unworthy of having love and pleasure unless they literally and figuratively pay for it.

Over 200 years ago, German philosopher Immanuel Kant wrote in *Critique of Practical Reason*:

> Morality is not properly the doctrine of how we make ourselves happy, but how we make ourselves worthy of happiness.

Emotional honesty and its defenses deny our true feelings by disavowing our emotional reality. When we devalue painful and shameful feelings because they "reveal our shameful vulnerability," we may also distrust happiness and the loving feelings others give us. *Feeling unlovable and unacceptable is much more painful than just feeling unloved or unaccepted. The latter is a present, painful state; the former a terrible character flaw!*

Trying to rid ourselves of troubling feelings by blaming others for what we feel distances us from our feelings. Emotional dishonesty often involves "giving" others the power to control what we feel. If others control our hurt feelings (they are "at fault"), they also determine our happiness. For that, too, is out of our hands. In *The Language of Feelings* (Appendix IV), David Viscott states, "There is no way of avoiding pain if you wish to be open to pleasure." *When we feel like a fake, we can't love ourself for who we really are. We also can't believe that someone who loves us, values us for ourself.*

An attorney friend of mine recently disclosed his difficulty with being emotionally honest and how it affected holding onto happiness and fulfillment in his work. With a sad smile he acknowledged that something prevented him from experiencing personal satisfaction, though he was skillful and capable of helping others through his law practice. He described his mission as helping clients to overcome legal problems so they could achieve freedom. Likening himself to Moses, he described his work as leading clients to the promised land and helping them achieve their dreams. But, he mournfully acknowledged, "I can never go along."

Barriers to love and intimacy

Accepting joyful feelings is the gift of happiness we give ourself. No matter how much genuine love and caring someone offers, the defended person cannot receive it without scrutiny. *When we love people who do not own their feelings, true intimacy is impossible.* Intimacy requires the ability to own feelings and vulnerability so that we can share them.

We all want unqualified love, but sometimes don't feel qualified to have it. Love and happiness can never be genuinely enjoyed nor fully experienced if we lack the courage to lower defenses and risk being emotionally honest and vulnerable. Emotional honesty, though difficult and risky, enables us to experience our full range of feelings without censure. By lowering defenses that protect us by disowning our hurt, we can also remove barriers that prevent us from deserving and owning feelings of love and happiness.

John Amodeo and Kris Wentworth, in *Being Intimate* (Appendix IV), explain that "By 'accepting' or 'honoring' feelings, we mean the ability to be open to the direct experience of such feelings – the capacity to tolerate without trying to diminish, exaggerate, or dismiss whatever happens to present itself in any given moment." The therapists describe how being free to feel opens us to personal growth and healing:

> The real experience of forgiveness cannot occur through a
> mental decision – it results from experiencing and being re-
> leased from our resentments and the underlying pain and hurt
> . . .The path toward a richer life does not predominantly

involve feeling 'happier' but, rather, feeling more . . .As we open to feeling more, we generally begin to feel better. However, expecting personal growth to mean perpetual happiness would be to sadly miss the point. As we grow, we feel more, which includes more joy and love, as well as more hurt and sorrow . . .Gently opening to the experience of sorrow assumes a vastly different felt quality than the chronic pain associated with resisting our real feelings.

Removing barriers to being emotionally present

Early in life, many of us probably learned to quiet our emotional anxiety and fear by denying our hurt. The danger is this: When we survive emotionally only by distancing ourselves from our feelings, we sacrifice our emotional truth and presence. Defenses protect our emotional pain from the past and keep us on guard in perpetual anxiety against more potentially wounding experiences. The result is that we spend little time living emotionally in the present. In her 1997 book, *Don't Take it Personally!*, Elayne Savage describes children who felt ignored, betrayed, or abandoned by parents, who later in life associate being loved by anyone with feeling anxiety about their vulnerability: "It's not a question of *if* they'll get hurt, but *when* it will happen." These individuals are sentenced to being perpetually on guard, fearfully watching out for painful experiences they feel incapable of handling.

Emotional dishonesty is not a discriminating disability. It devalues positive and affirming feelings just as it discounts painful ones. It is a masquerade that makes a mockery of our emotional reality. What a price we pay for this protection! *We feel "safe" only when we distance ourselves from our feelings and disguise what we truly feel.* Being emotionally present or distant comes down to whether or not we are able to accept our feelings. Emotional dishonesty and distancing creates a time-warp problem. When we are emotionally honest and less fearful about what we are feeling in the present, we can savor joyful and painful feelings as they occur.

Emotional experiences cannot exist in the present when we

habitually disavow our true feelings by denying their presence. Post-traumatic stress syndrome, or "battle fatigue," occurs during war or life-threatening emergencies when we put aside feelings of fear, horror, or pain during a traumatic event, only to experience them later disguised in some other form of emotional distress or destructive behavior.

Emotional honesty requires living in the present and learning to put aside censoring devices that sort out which feelings are real and which are not. By questioning our emotional responses to both joy and pain, we become preoccupied with judging if feelings are genuine or false, rather than just experiencing them. *All of our feelings are real and part of us, even if we deny them.*

By maintaining emotional presence, feeling what we feel when we feel it without judgment, we carry less "baggage"of stored hurt from the past into each new life experience. Anxiety is the denied and unattended wounds of the past fearfully intruding in the present. Fear of being caught emotionally "off guard" is so terrifying that we post sentries to guard against painful feelings, past and future. This leaves little energy or awareness for present feelings. While carrying the pain from past losses, for example, and being preoccupied with anticipating future ones, we have little remaining energy or capacity to experience our emotional reality in the present moment.

The following poem is my way of expressing the way defenses keep us prisoners of emotional dishonesty and prevent us from being emotionally present.

My Faithful Sentries
by Ronald R. Brill

The hurt, the pain, cuts to my core
The wound ignites a familiar horror
I must be flawed to hurt so much
unlovable, unacceptable as such
Again and again I disguise my pain
"It doesn't hurt," goes my refrain
To deny my wound, to never cry

To bury my pain and let it die
Sentries posted to my front and rear
Guard past hurt and future fear
It's such vigilance that keeps me free
From frightening feelings I dare not see
My perfect defense is costly you say
But I gladly pay to stay this way
To keep my fears and pain at bay
While I live in tomorrow and yesterday
One day, unbearable pain may defy my game!
This masquerade no longer hide my shame
I'll need more sentries to fortify defenses
To double my guard and strengthen pretenses
Or, maybe my hurt just wants to be named
So no one, including me, needs to be blamed
What if there's no need to fear each wounded feeling?
Then I could embrace my pain and begin the healing

V. Finding Forgiveness and Personal Peace

We are healed of suffering only by experiencing it to the full.
–Marcel Proust

Forgiving, as philosopher and author Lewis Smedes (Appendix IV) says, begins when we start owning our pain. Forgiveness is more for ourselves than the person we forgive. Emotional dishonesty (EDH) tricks us into a blame-and-shame syndrome whenever we are emotionally wounded. By forgiving ourselves for shaming our feelings, denying our vulnerability, and being emotionally dishonest with ourselves, we can learn to release the pain that otherwise deepens into self-loathing. Any devaluing of ourself leads to anger and resentment toward others.

Smedes believes that "Eighty percent of what we see when we look at a person who recently wronged and deeply wounded us is the memory of our pain . . .He becomes the wrong he did." And we become the victim. Forgiving others for doing or saying things that caused our feelings to hurt helps to release the pain and shame associated with feeling unlovable or unacceptable. He says, "To give forgiveness requires nothing but a desire to be free of our resentment." When we forgive others, we have no need to avenge emotional wounds, since we have taken the charge off of our pain and removed its stigma. Once we recognize that hurt feelings are neither deserved nor something to be blamed on others, our self-acceptance grows. "Forgiveness is the only way to get ourselves free from the trap of persistent and unfair pain," says Smedes.

Relationships deepen when they are centered on people being emotionally honest with themselves and being emotionally free to be in the present. Family therapist John Amodeo, in *Love & Betrayal* (Appendix IV), states, "I often hear clients say, 'I've had enough hurt' and no longer allow themselves to experience it." He says that "By cleverly dodging the emotional aches that are part of life, we pay the tragic price of betraying ourselves." Amodeo quotes Long Beach, California marriage and family therapist Maggie Kline, who makes a distinction between pain and suffering: "We can release our pain only when it is honestly faced . . .Chronic emotional suffering is the consequence of not facing our pain. It is a self-victimization through which we avoid uncomfortable feelings."

In *Emotional Resilience* (Appendix IV) David Viscott observes:

> Most of your problems come from not wanting to see things as they are. When you resist being honest, you defeat the natural healing process. The defensive attitude you adopt to protect yourself gives you no peace. You are always expecting some undeniable truth to cut through your facade and remind you of how you truly feel.

Lying to yourself about your feelings is more damaging to your well-being than lying to others, for it distorts your emotional reality – the basis for your self-acceptance and acceptance of others. Hiding your hurt allows it to manifest in some disguised, destructive form such as anger or depression; or even makes you into a victim who uses misfortune or pain as a way of getting attention that you otherwise feel you don't deserve. *When you're emotionally wounded, it's not your anger about the hurt you need to "get in touch with" and express. It's the meaning of the hurt itself.*

Discounting your feelings is discounting and devaluing your self. You may be unable to directly ask for love and acceptance, although it is your eternal desire to have them. You must first believe you deserve love and acceptance to have and hold them. We all have the *power* to choose to be emotionally honest, but not everyone has the *courage*. Emotional dishonesty is self-betrayal, for it disables and disconnects us from our feelings. And when we disrespect what we feel, we disrespect ourselves. Emotional honesty can also enable us to forgive ourselves when we lack the courage to end our pretenses and self-deception about our feelings.

Emotional dishonesty is not a dirty word

I often encounter a predictable pattern of negative responses to my use of the term "emotional dishonesty." People insist that I should use another term – anything but dishonesty. Perhaps their reaction is caused by the shame we feel in acknowledging that we routinely engage in pretenses and self-deception to protect ourselves from our real feelings. Resistance to my use of the word "dishonesty" may tell us why we have so much difficulty recovering from emotional distress. When we are in pain, we resist admitting that we want to escape from it without having to acknowledge it – and without ever admitting our emotional subterfuge!

In his 1990 book, *Resolving Resistances in Psychotherapy*, Herbert Strean says that people who are controlled by their emotional dishonesty fear that therapy will "blow their cover." They cannot afford to risk exposing both their betrayal of self and their fear of being unlovable and unacceptable. "What frightens many prospective clients about therapy," Strean writes, "is the possibility that their secret will be discovered and condemned." EDH is addictive, for it is a process by which we are able to deny our emotional lies.

The punishment we inflict upon ourself for distrusting and betraying our real feelings is far more painful than any torture someone else might inflict upon us. The lies of emotional dishonesty are far more harmful to ourselves than to others. *Not only do we distrust and devalue our feelings, but we then become ashamed of our self-betrayal.* Recovering from the addictive practice of EDH is one of life's most difficult tasks. This is why we need others who understand these emotional games to help us identify them and develop confidence to stop them by honoring and valuing our emotional truth.

Overcoming fear of the unknown

Emotional honesty is a necessary risk, one that people in therapy must confront every day to recover from emotional distress. This fear of exposing our lies about painful feelings is the reason so many cannot tell the truth about them, even in the protective environment of therapy. This is the fear that patients of the late psychiatrist David Viscott realized as they listened to themselves on therapy session tapes telling lies about what they felt. His patients reported being surprised at how often they lied about what they were really feeling, even in these private sessions.

How do we find the courage to confront, identify, and release our addiction to EDH? Adults, like children, are frightened of the unknown because it tends to magnify the mysterious. Hiding denied feelings in the dark den of denial actually makes them more frightening. Once we understand and specifically name our painful feelings – going into the darkness and bringing the hurt into the light to examine it – our pain becomes more specific, tangible and demystified. Once frightening feelings become more real, they also become more acceptable and manageable.

Children's fairy tales often contain frightening encounters with wild and potentially dangerous animals, playing on the infant's primitive survival fears. Fairy tales are one way of demystifying and making tangible those formless terrors that frequently occupy a child's imagination and dreams. Adults also have hidden, mysterious, and unidentified terrors that threaten their safety and security. In therapy, during the process of healing, there comes a time when people realize that it is their protective, emotional defenses that keep them from naming and facing their unthinkable fears. It is then that the mystery of their distress is revealed.

Once we become committed to being as emotionally honest as we can, no one can take that power away from us! Even when we fail in this task, we can forgive ourselves and try to be more truthful about our feelings the next time we are hurt. Each time we honor our ability to accept what we feel, we gain strength that enables us to recover from the next wounding experience. No matter how our parents or our society conditions us to dishonor and neglect our hurt and disappointment, we know better. We won't permit ourselves to engage in this self-deception because we realize its dangerous consequences.

The best time to seek therapy and assistance to stop this cycle of self-betrayal and emotional dishonesty is when our vulnerability and pain seem unbearable. When we can no longer avoid the pain nor tolerate our continuing denial of it, we become motivated to risk confronting our deepest fears. *The only pathway out of pain is through it.*

Therapy, self-healing, and self-awareness all involve increasing our capacity to be emotionally honest. All three are part of the process of identifying the true source of our pain and fear. By naming and taming the painful feelings that threaten our well-being we can overcome the fear of vulnerability that our defenses try to hide. This process, long considered a mystery, requires a new language to help us understand what prevents healing of hurt feelings. Just learning the language of emotional honesty gives us a powerful tool for recovering from, and preventing, emotional distress.

In his 1988 book, *The Betrayal of Self*, Arno Gruen discusses the sense of autonomy we experience by living in full harmony with our feelings: "Having access to life-affirming emotions, to feelings of joy, sorrow, pain – in short to a sense of being truly alive – is essential . . .The history of our culture is to a large extent one of avoidance, rejection, and suppression of these feelings . . ." Robert Burney (Appendix IV) describes the personal transforming power of emotional honesty: "Each time that I need to grow some more – need to surrender some more of who I thought I was in order to become who I am – I get to peel another layer of the onion. Each time this happens, I get to reach a deeper level of honesty and see things clearer than I ever have before."

One of the saddest tragedies of emotional dishonesty is feeling unlovable, even in a loving relationship. To remain cursed by the Faustian bargain of EDH is a diabolical exchange in which we disable our deepest affirming feelings in order to avoid feeling pain. In the bargain, we give away our most precious birthright – our right to be hurt, as well as our right to be loved, and to be at peace with ourselves.

When we are able to reclaim the right and freedom to have and honor our feelings, we become more self-accepting and more resistant to being devastated by emotionally wounding experiences. Emotional honesty is a journey, not a destination. The journey starts with self-awareness. *There are many sources of wisdom, inner strength, and healing. They all start with self-awareness and end in self-acceptance.*

APPENDIX I.

Glossary of Emotional Honesty Terms

1. Instinctive emotional survival fears
- Fear of being abandoned/unwanted because of being unacceptable or unlovable
- Fear of emotional vulnerability as being devastating
- Fear and shame that we deserve our pain
- Fear that hurt feelings are a punishment that validates our unworthiness

2. Anatomy of our inner reactions to wounded feelings)
- Experiences (physical and emotional; in the here and now)
- Behavior (physical, often instinctive, responses to experiences)
- Thinking (Considering appropriate physical/emotional responses; problem-solving)
- Values and beliefs (rules for good/bad; right/wrong feelings)
- Emotional defenses (protect self from emotional danger; lies about our feelings)
- Inner sense of self (monitors vulnerability, lovability and acceptability; repository for feeling worthy, deserving, emotionally safe)

3. Feeling unacceptable or unlovable
- Unworthy/worthless/undeserving
- Not good enough
- Wrong/stupid

- Incapable/incompetent
- Unimportant/insignificant
- Not OK
- Defective/flawed (permanently)
- Bad/Evil

4. Emotional Defenses (what we do with unacceptable hurt feelings)
- Deny/Dismiss
- Deflect
- Distort/Disguise
- Devalue ("I don't care")
- Delay (e.g., post traumatic stress syndrome)

5. Types of Emotional Wounds
- Losses (see #6 below)
- Abandonment/desertion/unattended/unwanted
- Social rejection/ignored
- Public humiliation/embarrassment (bullying, harassment)
- Betrayal (being lied to, loss of trust, loss of respect)
- Being criticized (told we're wrong, not good enough)

6. Types of Wounding Physical Losses
- Of parent
- Of family member
- Of loved one (friend, relationship)
- Of physical or mental functions, of parts of body (health)
- Of job, position, income or money (investment)
- Of valued possession (home, car, memorabilia)
- Of innocence (child abuse, rape, etc.)

7. Disguised Behavioral Responses to Emotional Wounds
- Depression/withdrawal
- Anger/violence
- Blaming and criticism of others
- Being a victim or martyr

- Emotional numbing (alcohol, drugs, workaholism, compulsiveness)
- Sexual obsessions
- Eating disorders
- Self-injury
- Suicide wishes or acts

8. Resulting disabling effects of emotional dishonesty
- Inability to accept self and trust our feelings
- Inability to accept and trust feelings of others
- Inability to feel compassion and empathy
- Inability to reveal true feelings when we want to
- Inability to feel safe enough to reveal vulnerability and experience intimacy
- Inability to experience feelings in the present; loss of spontaneity
- Inability to feel deserving of love, happiness, achievements

9. Healing qualities of emotional honesty
- Owning hurt feelings without judgment, blame or shame
- Acknowledging feelings by naming our hurt
- Trusting feelings and taking responsibility for healing our hurt
- Honoring feelings as a valuable part of who we are
- Experiencing feelings in the moment; expressing real feelings
- Appropriate risking/sharing of vulnerability (intimacy)
- Forgiving ourselves and others for our pain
- Accepting our feelings; accepting ourselves

10. Emotional distress components
- Feeling overwhelmed or devastated; powerless to recover
- Feeling vulnerable and weak
- Feeling helpless and hopeless
- Fearful anxiety that something worse will happen
- Fear that our mask of pretense will being removed and self-deception exposed

APPENDIX II.

Questions and Applications of Emotional Honesty

1. **What does emotional honesty and self-acceptance have to do with preventing violence?**

    Self-accepting people have no need to harm themselves or others. A commonly acquired functional disability, emotional dishonesty (EDH), may lead to replacing denied feelings of pain with angry behavior. This self-deceptive process converts hurt feelings into destructive behavior ranging from depression to violence. Secretly embedded in each wounding event is a corrosive fear that we deserve to suffer for being an unworthy person. If we are unaware of this process, EDH uses defenses and pretenses to deny our pain, hide our secret shame, and then disown our hurt by hurting others. Emotional honesty allows us to honor and accept our painful feelings. By doing so we thereby accept ourselves. We do not blame others for the pain and shame we feel when we are hurt. We do not punish others for our own feelings.

2. **The term "emotional dishonesty" seems like a character flaw. Isn't there another term we can use?**

    Emotional dishonesty is more than a term, it describes a process that corrupts our feelings by disguising and distorting their real meaning. Emotional dishonesty is not a character issue involving being a "bad" person, since all of us are emotionally dishonest sometimes. While pretenses and defenses appear to protect us, this self-deceptive process has potentially dangerous consequences. Emotional dishonesty disconnects us from what we feel. These lies produce an emotional disability that makes it difficult to recover from everyday wounding experiences. Since the dishonesty keeps us from our emotional truth, we cannot trust what we really feel. These inner lies undermine self-acceptance and prevent us from developing close and trusting relationships.

3. Is emotional honesty telling people what we really think of them?
Emotional honesty refers to what we feel about *ourselves*. It is different from lying to others about how we feel about them. It is a self-deception. When we feel unsafe, ashamed or vulnerable because of our hurt feelings, it is emotionally dishonest to react by blaming others for the hurt we feel. Emotional honesty keeps us from becoming over-critical and judgmental of ourselves and others when we are emotionally wounded. Emotional honesty allows us to own, acknowledge, trust and honor what we really feel.

4. Isn't it impossible to be emotionally honest all the time? Aren't there situations when being vulnerable is truly not safe?
No one is emotionally honest all the time. We use emotional defenses as a way of coping with unbearable, painful feelings. But when we are aware of our defenses and emotional dishonesty (EDH) we are capable of choosing when it feels safe to drop emotional pretenses that disguise our real and vulnerable feelings. Without this awareness of EDH, we may automatically censor feelings we believe we "should" not have and substitute those which are more safe and acceptable. We may become addicted to emotional dishonesty and feel insecure in revealing any deep feelings of hurt, joy or love. While there may be unsafe situations for our emotional honesty, the goal of emotional education is to develop freedom of choice when and where we can and should be honest about our feelings with ourselves and others. By being aware when we are emotionally dishonest, we can exercise discretion when to use it to reduce unreasonable anxiety and pain.

5. **Isn't self-acceptance just another term for self esteem or self-confidence?**

Self-acceptance is related to self esteem and self-confidence, but is more critical to our emotional health. Being emotionally honest and accepting our feelings allows us to be more self-accepting. We can appear to have self-confidence, be successful in life, yet spoil it because of emotional confusion that leads us to question which of our feelings are true and which are false. Emotional defenses are nature's protective devices that sometimes get out of hand by making us deny what we really feel. It is hard to have self-acceptance when we reject our feelings. Even our sense of accomplishment and ability to experience intimacy is spoiled when we cannot trust our feelings. Self-accepting persons are emotionally free and more accepting of others and their feelings. Being capable in what we do does not mean being capable of trusting and being honest about what we really feel.

6. **How do we know when we're emotionally dishonest since our defenses are self-deceiving?**

Only the person who experiences feelings can determine if they are genuine or not. The main signs of emotional dishonesty are judging feelings as good or bad, being uncertain if we are entitled to feel the way we do, and being fearful of revealing what we really feel. When we feel hurt and we cannot identify the specific losses, rejection, betrayal or humiliation that cause the injury, we may react with general anger or depression without seeing the connection between our behavior and our hurt feelings. With practice, adolescents and adults can develop this awareness and learn to recognize their particular pattern of emotional dishonesty.

7. **Some people seem just fine being emotionally dishonest and unaware of deeper hurt feelings. Why do they need to know about emotional honesty?**

Emotional honesty affects our self-acceptance, tolerance and acceptance of others, as well as our capacity for emotional intimacy and feeling in the present. Even if we are not concerned about improving our relationships with others, we need to understand how defenses keep us distanced from our feelings. When we are in emotional pain, but deny and bury it in silent shame, we may secretly feel we deserve our emotional wounds as punishment for being unworthy. Whenever we sense being emotionally vulnerable we may be too frightened to reveal these "shameful" feelings. Outwardly we may seem unaffected by experiencing a rejection or loss, for example. But using defenses and pretenses to ignore the feelings may lead disguising and acting out emotional pain in destructive ways toward ourselves and others.

8. **Is there something wrong with me when I am emotionally dishonest?**

    Emotional dishonesty is not about being "wrong". It is about needlessly suffering from our self-deception. Specifically, by not owning our painful feelings, it is more difficult to heal and recover from emotional wounds. Stored pain rises and haunts us the next time we are wounded. Emotional distress is needlessly prolonged or deepened. We may sabotage relationships and be consumed by energy-sapping defenses, rage or emotional withdrawal. This behavior masks our painful feelings, but doesn't allow us to recover from them. We become caught in an emotional protection racket. Chronic emotional dishonesty disables our ability to attend to hidden emotional pain. Allowed to accumulate, it may eventually surface as self-destructive behavior or violent acts against others.

9. **Is there an appropriate age to begin teaching children about emotional honesty?**

    Parents who demonstrate and model emotional honesty are far more influential in teaching their children than telling children what to do when their feelings are hurt. Children learn more from parents by example than by what they say. Parents first need to understand the principles of emotional honesty so they can model healthy ways for children to effectively overcome emotional pain. Long before children are old enough to comprehend the language of emotional honesty or learn through formal "lessons", they learn by observing how their parents deal with their own emotional wounds. Those parents who would like to explain emotional honesty principles to preadolescent children, aged 8 to 11, will be assisted by the author's next book, *Emotional Honesty for Kids*, which is being written as a read together book for children, their parents and teachers. The storybook uses allegories to illustrate how emotional honesty helps to avoid emotionally distressing and disabling pretenses about feelings that are common during adolescence.

10. Why emphasize emotional education for adolescents? Don't younger kids also need it?

Without question, all parents and children can benefit from emotional health education which helps them understand the healing power of emotional honesty, and the high costs of emotional dishonesty (EDH). Prior to their adolescence, children's most important teachers are their mothers and fathers. In addition to modeling honesty in dealing with their own hurt feelings, parents can discuss with children the dangers of not honoring their feelings and those of others. As adolescents seek separation and individuation from parents their learning shifts from inside the home to outside. During this period of rebellion from parental influences, lessons of emotional honesty can be reinforced by teachers and other influential adults. Adolescence is a time of testing one's acceptability outside the family. Since normal, emotionally insecure teens hunger for respect and acceptance, they also need to know how to deal openly and honestly with their emotional responses to wounding events so they can strengthen their self-acceptance. This education can take place in schools with trained facilitators and teachers. It can become a component of school sex and life education classes. Normal but emotionally insecure and confused teens are at risk of denying their hurt feelings and expressing their hidden pain with destructive behavior toward themselves and others. There is no more vital time for learning about the dangers of emotional self-deception than during the turbulent transition years of adolescence when emotional vulnerability and EDH is at its zenith.

**11. How can I be helpful to a child or mate who is having diffi-
culty acknowledging their hurt or articulating their feelings?**

Those children or partners who have trouble explaining what
they are feelings may be helped by a caring person who helps
them acknowledge and honor their pain and fear. *One of the most
common mistakes made in this situation is attempting to alleviate their
distress by trying to talk them out of their pain.* We honor someone we
love when we can truly empathize that "I know how painful it
must be when your feelings are deeply hurt." When misfortune
befalls a child or mate, reassure them that they do not deserve the
pain they feel. It helps to be reminded when we are feeling sad and
forlorn that we are a lovable or acceptable person even though
we're in emotional pain. Help them avoid the trap of making judgments that having the bad feelings about themselves is a sign of
something terrible or bad. Help them avoid blaming others or
being ashamed of their distress. See chapter 11 for how to keep
and use an Emotional Honesty Journal as a way of becoming more
aware of emotional dishonesty and discussing hurt feelings.

12. Are emotional defenses a learned or an instinctive process?

They are probably both. Infants have a self-protective, innate
survival fear of being abandoned which is triggered by a failure of
parents to respond to their cries when their physical needs go unattended. As children develop, they first learn from parents and then
from siblings, peers, teachers and care givers who may model how to
hide threatening"hurt feelings". Adolescence is a time of testing one's
identity, acceptance and lovability in the world. By the time youngsters reach adolescence, they are typically well-armed with an array of
defenses to keep from being emotionally "devastated" when their feelings are hurt by loss, rejection, betrayal and humiliation.

**13. What is so horrible about the sense of being unacceptable or
unlovable that keeps us from being emotionally honest?**

One reason for denying our feelings when we experience emotional pain is that we seem threatened and become overwhelmed
by a fear that we are being punished because we are not lovable or

acceptable. We have a vulnerable core that warns us when we are in danger of being emotionally "devastated." We become so terrified and confused by anxiety that we must be an unworthy person to hurt so much. We then distance our self from such unbearable feelings since attempting to deny terrifying pain seems like a "life or death" issue. These innate fears serve helpless infants as a survival warning system that they are in danger of being abandoned. However, as we mature and develop more complex social and relationship needs, these warnings alert us to more generalized threats. We suffer more from our emotional wounds when they are taken as evidence that we are a flawed person.

14. How does the growing incidence of school killings and violence by adolescents relate to the need for emotional education for youth?

Americans are shocked and dismayed that so many "good" kids, even students in junior high school feel a need to take up arms to kill their peers and teachers. What is turning schools into tragic scenes of violence? The one question rarely asked is: *What kind of driving pain and fear must kids be feeling that causes them to take up guns to kill schoolmates?* These tragic killings are not acts of gangs or ritual warfare. They are the acts of despair by emotionally insecure youngsters who feel helpless and powerless to otherwise deal with their emotional pain. Their problems arise around issues of self-acceptance, acceptance by peers, public humiliation, rejection and embarrassment – emotionally wounding experiences that may be too painful and too shameful to acknowledge and heal. This is the type of distress that triggers emotional defenses and dishonesty. Overwhelming, painful feelings and fears of being unlovable or unacceptable may cause emotionally wounded adolescents to express their unspeakable pain through self-destructive acts or violent revenge. Given the potential danger of destructive acts by teens, we have a public responsibility to help young people find safe and effective ways of dealing with their common but troubling pain. Otherwise, it may have no outlet except through retaliation against schoolmates or teachers.

15. Does emotional dishonesty differ in males and females?

The process of developing defenses, denying hurt feelings, and acting out destructive responses to emotional wounds is common to males and females. The hurt feelings both sexes suffer may be triggered by different types of experiences, but the defenses used are often the same. Males tend to keep from acknowledging hurt feelings because they have been conditioned to see being vulnerable as a shameful sign of weakness. Females may be more sensitive to criticism and fear of being unacceptable because of their physical appearance. Males tend to hide hurt feelings with aggressiveness, and females with self-punishing depression or self-injury. The World Health Organization reports women have twice the rate of depression as men. However, men have seven times the risk of suicide following significant losses, such as death of a spouse or loss of a job. In addition, every culture prescribes separate roles for males and females – what is and is not acceptable in behavior, thoughts, feelings and appearance. In America, and in many advanced societies around the world, there is decreasing gender differentiation regarding emotions. Our grandmothers may have been emotionally dishonest because of rigid and repressive Victorian social rules. Today, males and females are equally likely to be aggressive and depressive. One example of changing gender roles is women holding more responsible positions in the work force. Therefore, workaholism is becoming as common a distraction from emotional pain for women as it has been for men. Changing gender roles in work and household responsibilities now give men with more child-rearing responsibilities. These new roles blur previous gender distinctions and emotional relationships between mothers, fathers and their children. They also create new stress factors which increase the emotional burdens and insecurity for both sexes.

16. Are there cultural differences about emotional dishonesty and honesty?

This book is written from the author's perspective of living in American culture. Cultural differences, religious backgrounds, prescribed roles of parents, and values around expression of feelings, all have a bearing upon principles and applications of emotional honesty. Each culture or faith prescribes personal acceptability and lovability within the context of its own beliefs and rules. Comparing attitudes and practices of emotional honesty among different religious groups, countries and cultures is a valuable area for further research and development. Despite cultural differences, people throughout the world still have the same basic human emotional needs. They share many of the same emotional defenses even though their typical forms of emotional distress may differ. People throughout the world manifest similar defenses for hiding shameful pain. They also engage in similar destructive behavior though in varying degrees.

17. How does emotional honesty work when others intend to harm us?

Physical and emotional abuse is a serious problem which requires intervention and prevention strategies beyond the scope of this book. This book addresses dealing with our own emotional hurt, which is a different issue than stopping others from intentionally physically or emotionally abusing and wounding us. With emotional wounds, we can never be sure about another's intent. It is also difficult to know where a cycle of criticism and rejection began. Another question about determining intent is whether we are being singled out for emotional abuse by tyrannical boss, for example, or is the boss engaging in a general pattern of abusiveness toward others? While we cannot always be sure of an intent to specifically harm us, *the way we deal with resulting emotional wounds is the same whether they are intentional or not.* An advantage of emotional honesty is that it helps us to know when to leave an abusive relationship or situation. How we respond to being emotionally hurt is generally more important than determining if someone actually meant to hurt us. We may be incapable of preventing someone from harming us, but we can learn to heal pain that we own rather than externalize it through self-destructive or violent, retaliatory behavior. Certainly, at times people do intend to harm us. There are several strategies for dealing with emotional wounds from bullies, for example. One strategy is to aggressively punish bullies to try and prevent further harassment. Another is to strengthen our ability to honestly deal with and heal the predictable emotional distress that this type of experience produces. Both approaches are needed. This book addresses the largely neglected second strategy.

18. Are the principles of emotional honesty used in this book based on any particular school of psychology?

No. The author writes from the perspective of an educator, rather than a psychologist or therapist. This is a unified, broad ranging, interdisciplinary approach which includes the author's insights. These principles provide a comprehensive perspective about the components of emotional honesty and what gets in the way of achieving it. These are concepts that can be taught by parents and teachers and easily discussed by adults. Rather than use traditional psychological terminology, the book is written in non-technical language. Since understanding and practicing emotional honesty requires having a language to describe feelings, the appendix of this book contains a glossary of terms as used by the author.

19. What is meant by "healing" painful wounds with emotional honesty?

To recover from emotional wounds, we must attend to our hurt feelings by naming, honoring and accepting our pain. Recovery from emotional distress is one of the primary outcomes from learning and using emotional honesty. When we attend to each emotional wound as it happens, we are doing healing work. This healing process keeps wounding events "contained" to the specific experience which caused them, rather than protecting against feeling pain, allowing it to become a generalized, shameful indictment of one's worthiness. By dealing with painful feelings in this manner we become free to put them in their place. We resist self-destructive acts or violence toward others. Emotional honesty is also healing in the sense that it is an essential process for developing greater self-acceptance.

20. How does emotional honesty and emotional health relate to the concept of emotional intelligence?

There are some related basic premises between the two concepts which include the critical importance of emotional self-awareness to our well being, and recognizing the role of feelings in relationships. Additionally, Daniel Goleman's work on emotional intelligence and this book on emotional honesty both acknowledge that we can *learn* to develop our emotional capabilities that allow us to more effectively manage our emotional responses to experiences. Emotional honesty focuses on being responsible for, trusting, owning and accepting our feelings so that we can be more self-accepting. Self-accepting people are more capable of accepting others. The result is that we naturally develop more healthy and honest relationships. Furthermore, emotional honesty is essential to our emotional health for it allows us to develop the strength and courage to confront our self-deception in order to recover from emotional distress, as well as to resist both self-destructive behavior as well as harmful acts toward others. Without awareness (or "intelligence") of our emotional truth, particularly our painful feelings, we are more likely to substitute anger for our pain and suffer from increased or prolonged emotional distress.

APPENDIX III.

Healing Together:
Emotional Honesty Discussion Groups

In his book, *Love and Survival* (1998), Dr. Dean Ornish, one of the nation's leading medical researchers in prevention of heart disease, writes about the epidemic of "emotional heart disease," the profound sense of loneliness, isolation, alienation and depression that are so prevalent today. In his chapter in Bill Moyer's 1993 book, *Healing and the Mind*, based on the PBS television series, Ornish shared what he had learned by observing heart disease recovery groups:

> Most people, including me, are frightened to take part in a group and talk about their feelings. At the same time, most of us have been betrayed and hurt very badly, and we have learned to build defenses, which, at some stage of our life, were essential to our survival..We try to create a place that feels safe enough for people to let down their defenses and share more of who they really are..The same walls and defenses that protect us can also profoundly isolate us if the walls are always up, if we have no one or no where that feels safe enough to let them down.

The function of Discussion Groups

By discussing the principles of Emotional Honesty and sharing personal experiences, participants can learn skills that help them become better parents, teachers, friends and relationship partners. The group experience is intended to encourage members to take necessary risks to recognize their own emotional dishonesty processes. Groups work mainly by strengthening individual confidence and capability to remain connected with their feelings, by sharing feelings in an open and honest manner with their peers in a non-judgmental environment.

This book and the author's Emotional Health Education consulting and training services are resources for broadening an understanding of the healing power of emotional honesty for recovering from disabling defenses, fears and pretenses that otherwise keep us trapped in emotional distress. In addition, we need planned opportunities to safely risk exposing our vulnerability so we can confront painful feelings we conceal from ourself. There are few safe and supportive ways, outside of therapy, for practicing the application of emotional honesty principles by one's self or with others. Helen Lynd, in her 1958 book, *On Shame and the Search for Identity*, writes about needing to find support to recover from shame from what we feel: "The very fact that shame is an isolating experience also means that if you can find ways of sharing and communicating it, this communication can bring about closeness with other persons and other groups."

Jane Middleton-Moz, author of *Shame and Guilt: Masters of Disguise* (Appendix IV), refers to the difficulty of talking about hurt feelings, without having a safe group of peers with whom we can share our vulnerability: "Acknowledging [hurt feelings] to another means self-acknowledgment. Self-acknowledgement requires us to feel not only the pain . . .but the mask that we have hidden behind for a lifetime." When a topic is too painful for us to deal with directly, we can benefit from being with others and sharing the challenge of trying to deal with the same problem. Healing may occur even when curing is not possible. Teens, in particular feel much more safe revealing their shameful and troubling feelings with peers who have the same type of pain.

The author encourages teens and adults to join autonomous, local Emotional Honesty Discussion Groups. A group is effective if comprised of peers. For example, separate Discussion Groups work best for: parents, educators and counselors, individual adults, couples, adolescents, mental health professionals, etc. Members of each peer group, typically five to eight persons, periodically gather to deepen their individual understanding of emotional honesty by sharing their problems and successes as they apply the principles to their individual experiences. Emotional dishonesty and the resulting distortion of feelings can be overcome by regaining the courage to trust feelings and risk accepting our vulnerability to being hurt, as well as recognizing how specific experiences trigger our defenses and pretenses. A group setting of peers is an effective method for learning how to accurately identify and manage emotional self-deception that otherwise prevents healing.

This group setting allows the practice of emotional honesty "in real time" with ourselves and others. Small groups provide an opportunity to observe and encourage others as they share their processes for dealing with vulnerability and hurt feelings. This group process helps to overcome cultural beliefs that keep us from seeing the meaning of painful feelings that we might otherwise overlook. Group participants build confidence by supporting each other in their quest for greater emotional honesty and self-acceptance. Group members are encouraged to use a common language and framework, such as that suggested in this book, so they are able to compare and share their insights.

Emotional honesty groups and training classes create an open dialogue to remove the shameful stigma associated with having hurt feelings. Harriet Lerner, in *The Dance of Deception* (1993), discusses the particular importance for women to have a safe place for truth-telling about painful feelings: "Until she shares her secret [feeling] she can't begin to understand and assimilate its meanings, look it in the eye, cut it down to size, neutralize it, and drain it of its destructive power." A group is an ideal setting in which to experience and deal with the negative self-messages that painful experiences often etch inside us.

Discussion Group leaders

Each group is a "community of learners," equals searching for greater emotional truth. The leader is a co-learner within the group and need not be a therapist or mental health professional. Usually one or two people are organizers of each group. Initially this person is referred to as the "group leader" for the logistics of meetings. Group leaders may enroll in the author's Emotional Health Education training program. (For contact information see the end of this article.) Individuals interested in forming a discussion group are encouraged to utilize the emotional honesty leader training workshops. These workshops familiarize potential leaders/participants with the concepts of emotional honesty as well as discuss ideas for group topics, exercises and processes. Trainees participate in workshops broken into small groups so they become familiar with the operation of actual Discussion Groups. Trained Discussion Group leaders play an important role in bringing peers together for mutual learning and practicing of emotional honesty.

Services for group leaders

1. To help launch new groups, potential group leaders are encouraged to hold informational gatherings to introduce potential Discussion Group participants to the process. Consultant and trainer Ronald Brill may be requested to attend these information sessions to explain the group process and answers questions about the principles and applications of emotional honesty. He is also available to facilitate the first meeting of a new group. The author also maintains a geographical list of persons interested in Emotional Honesty Discussion Groups. Individuals interested in forming a new group or joining an existing one in their area may contact the author at the address below to join existing groups, find the location of new groups being formed, and how to contact the nearest group leader. All group member lists are strictly confidential. No individual names and are sold or made public.

2. Half-day group leader basic training programs are offered periodically for those who wish to organize/lead new groups. In

the future, training may be available through a self-directed learning station on the web site: **emotionalhonesty.com.** Training includes a review of emotional honesty principles, participation in exercises and processes to encourage effective group interactions. Announcements of conferences, training and other information useful for group leaders and participants is also available on the web site "Articles & News" page, and particularly in the "Emotional Education Perspective" newsletter.

3.   Registered group leaders who have completed the basic training program will regularly receive group leader tips and suggestions for Discussion Group topics and activities, as well as descriptions of resources and ideas submitted by other groups.

4.   Regional meetings of Discussion Group leaders may be available in your area. These meetings are particularly helpful for leaders who would like help with questions, problems and opportunities for applying emotional honesty principles. Discussion Group *participants* may also attend the regional meetings.

5.   Conferences and regional meetings may feature noted authorities and authors on various aspects of emotional honesty. Conference topics may include, but are not limited to: Parenting with Emotional Honesty; Emotional Honesty in Relationships; Emotional Honesty at Work; Emotional Honesty for Adolescents; and Teaching Emotional Honesty for Kids (pre-adolescents).

Questions about the Discussion Group program

1.   **Is there a cost to participate in Discussion Groups?** Each group develops its own procedures, including fees (if any), types of participants desired, meeting schedule and operation. There is a charge for group leader training workshops, books, conferences and some publications. Travel reimbursement is required for the author's site visits with leaders or groups.

2.   **What types of materials and resources are available to groups?** In addition to the web site: **emotionalhonesty.com,** which will include a resource section devoted to Discussion Groups, most information will be available through recommended books, ar-

ticles and audio-visual materials. The author's newsletter, "Emotional Education Perspective," which includes information about new books, articles and other developments related to emotional health education, is also available in hard copy form by separate subscription. Group members may also receive discounts for quantity orders of selected books and publications.

    3. Are Discussion Groups a form of group therapy? Discussion Groups are an informal learning environment. Their purpose is to help individuals gain a greater understanding of emotional honesty principles and practices by sharing their experiences, problems and successes. While some may consider this "therapy," the intent of Discussion Groups is to encourage individuals to explore opportunities for using emotional honesty in their life. Groups can be useful to help individuals clarify further inner work, and more clearly identify the type of further assistance they may need from mental health professionals or community agencies.

    For further information about joining or starting an Emotional Honesty Discussion Group in your area contact Emotional Health Education consultant and trainer Ronald Brill at:

448 Ignacio Blvd., # 214
Novato, CA 94949-6085
E-mail: rbrill@earthlink.net
Web site: emotionalhonesty.com

APPENDIX IV.

Recommended Reading and References

Listed alphabetically by author

John Amodeo, Ph.D., *Love & Betrayal*, Ballantine Books, New York (1994)

John Amodeo and Kris Wentworth, *Being Intimate*, Arkana, New York (1986)

Laurie Ashner, Mitch Meyerson, *When is Enough, Enough?* Hazeldon, Center City, Missouri (1996)

Robert Burney, *Codependence – The Dance of Wounded Souls*, Joy to You and Me Enterprises, Cambria, CA (1995)

Milton R. Cudney, Ph.D. and Robert E. Hardy, Ed.D., *Self-Defeating Behaviors*, Harper San Francisco (1991)

James Gilligan, M.D., *Violence – Reflections on a National Epidemic*, G.P. Putnam Sons, New York (1997)

Daniel Goleman, Ph.D., *Vital Lies, Simple Truths: The Psychology of Self-Deception*, Simon and Schuster, New York (1985)

John Gray, Ph.D., *What You Feel, You Can Heal*, HEART Publishing, Mill Valley, CA (1984)

Rabbi Harold S. Kushner, *How Good Do We Have to Be?* Little, Brown & Co., Boston (1997)

Jane Middleton-Moz, *Shame & Guilt: Masters of Disguise*, Health Communications, Inc., Deerfield Beach, Florida (1990)

Andrew P. Morrison, M.D., *The Culture of Shame*, Ballantine Books, New York (1996)

Michael P. Nichols, Ph.D., *No Place to Hide – Facing Shame So We Can Find Self-Respect*, Prometheus Books, Amherst, New York (1991)

Jay B. Rohrlich, M.D., *Work and Love: The Crucial Balance*, Simon & Schuster, New York (1980)

Lillian B. Rubin, *Intimate Strangers – Men and Women Together*, Harper & Row, NewYork, (1983)

Antoinette Sanders, *The Stress-Proof Child*, Holt, Rinehart & Winston, New York(1984)

Sidney B. Simon, Ph.D. and Suzanne Simon, *Forgiveness: How to Make Peace with Your Past and Get on With Your Life*, Warner Books, New York, (1990)

David Viscott, M.D., *Emotional Resilience*, Three Rivers Press, New York (1996)

David Viscott, M.D., *The Language of Feelings*, Arbor House, New York (1976)

Recommended Web Sites:

http:www.emotionalhonesty.com
This is the site for news and information about emotional honesty publications, Emotional Honesty Discussion Groups, author Ronald Brill's presentations and workshops, as well as information about emotional health education programs and resources.

http:www.casel.org
The Collaborative to Advance Social and Emotional Learning (CASEL), founded in 1994, is a network of educators, researchers and others concerned with promoting school-based social-emotional education. It is based at the Psychology Department of University of Illinois at Chicago.

http:www.divorceasfriends.com/healhurt.html
This site by author Bill Ferguson (Heal the Hurt That Runs Your Life) contains brief but wise statements about the importance of attending to hurt feelings.

http:www.parenting.process.com/longtran.html
This web site offers information relative to emotional honesty in parenting and includes topics on emotional development.

http://joy2meu.com
This is the site for Robert Burney, author of the above recommended book. He shares provocative insights about healing, codependence and emotional honesty.